CROSSING BORDERS BETWEEN
THE DOMESTIC AND THE WILD

DNI Supplements

1

General Editor
Dalit Rom-Shiloni, General Editor (Tel Aviv University, Israel)

Editorial Board
Mark J. Boda (McMaster Divinity College, Hamilton, Ontario, Canada)
Kathe P. Darr (Boston University, USA)
Christian Frevel (Bochum University, Germany)
Paul M. Joyce (King's College London, UK)
Hanne Løland Levinson (University of Minnesota, USA)
Andrew Mein (University of St. Andrews, UK)
Christophe Nihan (University of Münster, Germany)
Hans U. Steymans (University of Fribourg, Switzerland)
Beth Stovell (Ambrose University, Calgary, Alberta, Canada)

CROSSING BORDERS BETWEEN THE DOMESTIC AND THE WILD

Space, Fauna, and Flora

Edited by
Mark J. Boda and Dalit Rom-Shiloni

LONDON • NEW YORK • OXFORD • NEW DELHI • SYDNEY

T&T CLARK
Bloomsbury Publishing Plc, 50 Bedford Square, London, WC1B 3DP, UK
Bloomsbury Publishing Inc, 1359 Broadway, New York, NY 10018, USA
Bloomsbury Publishing Ireland, 29 Earlsfort Terrace, Dublin 2, D02 AY28, Ireland

BLOOMSBURY, T&T CLARK and the T&T Clark logo are
trademarks of Bloomsbury Publishing Plc

First published in Great Britain 2024
Paperback edition published 2025

Copyright © Mark J. Boda, Dalit Rom-Shiloni, and contributors, 2024

The authors have asserted their right under the Copyright, Designs and Patents Act, 1988, to be identified as Authors of this work.

All rights reserved. No part of this publication may be: i) reproduced or transmitted in any form, electronic or mechanical, including photocopying, recording or by means of any information storage or retrieval system without prior permission in writing from the publishers; or ii) used or reproduced in any way for the training, development or operation of artificial intelligence (AI) technologies, including generative AI technologies. The rights holders expressly reserve this publication from the text and data mining exception as per Article 4(3) of the Digital Single Market Directive (EU) 2019/790.

Bloomsbury Publishing Plc does not have any control over, or responsibility for, any third-party websites referred to or in this book. All internet addresses given in this book were correct at the time of going to press. The author and publisher regret any inconvenience caused if addresses have changed or sites have ceased to exist, but can accept no responsibility for any such changes.

A catalogue record for this book is available from the British Library.

Library of Congress Cataloging-in-Publication Data
Names: Boda, Mark J., editor. | Rom-Shiloni, Dalit, editor.
Title: Crossing borders between the domestic and the wild : space, fauna, and flora / edited by Mark J. Boda and Dalit Rom-Shiloni.
Description: London, UK ; New York, NY, USA : T&T Clark, 2023. | Series: DNI supplements ; 1 | Includes bibliographical references.
Identifiers: LCCN 2023025292 | ISBN 9780567696359 (hardback) | ISBN 9780567712639 (paperback) | ISBN 9780567696366 (epdf) | ISBN 9780567696380 (epub)
Subjects: LCSH: Animals in the Bible. | Bible–Geography. | Plants in the Bible. | Animals–Religious aspects. | Domestic animals–Religious aspects.
Classification: LCC BS1199.A57 C76 2023 | DDC 220.8/59–dc23/eng/20230818
LC record available at https://lccn.loc.gov/2023025292

ISBN: HB: 978-0-5676-9635-9
PB: 978-0-5677-1263-9
ePDF: 978-0-5676-9636-6
ePUB: 978-0-5676-9638-0

Series: DNI Supplements, volume 1

Typeset by Integra Software Services Pvt. Ltd.

For product safety related questions contact productsafety@bloomsbury.com.

To find out more about our authors and books visit www.bloomsbury.com and sign up for our newsletters.

CONTENTS

List of Figures	vii
List of Tables	ix
DNI Bible Supplements, Introduction	x
List of Abbreviations	xii

INTRODUCTION   1
    Mark J. Boda and Dalit Rom-Shiloni

Chapter 1
IT'S A JUNGLE IN HERE: WILD ANIMALS, PLANTS, AND PLACES IN THE
BOOK OF AMOS   9
    Alexander Coe Stewart

Chapter 2
OUTSIDE THE WALLS: THE PORTRAYAL OF WILD ANIMALS IN
THE HEBREW BIBLE   31
    Dorit Pomerantz

Chapter 3
FLORA AND FAUNA IN THE METAPHORICAL LANDSCAPES OF
THE SONG OF SONGS   43
    Martien A. Halvorson-Taylor

Chapter 4
WILDSCAPES, LANDSCAPES, AND SPECIALIZED LAND MANAGEMENT:
THE IMPACT OF THE ASSYRIAN RULE OVER LAND EXPLOITATION IN
THE KINGDOM OF JUDAH   57
    Dafna Langgut and Yuval Gadot

Chapter 5
THE WILDERNESS AND THE SOWN IN THE LAND OF ISRAEL:
HISTORICAL MAPPING, THE HUMAN FOOTPRINT, AND
REMOTE SENSING   93
    Noam Levin

Chapter 6
SPATIAL LANGUAGE OF THE WILD: *YAʿAR, MIDBAR, AND ŚĀDEH*   121
    Dalit Rom-Shiloni

Chapter 7
NATURE AND CRITICAL SPATIALITY: A RESPONSE 147
    Jon L. Berquist

Chapter 8
BEYOND THE NATURE-CULTURE DIVIDE: A RESPONSE 151
    Anselm C. Hagedorn

Index of Authors 161
Index of References 165

FIGURES

1.1	Illustrating wild versus domestic spheres	10
1.2	Seal impression with lion and Samarian ivory with lion and bull	18
1.3	German Bible Society, "Hemlock and Wormwood"	25
2.1	"The high mountains are for wild goats" (Ps. 104:18a)	33
2.2	"Her leaders were like stags that found no pasture" (Lam. 1:6b)	33
2.3	"The lion of the forest strikes them down, the wolf of the desert ravages them" (Jer. 5:6)	36
2.4	"Can the Cushite change his skin, or the leopard his spots?" (Jer. 13:23)	37
4.1	(a) The Kingdom of Judah in the eighth to seventh centuries BCE, together with rainfall isohyets. (b) Vegetation zones of the southern Levant	58
4.2	Iron Age wine press in the Jerusalem highlands characterized by the presence of two small niches that were usually etched in the vertical rock wall at the back of the treading surface	62
4.3	The locations of surface samples collected from the thirty-four vegetation stations from the Baruch study	67
4.4	Simplified pollen diagrams of the Dead Sea (Ze'elim) record presenting paleo-environmental reconstruction for the c. 2500–500 years BCE time interval	68
4.5	The location of the Repha'im and Soreq Valleys and their tributaries, the watershed, Jerusalem as well as other sites mentioned in the text	69
4.6	Wine press I and the southwest room of Building II at Kh. Er-Ras	74
4.7	A stone pile at Nahal Shemuel	75
4.8	Remains of a structure at Nahal Shemuel	75
4.9	Harvesting of grapes growing along the ground in soil pockets in the Hebron Mountains	77
5.1	The location of towns and some of the twelve tribes according to the book of Joshua, combined with average annual rainfall (for the years 1970–2000)	99
5.2	(a) Kiepert's (1875) map showing winter areas of grazing by nomads in desert areas in yellow; (b) Fischer's 1911 map showing the "current limit of permanent settlement" in a red line; (c) PEF (1880) land cover classes, overlaying the 1946 British census of	

	Bedouin tents; (d) The British Mandate 1946 "Tentative Land Classification Map"	102
5.3	A comparison of approaches for mapping wilderness: (a) the wilderness continuum of Lesslie; (b) the human footprint of WCS, CIESIN; (c) the global human modification layer of Kennedy et al.; (d) the landscape continuity	105
5.4	Köppen-Geiger climate zones, overlaid by annual rainfall isohyets of 200 mm	107
5.5	Land cover and vegetation maps of Israel: (a) Israel vegetation according to Zohary; (b) land cover of Israel, based on the MAARAG (2018), as of 2018; (c) temporal variability for 2000–19 in the 16-day values of the Normalized Difference Vegetation Index (NDVI), based on MODIS data	111
5.6	(a) VIIRS nighttime lights; (b) protected areas and military land uses, and the overlaps between them; (c) strava heatmap showing areas frequently used by hikers and runners; (d) strava heatmap showing areas frequently used by bikers (bicycles)	112

TABLES

4.1	The fifty-seven excavated and surveyed wine presses along the Repha'im and Soreq Catchments dating to the late Iron Age	72
6.1	Seven parameters of "the wild": יער, מדבר, and שדה	126
6.2	Seven parameters of "the wild": שדה as cultivated field	130
6.3	Seven parameters of "the wild": שדה as territory, possession	132
6.4	Seven parameters of "the wild": שדה as wild steppe	133

DNI BIBLE SUPPLEMENTS, INTRODUCTION

DNI Bible Supplements is a platform for monograph-length, in-depth, and multidisciplinary studies and edited volumes on specific topics within the broad spectrum of nature and nature imagery in the Bible, in five fields of nature: fauna, flora, landscape characteristics, climate systems, and water sources.

This supplement series accompanies the DNI Bible project, the **D**ictionary of **N**ature **I**magery of the Bible (http://dni.tau.ac.il/). The DNI Bible project is designed to expand the exegetical toolbox by becoming a recognized device that Bible scholars, students, and clergy can turn to when explaining aspects of nature and landscape as part of their scholarly work and study. The point of departure for this project is the recognition that knowledge of diverse aspects of life and natural sciences; acquaintance with broad ecological systems (geography, climate, and more) mentioned in the biblical literature; and study of evidence from the material culture of the second and first millennia BCE (with specific interest in archaeobotany, archaeozoology, and iconography), are all *essential* for biblical exegesis. The DNI Bible project is aimed at studying each nature reference of the five fields of nature (above) in six sections: (a) biblical data, (b) history of identification, (c) life & natural sciences as well as their ecological backgrounds, (d) material culture findings, (e) exegetical studies of specific biblical passages that utilize nature images, and finally, (f) the reception history developed concerning diverse interpretive traditions of each nature reference. Integrating all this information concerning each nature reference is to serve biblical scholars to produce better informed exegetical studies of the Bible.

The DNI Bible project is a highly multidisciplinary and international enterprise. It employs the rich and varied critical methodologies of biblical studies, and brings experts from a wide range of disciplines to contribute each in their field of expertise. In terms of time, the project focuses on second and first millennia BCE literary, pictorial, and material sources, and in terms of geography the project focuses on the land of Israel, the Levant, the eastern Mediterranean regions, and the ancient Near East.

DNI Bible Supplements is aimed at broadening and deepening scholarly discussions on selected topics, themes, and natural phenomena. Each volume involves collaborations between scholars. If written by a single author, the author consults with relevant scientific experts in the course of preparing the monograph. In volumes with at least two co-authors, a biblical scholar joins another scholar or scholars from the other field(s) required by the topic. Discussions shed light on the biblical nature imagery and define what we gain from the biological/ecological subfields that might produce a better understanding of specific biblical texts and themes.

DNI Bible Supplement volumes treat a wide range of topics concerning nature references in the Bible, related to the five fields of nature: fauna, flora, landscape characteristics, climate systems, and water sources; or integrating several of these together. Imagery and metaphorical language of nature are of great interest as also are comparative studies on nature imagery in the Bible, in ancient literature, and in iconography. Monographs or edited volumes may address methodological considerations, questions of identification and taxonomy (including history of identifications), as well as conceptions of nature in biblical literature, in other ancient literatures, and up to modern conceptions of nature that were informed by the Bible.

DNI Bible Supplements is nurturing a home for multi-disciplinarity in the study of the Bible. Monographs, PhD dissertations, and co-edited volumes are invited and will be considered for publication by the Editorial Board. Furthermore, the series is the publication venue of thematic and methodological discussions developed by the SBL section "Nature Imagery and Conceptions of Nature in the Bible," established in 2019.

DNI Bible Supplements sets new horizons for scholarly cooperation and is aimed at both professional and general audiences that share an interest and curiosity in natural reality and in nature imagery language within the Bible.

Dalit Rom-Shiloni
General Editor

LIST OF ABBREVIATIONS

AB	Anchor Bible
AOAT	Alter Orient und Altes Testament
AYB	Anchor Yale Bible
ATD	Das Alte Testament Deutsch
BARev	*Biblical Archaeology Review*
BASOR	*Bulletin of the American Schools of Oriental Research*
BETL	Bibliotheca ephemeridum theologicarum lovaniensium
BZAW	Beihefte zur ZAW
ConBOT	Coniectanea biblica, Old Testament
CoS	William W. Hallo and K. Lawson Younger (ed.), *Contexts of Scripture* (4 vols.; Leiden: Brill, 2003)
DNI	Dictionary of Nature Imagery (DNI Bible: https://dni.tau.ac.il/)
FAT	Forschungen zum Alten Testament
HALOT	*Hebrew and Aramaic Lexicon of the Old Testament*
HThKAT	Herders theologischer Kommentar zum Alten Testament
ICC	International Critical Commentary
IEJ	*Israel Exploration Journal*
IEKAT	Internationaler Exegetischer Kommentar zum Alten Testament (International Exegetical Commentary on the Old Testament)
JAAR	*Journal of the American Academy of Religion*
JAOS	*Journal of the American Oriental Society*
JBL	*Journal of Biblical Literature*
JCS	*Journal of Cuneiform Studies*
JNES	*Journal of Near Eastern Studies*
JPS	*Jewish Publication Society*
JSOT	*Journal for the Study of the Old Testament*
JSOTSup	Journal for the Study of the Old Testament, Supplement Series
LHBOTS	Library of Hebrew Bible/Old Testament Studies
MAARAG	HaMaarag: The National Program for Assessing the State of Nature in Israel (https://hamaarag.org.il/)
NCB	New Century Bible
NICOT	New International Commentary on the Old Testament
NJPS	*The New Jewish Publication Society of America*
OBO	Orbis biblicus et orientalis
OTL	Old Testament Library
OTS	*Oudtestamentische Studiën*
PEQ	*Palestine Exploration Quarterly*
SBL	Society of Biblical Literature

SBLSS	SBL Semeia Studies
SBS	Stuttgarter Bibelstudien
TDOT	*Theological Dictionary of the Old Testament*
TWAT	G. Johannes Botterweck (ed.), *Theologisches Wörterbuch zum AltenTestament* (Stuttgart: Kohlhammer, 1978-1984)
UF	*Ugarit-Forschungen*
UNESCO	The United Nations Educational, Scientific and Cultural Organization (https://www.unesco.org/en)
VT	*Vetus Testamentum*
VTSup	*Vetus Testamentum, Supplements*
WBC	Word Biblical Commentary
ZAW	*Zeitschrift für die alttestamentliche Wissenschaft*

INTRODUCTION

Mark J. Boda and Dalit Rom-Shiloni

Should the borders crossed be from the Wild to the Domestic, or from the Domestic to the Wild? This has been one of the issues we struggled with throughout work on this volume. The difference seems to be one of directionality. Humans cross from the domestic to the wild, leaving the familiar human realm of activity only to rarely enter the unknown space; non-humans within the wild (fauna and flora) take the opposite direction, and often threaten humans and their domesticated animals and crops. God, however, crosses, extends, transforms the wild at the expense of the domestic (or vice versa), being free to move between them. Hence, the decision about the title of this book was not easy to make and could continue to be debated.

Debates over definitions of "wild" and "wilderness" have long characterized several disciplines within the Social Sciences, e.g., Geography and Sociology; Life & Natural Sciences, e.g., Zoology, Botany, Ecology, etc. A point of consensus is the convention that the "wild" (or "wilderness") designates a realm beyond human reach and thus (supposedly) beyond human intervention.[1] However, geographers, sociologists, and other specialists have recognized that there are not really clear borders between the domestic and the wild. Rather, the relative proximity of these two realms (which in the Levant and the Land of Israel is often dynamic and ever changing), as well as the interactions between them, are among the most intriguing issues to investigate. Interjecting a humanities perspective, and particularly that of Hebrew Bible (HB) Studies, into this multidisciplinary discussion accentuates the anthropological-cultural and the theological dimensions of these terms,[2] and challenges us, HB scholars, with the questions: How did biblical authors, that is, the producers of ancient texts in the Levant during the first millennium BCE,

---

1. For definitions of wild/wilderness, see Roderick F. Nash, *Wilderness and the American Mind* (New Haven and London: Yale University Press, 1967), 1–7.

2. See Laura Feldt, "Wilderness in Mythology and Religion," in *Wilderness in Mythology and Religion: Approaching Religious Spatialities, Cosmologies, and Ideas of Wild Nature*, ed. Laura Feldt, Religion and Society 55 (Berlin: de Gruyter, 2012), 1–24.

define the wild around them? What did they actually know about it? How did they portray human interactions with the wild?

The investigation of the HB to expose its ancient conceptions of the wild is methodologically complicated by premodern, modern, and even postmodern definitions of the wild, which themselves were heavily influenced by interpretive biblical traditions. Thus, the danger of circular argumentation is ever present. Methodologically, the study of the wild (and wilderness) participates in a lively (and fairly recent) discussion in biblical scholarship, drawing on Social Spatiality Studies, as formulated by Henri Lefebvre (from the 1970s and into the 1990s) and by Edward W. Soja (in the 1990s).[3] Jon Berquist, among several other scholars, has brought those valuable perspectives of social spatiality into HB studies, and defined critical spatiality in its postmodern framework for the context of biblical studies.[4] Berquist argued that "critical spatiality understands all aspects of space to be human constructions that are socially contested."[5] He furthermore accentuated the unique status of postmodern geographies that still have not lost their realistic anchor:

> Space has a genealogy and a history; it exists as a constructed category within the framework of human experience. Space is something we make, create, shape, reshape, form, inform, disform, and transform. All these human activities are operations upon space, leaving traces that mark its history and its shape.[6]

---

3. Formative for social spatiality studies, and constructive for the biblical angle have been Henri Lefebvre, *The Production of Space*, trans. Donald Nicholson-Smith (Malden, MA: Blackwell, 1991 [1974]); followed by Edward W. Soja, *Thirdspace: Journeys to Los Angeles and Other Real-and-Imagined Places* (Malden, MA: Blackwell, 1996); Edward W. Soja, *Postmodern Geographies: The Reassertion of Space in Critical Social Theory* (London; New York: Verso, 1989).

4. See Jon L. Berquist, "Critical Spatiality and the Construction of the Ancient World," in *"Imagining" Biblical Worlds: Studies in Spatial, Social and Historical Constructs in Honor of James W. Flanagan*, ed. David M. Gunn and Paula M. McNutt, JSOTSup 359 (Sheffield: Sheffield Academic Press, 2002), 14–29. Berquist also mentioned the diverse scholarly fields connected by terminology and themes to critical spatiality. Claudia V. Camp, "Introduction," in *Constructions of Space II: The Biblical City and Other Imagined Spaces*, ed. Jon L. Berquist and Claudia V. Camp, LHBOTS 490 (New York: T&T Clark, 2008), 1–17; see further, Thomas B. Dozeman, "Biblical Geography and Critical Spatial Studies," in *Constructions of Space I: Theory, Geography, and Narrative*, ed. Jon Berquist and Claudia V. Camp, LHBOTS 481 (New York: T&T Clark, 2007), 87–108, esp. 105; Mark K. George, "Space and History: Siting Critical Space for Biblical Studies," *Constructions of Space* I, 15–31; idem, "Introduction," in *Constructions of Space IV: Further Developments in Examining Ancient Israel's Social Space*, ed. Mark K. George, LHBOTS 569 (New York: T&T Clark, 2013), 1–22.

5. Berquist, "Critical Spatiality," 15. Berquist also mentioned the diverse scholarly fields connected by terminology and themes to critical spatiality.

6. Berquist, "Critical Spatiality," 14–15.

Inspired by those observations on "human activities," the present volume searches for different biblical perceptions of the wild, paying particular attention to the significance of fluid boundaries between the domestic and the wild, and to the options of crossing borders between them.

The negotiation between those domestic and wild arenas may be more complex than two opposing spaces. To quote Mark George:

> Space also [has] meaning and significance. People, individually and corporately, give meanings to spaces as part of their interaction and relationship with it. These meanings are not merely logical expressions of space. They articulate something in addition to, or beyond, the logical and conceptual.[7]

The diverse interactions with the different wilds in the HB indeed bring articulations that are beyond the logical and the conceptual. Our theme of "Crossing borders between the domestic and the wild" is a great opportunity to discuss this antagonism presented in recent scholarship of biblical spatiality studies. The studies below address various ways that biblical authors defined the wild—as real or imagined—and often as a realistic ground that serves metaphoric-imagery language and theological proclamations.

This collected volume containing six chapters is the first written product of two consecutive years (2019, 2020) of discussions at the Society of Biblical Literature (SBL) Annual Meeting section, "Nature Imagery and Conceptions of Nature in the Bible," a section we co-founded and for which we serve as co-conveners as of 2019. Four of the chapters were written by HB scholars, one co-authored by an archaeologist and an archaeobotanist, and one by a geographer. The chapters are accompanied by two responses from HB scholars. This multidisciplinary collaboration within the community which we have now in writing is one of the great challenges our SBL section and the DNI Bible project in general (https://dni.tau.ac.il/, accessed May 4, 2023) have aimed to address. The present volume calls us to look at the entire spectrum of real, imagined, metaphorized, and conceptualized forms of the wild appearing in biblical sources, but also in the material culture and agriculture of ancient Israel, and to some extent observe the great gap between biblical observations and modern studies of geography and of mapping that marks the distinctions between "the wilderness" and "the sown."

Alexander Coe Stewart, in "It's a Jungle in Here: Wild Animals, Plants, and Places in the Book of Amos," argues that no space is safe from divine judgment in Amos, and the nature imagery throughout the text presents a jungle of wild animals, plants, and places that threaten the human realm and expose the injustices of the ancient Israelites. He shows how the wild community encroaches on the domestic community at key parts of the book, and focuses on the references to plants, animals, and places that comprise "wild" spaces and faces in tension with the humanly managed spaces and faces portrayed in Amos. By contrast, domesticated

---

7. George, "Introduction," 12.

animals and their products typically belong within the "safe" spaces of the human community and are considered when threatened by wild creatures (Amos 3:12) or when out of place (Amos 6:12). Likewise, cultivated plants and their yields are not considered wild in the Hebrew cosmos, though these can be threatened by outside creatures too. Using the book of Amos to showcase the prophetic contribution concerning the wild in the Old Testament, Stewart demonstrates that the wild creatures and features in Amos convey a world in which it is not safe for abusers to act with impunity. Yahweh sides with the wild animals against exploitative people in such times.

In "Outside the Walls: The Portrayal of Wild Animals in the Hebrew Bible," **Dorit Pomerantz**'s point of departure is that exposure to the wilderness and to wild animals allowed biblical authors to portray the animals in narratives, similes, and metaphors in order to derive a deeper meaning of the text and affect the readers' emotional span of fear, excitement, awe, and admiration. She addresses the interaction between biblical authors and wild animals in two parts. First, she asks: how familiar were the authors with wild animals based on the description of the habitats, appearance, and behavior of the animal? A case study of the leopard details the occurrences in the HB where the animal appears, describes the context in which it is mentioned, and focuses on how the animal's characteristics enable authors to portray the wild carnivore as a dangerous and unexpected attacker on Israel. Second, she broadens the spectrum to discuss presentations of carnivores portrayed as predators in their interaction with people in four spheres: hunting, "zoological gardens," war, and herding flocks. The four chosen spheres, which either initiated or forced contact of human and wild animals, produced the types of experience which left a strong impression and enabled the literary expressions. Moreover, while knowing the habitat and seeing the appearance of the animal is descriptive, it is the behavior of the animal that demonstrates to the reader the level of familiarity with the wild.

Martien Halvorson-Taylor, in "Flora and Fauna in the Metaphorical Landscapes of the Song of Songs," considers, through a treatment of the natural metaphors that are used in the Song of Songs, how landscape shapes identity and, in turn, how identity shapes landscapes. The lovers use metaphorical language borrowed from both their wild and their domestic spaces. The natural imagery, no less than the domestic, reflects at once the particularities of the lovers' Israelite identities and also is shaped by it—though the particularities may be lost in translation. This delicate interaction between landscape and identity occurs not simply in the allusions to the natural world that evoke the stories of the ancestors (tents, nomadic existence, wandering in the desert), but through the flora and fauna that the lovers choose to describe one another. How they incorporate the wild ("doves," "cedars of Lebanon," "lilies") into their descriptions and self-descriptions, and what constitutes the "wild" that they incorporate, reveals their distinctive identities. Finally, in the inevitable inversions that occur in metaphorical language, the lovers themselves recede into the natural images that they employ.

Dafna Langgut and **Yuval Gadot**, in "Wildscapes, Landscapes, and Specialized Land Management: The Impact of the Assyrian Rule over Land Exploitation in the Kingdom of Judah," demonstrate the massive influence of imperial rule on the Levantine landscape. They focus on the Judean Highlands and the hills to their west (the Shephelah) during the late eighth to seventh centuries BCE, when the region was under the hegemony of the Assyrian empire. Reconstructing the ancient landscape, Langgut and Gadot employ several proxies—archaeological finds of industrial installations (olive and wine presses), artifacts related to centralized storage and distribution of agricultural products (e.g., stamped jar handles), changes in the settlement pattern, and fossil pollen (mainly pollen grains that had originated in the Judean Highlands and became embedded in the Dead Sea). They claim that under Assyrian rule the regional economy shifted from a typical mixed Mediterranean to a specialized agriculture. While olive culture intensified in the Shephelah, viticulture flourished in the Judean Highlands. The archaeological record points to the exploitation of inhospitable rock terrain that had not previously been cultivated in the highlands and the dedication of most of the plots to the production of a single commodity: wine. Evidence of centralized storage and distribution of agricultural products were documented in both regions—the highlands with its viticulture and the Shephelah with its olive culture.

In "The Wilderness and the Sown in the Land of Israel: Historical Mapping, the Human Footprint, and Remote Sensing," **Noam Levin** examines the distinction between the wilderness and the sown land within the geographic context of the Land of Israel, and different approaches for mapping the wilderness, starting in the nineteenth century (using a historical geography approach), and moving into our modern space age (using a conservation-oriented and an environmental approach). He presents the agricultural revolution and the historical conflict between nomadic peoples (inhabiting desert and wilderness areas) and settled populations, as they appear in the HB. Levin then proceeds to demonstrate how the territories of nomadic and settled populations were mapped in Israel/Palestine by the late nineteenth century and during the period of the British Mandate. He moves on to describe modern approaches to mapping and delineating wilderness areas (remote areas with little impact by human intervention) and deserts, using spatially explicit datasets and satellite images. Whereas traditional mapping approaches often refer to wilderness areas as static, time series of meteorological data and of satellite-derived variables enable him to quantify the spatial and temporal variability of wilderness and desert areas. While desert areas may be defined climatically, the intensity of human modification of the Israeli landscape has greatly expanded human land uses to areas which were formerly scarcely inhabited. The chapter concludes with the question of whether there still remain any wilderness areas in modern Israel.

In "Spatial Language of the Wild: *Ya'ar*, *Miḏbar*, and *Śāḏeh*," **Dalit Rom-Shiloni** discusses three terms that designate "the wild" in the HB. The three differ substantially from one another because they refer to very different landscapes, and yet they do have at least one major characteristic in common—they denote territories beyond the borders of human residence. Methodologically, this chapter utilizes critical spatial theory. The goals of this study are twofold. The first goal is to explore these different "wilds" as perceived spaces in order to reconstruct the biblical definitions and portrayals of the wild. The study suggests seven parameters of the wild: four refer to geographical features (locations, landscape characteristics, flora formations, and fauna) and three refer to human interaction with the wild (human presence, human intervention, and the perception of the wild as threatening and dangerous to humans). Focusing on *śādeh* in its three biblical meanings: "cultivated field, territory, wild steppe," and specifically on the latter as the perceived "wild," allows Rom-Shiloni to offer some more general observations on the wild as conceived space (and even as Soja's other Thirdspace). The second goal is to discuss the implications of these portrayals of the wild for anthropological and theological conceptions of space and of nature in biblical literature, by looking at the fluidity of boundaries between the domestic and the wild.

The final part of this collection brings two HB scholars, **Jon Berquist** and **Anselm Hagedorn**, to reflect upon those studies and explore possible venues for further multi-disciplinary conversations among scholars on this topic, as recorded in ancient HB sources.

We are thankful to the above scholars for their brilliant contributions to this project. In addition, we want to express our appreciation to Dominic Mattos at Bloomsbury for believing in this volume and series. The professional editing team at Bloomsbury (especially Ayesha Hussain) and Integra (especially Anne Hunt) helped guide this project to completion. We also extend our thanks to two research assistants at McMaster Divinity College, Ambrose Thomson and Ki Hyun Kim, who assisted with editing and indexing. This collected volume is the first issue of the new series, DNI Bible Supplements—and, thus, we are thrilled to celebrate these new beginnings, and invite readers to join this field of study.

Mark J. Boda, Hamilton, Canada
Dalit Rom-Shiloni, Tel Aviv, Israel

Bibliography

Berquist, Jon L. "Critical Spatiality and the Construction of the Ancient World." In *"Imagining" Biblical Worlds: Studies in Spatial, Social and Historical Constructs in Honor of James W. Flanagan*, edited by David M. Gunn and Paula M. McNutt, 14–29. JSOTSup 359. Sheffield: Sheffield Academic, 2002.

Berquist, Jon L., and Claudia V. Camp. "Space and History: Siting Critical Space for Biblical Studies." In *Constructions of Space I: Theory, Geography, and Narrative*, edited by Jon L. Berquist and Claudia V. Camp, 15–31. LHBOTS 481. New York: T&T Clark, 2007.

Camp, Claudia V. "Introduction." In *Constructions of Space II: The Biblical City and Other Imagined Spaces*, edited by Jon L. Berquist and Claudia V. Camp, 1–17. LHBOTS 490. New York: T&T Clark, 2008.

Dozeman, Thomas B. "Biblical Geography and Critical Spatial Studies." In *Constructions of Space I: Theory, Geography, and Narrative*, edited by Jon L. Berquist and Claudia V. Camp, 87–108. LHBOTS 481. New York: T&T Clark, 2007.

Feldt, Laura. "Wilderness in Mythology and Religion." In *Wilderness in Mythology and Religion: Approaching Religious Spatialities, Cosmologies, and Ideas of Wild Nature*, edited by Laura Feldt, 1–24. Religion and Society 55. Berlin: de Gruyter, 2012.

George, Mark K. "Introduction." In *Constructions of Space IV: Further Developments in Examining Ancient Israel's Social Space*, edited by Jon L. Berquist and Claudia V. Camp, 1–22. LHBOTS 596. New York: T&T Clark, 2013.

Lefebvre, Henri. *The Production of Space*. Translated by Donald Nicholson-Smith. Malden, MA: Blackwell, 1991.

Nash, Roderick F. *Wilderness and the American Mind*. New Haven, CT: Yale University Press, 1967.

Soja, Edward W. *Postmodern Geographies: The Reassertion of Space in Critical Social Theory*. London; New York: Verso, 1989.

Soja, Edward W. *Thirdspace: Journeys to Los Angeles and Other Real-and-Imagined Places*. Malden, MA: Blackwell, 1996.

Chapter 1

IT'S A JUNGLE IN HERE: WILD ANIMALS, PLANTS, AND PLACES IN THE BOOK OF AMOS

Alexander Coe Stewart

Introduction

The book of Amos portrays wild things encroaching upon the domestic realm of settlements and buildings, even though the "jungle" is supposed to stay "out there" in the categories of the English saying and the Israelite worldview. It turns out that no space is safe from divine judgment in Amos. The nature imagery throughout the text presents a "jungle" of wild animals, plants, and places that threaten the human realm and expose the injustices of the ancient Israelites. This chapter will examine the references to animals, plants, and places that comprise wild spaces and faces in tension with the humanly managed spaces and faces in the book of Amos.

For wild animals, hunting scenarios with birds and lions imply a threat to the domestic realm as one series of rhetorical questions moves readers from rural to urban spaces (Amos 3:3-8). Blight, plague, and locusts sent by Yahweh, the God of Israel, are wild pests that cross into cultivated land to ruin crops and human health (Amos 4:9-10; 7:1-2). Wild animals feature as well in examples of future threats of devastation by divine judgment. Whether at the farthest limit of the cosmos (Amos 9:3), at the shepherding border of civilization (Amos 3:12), or in the most guarded of human residences (Amos 5:19), wild creatures can attack. Furthermore, Amos features wild plants as a threat to human society, specifically as the "forest" in which lions lurk (Amos 3:4) and in the plant imagery for social injustice in Israel (Amos 5:7; 6:12). The Israelites are accused of turning justice into "(bitter) wormwood" and "poison (hemlock)" (Amos 5:7; 6:12), again revealing a conception of nature and society in which some species (and some social actions) are outside the boundaries of what is good, life-giving, and acceptable. In addition, natural places that are wild spaces or liminal spaces include the "pastures of the shepherds" (Amos 1:2), the "forest // lair" (Amos 3:4), the "wilderness" (Amos 2:10; 5:25), and the "Rift Valley" (Amos 6:14). These places are not necessarily negative, but they are often under threat or at the edge of the domestic orbit managed by humans. While there were no tropical "jungles" in ancient Israel or in Amos, the natural imagery in the book often presents dangerous, unmanaged places to the audience.

Wild things in Amos contribute to the book's warnings, justifying the prophet's mission, revealing an inescapably negative future for ancient Israel, criticizing injustices, and characterizing violent enemies or the God of Israel in non-human ways. Using the book of Amos to showcase the prophetic contribution concerning the wild in the Old Testament, this chapter demonstrates that the wild creatures and features in Amos convey a world in which it is not safe for abusers to act with impunity. There is an order to the world; for people to go against that order only produces death and suffering. The boundaries between wild and domestic break down when there is injustice. Yahweh sides with the wildlife against exploitative people in such times. That said, let me briefly define what I mean by "wild" before explaining representative examples of this unruly jungle that we encounter in Amos.

Defining "Wild"

There are no Hebrew nouns corresponding to the exact connotations of the English phrases "wild animal," "wild plant," or "wilderness," nor is there a Hebrew adjective to modify such nouns. Despite this, the Hebrew texts do not lump all animals together, all plants together, and all places together with one term for each category. The writers treat some animals as dangerous and undomesticated and some plants as inedible, toxic, or unsuited for agriculture. Some places are comparatively lacking in resources and are portrayed as barren of life or hostile to human habitation. This is what I mean by "wild." I mean something beyond human control, management, or benefit, often some life-form dangerous to human health and social well-being. While the wild and domestic spheres overlap, they are distinguishable in their treatment by the biblical authors across many texts (see Figure 1.1).

Figure 1.1 Illustrating wild versus domestic spheres.

Similarly, ancient Hebrews did not categorize animals in Western scientific terms by biological traits.[1] The term מִין for each "kind" of creature in the Hebrew Bible or Old Testament is not always what Western science would label a "species," and some biblical texts classify animals by the zone in which they operate (i.e., in the sky, land, or water) and/or their method of movement (i.e., flying, crawling, or teeming).[2] For undomesticated land animals, we sometimes read of creatures called חית השדה (e.g., Gen. 2:19-20), meaning "animals of the field" or "wild animals."[3] Amos does not use this phrase, but the book does mention animals that match the description. Elsewhere in this volume, Dorit Pomerantz gives another spatial definition of wild animals: animals "outside the walls." Such animals in Amos include lions (Amos 3:4, 8, 12; 5:19), perching birds (Amos 3:5),[4] locusts (Amos 4:9; 7:1), bears (Amos 5:19), snakes (Amos 5:19), and even a sea serpent that is likely a reference to Leviathan in the ocean (Amos 9:3).

---

1. See Gene M. Tucker, "Rain on a Land Where No One Lives: The Hebrew Bible on the Environment," *JBL* 116, no. 1 (1997): 3–17; Theodore Hiebert, *The Yahwist's Landscape: Nature and Religion in Early Israel* (New York: Oxford University Press, 1996), 76–77. For example, we today might divide the cosmos into living and non-living things, whereas some biblical traditions draw that line within the animal kingdom itself such that some animals count as נפש חיה ("a living being" or "an animal life"; Gen. 1:20-21, 24, 28; cf. 1:30; 2:7) while plants and some other phyla of moving creatures are not called this (Bernhard W. Anderson, "Creation and Ecology," in *Creation in the Old Testament*, ed. Bernhard W. Anderson, Issues in Religion and Theology 6 [1983. Reprint, Philadelphia: Fortress, 1984], 162). See, generally, Richard Whitekettle, "Where the Wild Things Are: Primary Level Taxa in Israelite Zoological Thought," *JSOT* 25, no. 93 (2001): 17–37. However, we should not exaggerate differences in human *experience* of the natural world between then and now, even if ancient Hebrews classified creatures differently (John W. Rogerson, "The Old Testament View of Nature: Some Preliminary Questions," in *Instruction and Interpretation: Studies in Hebrew Language, Palestinian Archaeology and Biblical Exegesis. Papers Read at the Joint British-Dutch Old Testament Conference Held at Louvain, 1976*, by H. A. Brongers et al., OTS 20 [Leiden: Brill, 1977], 68).

2. See Gen. 1:20-30; 6:7, 20; 7:8, 23; 8:17, 19; 9:2; Lev. 11:46; 20:25; Deut. 4:17-18; 1 Sam. 17:43, 46; 2 Sam. 21:10; Job 12:7-8; Pss. 8:8-9 (Eng. 7–8); 79:2; 104:11-12; 148:10; Ezek. 38:20; Dan. 4:9 (Eng. 12); Hos. 2:20 (Eng. 18); 4:3; Zeph. 1:3.

3. Specific examples include snakes (e.g., Gen. 3:1, 14), jackals, ostriches (Isa. 43:20), bears, and lions (Hos. 13:8). For the distinction between wild and domestic animals, see Gen. 1:24-26; 2:20; 3:1, 14; Exod. 23:11, 29; Lev. 5:2; 25:7; 26:22; Pss. 8:8 (Eng. 7); 50:10; 104:11, 13; 148:10; Jer. 27:6; Ezek. 14:21; Hos. 13:8; Joel 1:18, 20; 2:22; Mic. 5:7 (Eng. 8). Compare also "bad animal(s)" in Gen. 37:20, 33; Lev. 26:6; Ezek. 5:17; 14:15, 21; 34:25.

4. "Does a bird swoop on a trap of the land when it has no bait? / Does a trap come up from the soil when it doesn't actually capture (anything)?" (Amos 3:5). The צפור ("bird") is a general term for perching birds, not raptors.

By contrast, domesticated animals can be managed inside the walls of settlements or houses.[5] In Amos, the following domesticated animals are mentioned or implied: sheep or goats, cows or oxen, and horses.[6] Because domesticated animals belong within the safe spaces of the human community, they will only be considered in this chapter when threatened by wild creatures (Amos 3:12) or when out of place (Amos 6:12). Likewise, cultivated plants and their yields are not considered wild in the Hebrew cosmos, though these can be threatened by outside creatures as well. For the most part, it is dangerous animals, plants, and places that are relevant in understanding the borders between "wild" and "home" in ancient Israel or Judah.

Examples from Amos

Let us consider some examples of wild animals first and then turn to plants and places in tandem.

Wild Animals in Amos

Amos 5:19 is a great example with which to begin, because three creatures appear in a single verse, and they have their usual rhetorical effect of threatening or illustrating divine judgment. The ancient audience apparently expects, in Amos 5, that "the day of Yahweh" would be a time of divine rescue from foreign enemies. Israel would be vindicated. They would all live peacefully. But no, the prophet declares, the day of Yahweh would actually mean something darker and more frightful for the Israelite kingdom. Amos 5:18-19 contains this use of animal imagery from the prophetic voice:

---

5. An overarching term for such livestock would be בהמה ("livestock, domesticated animal"), sometimes further divided into the בקר, the larger livestock like cows and oxen, and the צאן, the smaller livestock like sheep and goats. For the main division into large and small herd animals, see Lev. 1:2; Joel 1:18; Jon. 3:7. Cf. Deut. 28:4. For more specific kinds of livestock, lists in the biblical texts include donkeys, oxen, and sheep (Exod. 22:10), cattle, donkeys, and flocks (Num. 31:30), or oxen, sheep, and goats (Deut. 14:4). Various texts distinguish בהמה as non-human in status, abilities, and permissible treatment. See Exod. 13:15; 22:19; Lev. 24:21; Job 18:3; 35:11; Pss. 32:9; 49:13, 21 (Eng. 12, 20); 73:22; Dan. 4:13 (Eng. 16); 5:21. Contrast the pessimism or humility that blurs the distinctions between humans and livestock in Pss. 73:22; 49:13, 21 (Eng. 12, 20); Prov. 30:2; Eccl. 3:18-19.

6. Sheep or goats: Amos 1:1 (implied); 3:12 (implied); 6:4; 7:15; cows or oxen: Amos 1:1 (implied); 4:1; 6:4, 12; 7:14 (implied); and horses: Amos 2:15; 4:10; 6:12. Animal offerings for religious slaughter also implicitly assume the presence of various herd animals. See Amos 4:4-5; 5:22, 25.

הוי המתאוים את יום יהוה	5:18	Oh no for the ones who crave the day of Yahweh!
למה זה לכם יום יהוה		Of what real use to you is the day of Yahweh?
הוא חשך ולא אור		It is darkness and not light,
כאשר ינוס איש מפני הארי	5:19	just as a person would flee from the lion's presence,
ופגעו הדב		and the bear would attack them,
ובא הבית		and they would come to the house (of God),
וסמך ידו על הקיר		and place their hand on the wall (of the temple),[7]
ונשכו הנחש		and the snake would bite them!

Notice the three animals: the lion, bear, and snake (Amos 5:19). The syntax suggests that it is the same person escaping the lion and bear before the fatal snake bite. Although it is a hypothetical scenario, it is interesting to consider this: how likely would it be for an ancient Israelite to encounter each of these animals separately? Aulikki Nahkola has taken the time to collect various kinds of evidence to study this exact verse.[8] Based on studies of population density and territorial range for lions and bears, at least, Nahkola estimates that Israel might have contained about eighty to 100 lions, living in no more than twenty-five prides, and about twenty to thirty bears.[9] Due to a lion's nocturnal habits and a bear's hibernating habits—and since all three creatures avoid humans if they can—an Israelite would not encounter them personally on a regular basis. Crossing paths with one, let alone all three, would have been very rare but perhaps all the more frightening in the Israelite imagination due to that.[10] Here the "lion" (ארי) is a powerful threat, the "bear" (דב) is the height of animal aggression (cf. Hos. 13:7-8), and the "snake" (נחש) might illustrate "the suddenness of judgment."[11] There are at least five species of poisonous snakes found in modern Israel, at least some of which could have been around at the time of this text.[12] Whichever snake is intended, the snake in Amos 5:19 is likely poisonous, its bite fatal. There is a

---

7. All translations of biblical texts are mine unless otherwise noted. For reasons to understand the house and wall as temple architecture here, see Antti Laato, "Yahweh Sabaoth and His Land in the Book of Amos," in *Enigmas and Images: Studies in Honor of Tryggve N. D. Mettinger*, ed. Göran Eidevall and Blaženka Scheuer, ConBOT 58 (Winona Lake, IN: Eisenbrauns, 2011), 118 n. 7; Anthony I. Lipscomb, "'And He Leans His Hand against the Wall': A Cognitive Grammar Approach to an Overlooked Clause in Amos 5:19" (paper, Annual Meeting of the Midwest Region of the SBL, Bourbonnais, IL, February 8, 2015).

8. Aulikki Nahkola, "Amos Animalizing: Lion, Bear and Snake in Amos 5.19," in *Aspects of Amos: Exegesis and Interpretation*, ed. Anselm C. Hagedorn and Andrew Mein, LHBOTS 536 (New York: T&T Clark, 2011), 83–104.

9. Nahkola, "Amos Animalizing," 92–93.

10. Nahkola, "Amos Animalizing," 103–104.

11. Nahkola, "Amos Animalizing," 101, 102, respectively.

12. Nahkola, "Amos Animalizing," 90 n. 30. Specifically, the five species are the Palestinian Saw-scaled Viper (*Echis coloratus*), Field's Horned Viper (*Pseudocerastesfieldi*), the Desert Horned Viper (*Cerastes cerastes*), the Black Desert Cobra (*Walterinnesia aegyptia*), and the Israeli Mole Viper (*Atractaspis enganddensis*). Cf. Elazar Kochva, "Venomous Snakes of Israel: Ecology and Snakebite," *Public Health Review* 26 (1998): 209–32.

growing sense of horror instead of safety.¹³ Perhaps all three animals symbolize Yahweh directly,¹⁴ but the more likely point is that Yahweh is dangerous to his people in the way these wild animals are dangerous.¹⁵

Let us go backwards in the text to Amos 3:4 in order to focus more on lions. Indeed, lions are the most frequently mentioned wild animal in the entire Old Testament.¹⁶ In the Bible and in Amos, the king of the jungle takes the lion's share! Amos 3:4 asks,

הישאג אריה ביער וטרף אין לו	3:4	Does a lion roar in the forest when it has no torn prey?
היתן כפיר קולו ממענתו בלתי אם לכד		Does a young lion project its voice from its lair if it has not captured (anything)?

Typically not, is the expected answer. The first term, אריה ("lion"), is the most frequent for lions in the Old Testament. It refers to a male that is fully mature, able to hunt prey not only for itself but also for its "cubs" (גור) (Nah. 2:12-13).¹⁷ It is either the African lion (*Panthera leo*) or the Asian lion (*Panthera leo persica*), but the term and iconography from this part of the world are not specific enough to distinguish which species of lion is meant.¹⁸ The parallel term, כפיר ("young lion"), is an adolescent but older than a cub, because it is also able to hunt here and in other texts (cf. Judg. 14:5; Jer. 51:38; Ezek. 19:1-9).¹⁹ In a study of roaring and other lion behaviors in Africa in the 1900s, Schaller speaks of "at least nine more or less distinct expressions" of vocalizing among lion prides, only some of which are related to food.²⁰ In particular, although lions can roar or growl to warn others

---

13. Nahkola, "Amos Animalizing," 104.

14. So, Brent A. Strawn, "Material Culture, Iconography, and the Prophets," in *The Oxford Handbook of the Prophets*, ed. Carolyn J. Sharp (New York: Oxford University Press, 2016), 111–12.

15. David Jobling and Nathan Loewen, "Sketches for Earth Readings of the Book of Amos," in *Readings from the Perspective of Earth*, ed. Norman C. Habel, The Earth Bible 1 (Sheffield: Sheffield Academic, 2000), 83.

16. Brent Strawn wrote a monograph on them: *What Is Stronger than a Lion? Leonine Image and Metaphor in the Hebrew Bible and the Ancient Near East*, OBO 212 (Göttingen: Vandenhoeck & Ruprecht, 2005).

17. Strawn, *What Is Stronger than a Lion*, 300.

18. Strawn, *What Is Stronger than a Lion*, 29–32, 300. Cf. Oded Borowski, *Every Living Thing: Daily Use of Animals in Ancient Israel* (Walnut Creek, CA: AltaMira, 1999), 199–200, 226–27.

19. Strawn, *What Is Stronger than a Lion*, 309.

20. George B. Schaller, *The Serengeti Lion: A Study of Predator-Prey Relations*, Wildlife Behavior and Ecology Series (Chicago: University of Chicago Press, 1972), 103–15. Some examples (109–10) include: (1) to call one another and to advertise their presence; (2) to "avoid contact, by … delineating the pride area"; (3) to enhance "the physical presence of an animal by making it more conspicuous"; and (4) "to strengthen the bonds of the group."

away, when they are hungry, and when consuming food, they do not actually roar in the process of hunting their prey, since that would alert the prey to the danger.[21] You do not announce before you pounce! The scenarios in Amos 3:4 probably picture a warning growl to assert dominance and scare off other animals from prey already captured.[22] No, of course a lion would not roar unless it had captured something, at least not compared to roaring just before pouncing. Of course, such roaring would cause fear. In the same way, the prophet argues, a person cannot help announcing a divine message if God has "roared" a warning message of inevitable catastrophe to them (Amos 3:8).[23] The analogy suggests that Yahweh has already captured his prey (i.e., the kingdom of Israel), and it is as good as dead. Wild animals thus illustrate the natural order of cause-and-effect, adding to the case that the prophet's message is simply an effect following its cause, namely, the divine communication to him as prophet.

Wild animal rhetoric also plays a role back in Amos 1–2 to describe international violence and social oppression. First there is the anger of the nation Edom that "tore [טרף] continually"[24] and "kept watch" like a lion or similar animal stalking its prey (Amos 1:11).[25] Then we hear of the ferocity by the Ammonite soldiers who "shredded [בקע] the pregnant [women] of the Gilead region" (Amos 1:13), perhaps like a bear rips open its prey.[26] Finally, there are those in Israel "who sniff [שאף] (for food) on the dust of the land" like jackals or wild donkeys searching for food at "the head of poor

---

21. Edward R. Hope, "Problems of Interpretation in Amos 3,4," *The Bible Translator* 42, no. 2 (1991): 201–205; Strawn, *What Is Stronger than a Lion*, 35; Strawn, "Material Culture," 100–101. Contra Philip J. King, *Amos, Hosea, Micah: An Archaeological Commentary* (Philadelphia: Westminster, 1988), 129.

22. Strawn, "Material Culture," 100–101. Hear a sound clip of lions growling while feeding: Pro Sound Effects, "Lions Feeding," in *Sounds of Animals: Lions, Tigers and Bears* (Pro Sound Effects Library, 2012), https://www.youtube.com/watch?v=3JxOc6STpTY (accessed September 15, 2023).

23. Perhaps the rhetoric of Amos 3:3-6 also moves from rural to urban settings if the initial travelers are far from a city, for then the questions would concern space away from built environments (Amos 3:3), space where wild animals hunt (Amos 3:4), space where humans hunt birds (Amos 3:5), and finally urban space where calamity happens (Amos 3:6).

24. This verb is typically used for lions or other wild animals savaging their prey. See Gen. 37:33; 44:28; 49:27; Exod. 22:12 (Eng. 13); Deut. 33:20; Pss. 7:3 (2); 17:12; 22:14 (13); Jer. 5:6; Ezek. 19:3, 6; 22:25, 27; Hos. 5:14; 6:1; Mic. 5:7 (8); Nah. 2:13 (12).

25. See, more generally, Anselm C. Hagedorn, "Edom in the Book of Amos and Beyond," in *Aspects of Amos: Exegesis and Interpretation*, ed. Anselm C. Hagedorn and Andrew Mein, LHBOTS 536 (New York: T&T Clark, 2011), 41–57.

26. The term "shredded" may compare the savage military violence to that of a bear or a lion (see 2 Kgs 2:24; Hos. 13:8), although the verb is not solely used of animal violence. Among other uses, the term elsewhere describes the violent killing of women (2 Kgs 8:12; 15:16; Hos. 13:16) or men (2 Chron. 25:12) through military violence, which is the literal reference of the verb in Amos 1:13.

people" (Amos 2:7; cf. Amos 8:4).[27] When oppressive people are compared to domestic animals, it is usually for the sake of underscoring how vulnerable they are to death or exile (Amos 3:12; 4:1-3; 5:19). But when compared to wild animals, their actions are cast as inhumane, cruel, and beastly. In various ways, the foreign nations and the powerful people in Israel treated other societies or individuals as subhuman, as prey (Amos 1:11, 13) and a source of food (Amos 2:7).[28] This is a strategy of "othering" the violent nations in these oracles, portraying them as "other" than the audience is or should be, and the shocking thing is that Israel is "othered" along with the rest, criticized for oppressing its own citizens in a beastly way.

Finally, lion imagery is even used to portray Israel's God, Yahweh. This operates differently than it does for humans, because the violent power of God is understood to be legitimate, used to enforce justice in the cosmos. It is intriguing nevertheless that God is compared to a lion at least three times in the book. First, Amos 1:2 declares that Yahweh "will roar" (ישאג), using the verb we already saw in Amos 3 for a regular lion roaring (Amos 3:4) and soon after for a lion to whom Yahweh is

---

27. The ancient and modern versions struggle with translating this verb. My reason for translating it as "sniff" is that none of the biblical uses of the verb or similar-looking emendations have a preposition before the direct object if there is an object at all, meaning that the prepositions in Amos 2:7 likely introduce the locations of the action in parallel, not the direct object and then the location (cf. Amos 8:4). Even if the verb could be emended to mean "trample upon," following the Old Greek, the animal imagery arguably remains. Duane Garrett (*Amos: A Handbook on the Hebrew Text*, Baylor Handbook on the Hebrew Bible [Waco, TX: Baylor University Press, 2008], 58–59) suggests the sniffing is comparable to dogs but does not point to Jer. 14:6 in support, where the verb is indeed used of wild donkeys (פרא) whose panting or sniffing is comparable to that of dog-like jackals (תן). Cf. Job 24:5; Jer. 2:24; 14:6. The references to donkeys in Job 24:5 and Jer. 14:6 connote a search for food. That is why I understand the sniffing around in Amos 2:7 to convey the animal-like greed of the wealthy who demand a heavy quota or tax on the grain harvested by their workers (cf. Amos 5:11). These poor workers have nothing but scraps to eat, but the greedy "jackals" come sniffing around for the scraps anyway! The phrase "the dust of the land" shows the low socioeconomic position and perhaps the literal, physical position of some of these impoverished people (Amos 2:7). Alternatively, the verb in Jer. 2:24 has a sexual connotation, the religious infidelity of the nation being compared to a donkey sniffing the wind for signs of other sexual mates. So, in light of the sexual exploitation condemned at the end of Amos 2:7, the sniffing may instead connote that wealthy men in Israel are sniffing around for economically vulnerable women to exploit for sexual favors. Either way, the wealthy are acting in a beastly manner.

28. The Arameans treated other humans like grain (Amos 1:2). Other nations also treated people as commodities in human trafficking (Amos 1:6, 9), as decorating material (Amos 2:1), or as exchangeable for silver or sandals leading to debt slavery (Amos 2:6), but these examples do not mention wild animals, plants, or places as defined in this chapter.

compared or even metaphorically equated, in that Yahweh communicated or "roared" a message to the prophet (Amos 3:8).[29] The effect is to produce fearful reverence for this deity, for he is not to be trifled with or ignored. "Sure, but we will be rescued by our God," Israel may think. "Yahweh will be like a shepherd who snatches us from the jaws of the lion that is Assyria!" To that implicit objection, Amos the prophet has another oracle in chapter 3 to subvert their false hopes:

	3:12	"Thus Yahweh said:
כה אמר יהוה		
כאשר יציל הרעה מפי הארי		'Just as the shepherd rescues from the mouth of the lion two limbs or a piece of an ear,
שתי כרעים או בדל אזן		
כן ינצלו בני ישראל הישבים בשמרון		so the Israelites who reside in Samaria will be rescued—in the form of a corner of a bed and part from a leg[30] of a couch!'"
בפאת מטה ובד משק ערש		

Consider the lion iconography from this time period in Figure 1.2 as a way of picturing the strength of the lion and the popularity of this creature in Israelite art.[31]

---

29. The landscape in Amos 1:2 will respond by mourning (i.e., drying up), and the prophet will respond by preaching a message of mourning and tragedy in Amos 3:8.

30. The other ancient versions took this to contain a place name ("Damascus") and consequently struggled with the following word (see *Biblia Hebraica Quinta*). The Masoretic Text tradition vocalizes the form in question (ובדמשק) as a conjunction and an unattested lexeme. The best emendation is "and part from the leg of a couch" (וּבַד מְשֹׁק עָרֶשׂ), which rearranges only the word division and vocalization of the form in question (Isaac Rabinowitz, "The Crux at Amos III 12," *VT* 11, no. 2 [1961]: 228–31). Agreeing with Rabinowitz, Moeller ("Ambiguity at Amos 3:12," *The Bible Translator* 15, no. 1 [1964]: 34) notes that the emendation allows for better parallelism. The term בד likewise plays on בדל, and so the order of furniture is chiastic, a reverse parallelism compared to the order of the carcass of the sheep (A: limbs, B: ear, B′: corner, A′: leg), per Francis I. Andersen and David Noel Freedman, *Amos: A New Translation with Introduction and Commentary*, AB 24A (New York: Doubleday, 1989), 409–10.

31. The image on the left will be familiar to biblical scholars from the imprint on the JSOTSup and LHBOTS series (Bloomsbury T&T Clark). This image is also on the Israeli five pound coin (1978–84) and on the half-shekel of 1980–85. The original seal was discovered at Megiddo and mentions "Jeroboam," probably the same king of Israel about which the text of Amos is so critical. The image on the right depicts an ivory decoration from Samaria, Iron Age II (ninth or eighth century BCE), thus once again dating to the period of Amos 3:12, 15.

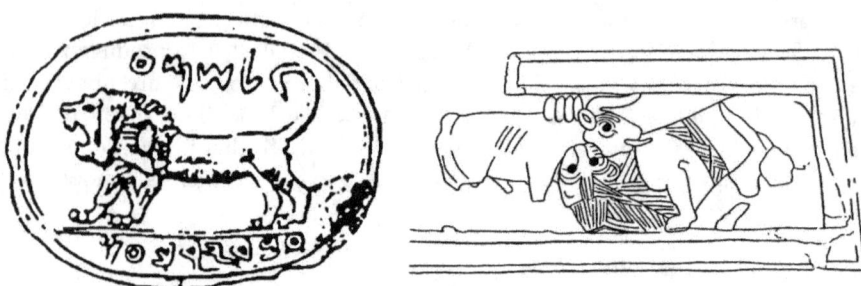

Figure 1.2 Seal impression with lion and Samarian ivory with lion and bull. Left: Strawn, *What Is Stronger than a Lion*, 403, fig. 3.96. Right: Ibid., 405, fig. 3.103.

The mangled animal in Amos 3:12 is probably a sheep.[32] The lion could stand for a human king or nation,[33] but given the earlier imagery associating Yahweh with a lion (i.e., Amos 1:2; 3:4, 8), this is probably another shocking reversal of expectations: Yahweh is not the shepherd king but the lion king.[34] Pierre Van Hecke puts it this way: "God, as a lion towards his own people … is to be explained as a conscious reversal of the traditional description of God as shepherd."[35] So, this is an ironic reversal of the divine shepherd motif. It is even more ironic historically, considering that lion carvings were used for protective symbolism and decorative

32. The mangled animal is likely a sheep, not a goat, given that the Old Testament associates the lion with sheep as its prey most often. See Strawn, *What Is Stronger than a Lion*, 354–55. Sirach 13:19 mentions wild donkeys as prey for lions, and iconographic drawings show gazelles as prey, among other wild animals. Mention of "the shepherd" confirms that it is domestic prey here in Amos 3:12, however. It was a custom for a shepherd to recover the mangled carcass of a sheep to confirm the loss of the livestock to some wild animal (Exod. 22:12 [Eng. 13]). See similar Mesopotamian laws cited in Shalom M. Paul, *Amos: A Commentary on the Book of Amos*, Hermeneia (Minneapolis: Fortress, 1991), 119. Cf. Gen. 31:39; 1 Sam. 17:34-35.

33. Either Assyria's king or Israel's rulers together, per D. Matthew Stith, "Whose Lion Is It, Anyway? The Identity of the Lion in Amos 3:12," *Koinonia* 11, no. 1 (1999): 103–18. Compare Ezek. 34:10, where Israel's rulers are compared to bad shepherds acting like lions against their flock.

34. Strawn, *What Is Stronger than a Lion*, 60. Compare Hugh S. Pyper, "The Lion King: Yahweh as Sovereign Beast in Israel's Imaginary," in *The Bible and Posthumanism*, ed. Jennifer L. Koosed, SBL Semeia Studies 74 (Atlanta: Society of Biblical Literature, 2014), 59–74. Not every element in the comparison needs to correspond to a specific referent, so it is equally possible that the focus should be on the destruction rather than the identity of the lion or shepherd.

35. Pierre Van Hecke, "'For I Will Be like a Lion to Ephraim': Leonine Metaphors in the Twelve Prophets," in *The Books of the Twelve Prophets: Minor Prophets—Major Theologies*, ed. Heinz-Josef Fabry, BETL 295 (Bristol, CT: Peeters, 2018), 401. The divine shepherd motif "was particularly in use in the Northern Kingdom" (401). Cf. Pss. 77:21 (Eng. 20); 78:52; 79:13; 80:2.

purposes in this century within Samaria.³⁶ Again, see the line drawing of the lion attacking a bull in Figure 1.2. "We will be rescued," thinks Israel. Well, only "rescued" in a pitiful mess that is no longer a kingdom, according to the prophetic message.

What is the effect of this zoomorphic language in Amos 1 and Amos 3? Terence Fretheim speaks of how such metaphors "temper" our human-centered God-talk: "God's transcendence is given a special lift by the use of such natural metaphors, for among other things they evoke wonder and awe in human beings."³⁷ Thus, not only do we see wild animals as symbols of judgment (Amos 5:19) or instructive lessons on natural causation (Amos 3:4), not only do we see them as "othering" techniques when portraying violent people or nations, we also see that Yahweh is "othered" so that he is not mistaken for being too similar to humans. He is not a flawed and limited king like Israel's king; and he is not human. Yahweh has royal power like a lion's power, and he is not a safe lion, to paraphrase C. S. Lewis.³⁸

Wild Plants and Places in Amos

Moving on from animals, let us consider plants and places together, since some places in the book of Amos are defined primarily by their plant life. Think of forests, for example. Neither plants nor places are called "wild" in Amos. Instead, readers require cultural information in order to understand whether a plant or place is wild in the sense of uncultivated, unmanaged, or dangerous. Dalit Rom-Shiloni's chapter in this volume focuses on the three primary land zones that make up the "spatial language of the wild," namely, "forest, field, and desert." The first words from Amos allude to two of these zones, specifically, forests and pasture fields:

ויאמר	1:2	And he [the prophet Amos] said:
יהוה מציון ישאג		"It is Yahweh who from Zion will roar,
ומירושלם יתן קולו		and from Jerusalem he will project his voice!
ואבלו נאות הרעים		So the pastures of the shepherds will dress mournfully,
ויבש ראש הכרמל		and the top of the Carmel Range will dry up!"

In this complex mixture of metaphors we can understand that Yahweh, from the domestic sphere (Zion // Jerusalem), affects some uncultivated regions of Israel and Judah. The "pastures of the shepherds" are the zones with minimal rainfall, perhaps the Judean wilderness near the prophet's hometown (Tekoa),³⁹ while "the top of the Carmel Range" could refer to one of two areas, either southeastern or northwestern

---

36. Helga Weippert, "Amos: Seine Bilder und ihr Milieu," in *Beiträge zur prophetischen Bildsprache in Israel und Assyrien*, ed. Helga Weippert, Klaus Seybold, and Manfred Weippert, OBO 64 (Freiburg: Universitätsverlag Freiburg, 1985), 15–18, 25.

37. Terence E. Fretheim, *God and World in the Old Testament: A Relational Theology of Creation* (Nashville: Abingdon, 2005), 247.

38. C. S. Lewis, *The Lion, the Witch, and the Wardrobe* (New York: HarperCollins, 1950), 79–80.

39. Compare Jer. 33:12 and the more common phrase "(the) pastures of the wilderness" (Ps. 65:13 [Eng. 12]; Jer. 9:9; 23:10; Joel 1:19-20; 2:22). Tekoa had grazing land nearby (2 Chron. 20:20; Neh. 3:5; Amos 1:1).

in location (Amos 1:2). There is a "Carmel" located south of Tekoa in Judah (Josh. 15:55; 1 Sam. 15:12; 25:2), and it was remembered for its flocks of livestock, but not particularly for its vegetation or elevation (1 Sam. 25:2-18).[40] There is also within the southeastern view "the carmel" in the general sense of fruitful land,[41] perhaps referring to the fruitful border of the Benjamin and Judean deserts. While these identifications of the term yield a poetic couplet that speaks of pasture grounds withering from low shepherding valleys to higher shepherding hills (or indicates identical, fruitful areas) within Judah, they do not adequately account for the mention of the "top" of Carmel, the rhetorical impact of the imagery, or the rhetorical target of most of the book. Instead, the northwestern option, the Carmel (Range) of Israel near the Mediterranean Sea, is preferable on these three counts. Amos mentions "the top" of this place (Amos 1:2; 9:3), and Israel's Carmel was higher than its capital city and famous for its "top" (1 Kgs 18:42; Song 7:6 [Eng. 5]).[42] It was also known for its dense forests and well-watered grazing grounds in association with other northern locations of similar fertility,[43] matching the rhetorical impact of the withering imagery in Amos 1:2 better, since a location on the border of the wilderness would hardly be remarkable if it withered. Finally, the rhetorical target in Amos is most often the northern kingdom of Israel, not Judah, so Carmel would more likely be in the north, hinting that Yahweh's roar would reverberate all the way into the northern kingdom in its effects. If both the shepherding pastures and the Carmel Range will wither at the coming earthquake (cf. Amos 1:1),[44] if both will turn brown in a figurative mourning ritual (אבל), then we see vegetation as the

---

40. It is true that the Judahite Carmel was somewhat elevated, since it is within the Judahite "hill-country" (Josh. 15:48-55) and people "went down" from there (1 Sam. 15:12; 25:20) or instructed others to "go up" there (1 Sam. 25:5), but it is a region characterized as "wilderness" (1 Sam. 25:7, 21) and steppe or "field" (1 Sam. 25:15), and it features almost nowhere else in the Bible.

41. Cf. 2 Kgs 19:23; 2 Chr. 26:10; Isa. 10:18; 16:10; 29:17; 32:15-16; Jer. 2:7; 4:26; 48:33; Mic. 7:14(?). Some uses of this term seem to mean fruitful land or orchards, refer to northern mountains (2 Kgs 19:23), or indicate less plant growth than the "forest" land (Isa. 29:17; 32:15) with which a northwestern Carmel is associated (Mic. 7:14).

42. Cf. 1 Kgs 18:19-20; 2 Kgs 2:25; 4:25; Jer. 46:18. It would be like referring to the heights of Denver. An audience in a North American context would know that this refers to Denver, Colorado, not Denver, North Carolina, even if the second were closer to some readers.

43. What is arguably this Carmel is often listed in association with other high and/or fertile regions like the Bashan region, the Lebanon mountains, or the Sharon plain (Isa. 33:9; 35:2; Jer. 50:19; Mic. 7:14[?]; Nah. 1:4). When the vegetation of Carmel is elsewhere mentioned as flourishing or withering, it appears to be the northwestern location (Isa. 33:9; 35:2; Nah. 1:4), with admitted exceptions that are not similar to Amos in wording (Isa. 10:18; 32:15; Jer. 4:26).

44. I interpret the roaring in Amos 1:2 as a prediction of the famous earthquake that functions as a warning message to the surrounding kingdoms. If one understands the imagery as a thunderstorm instead, then the location of Carmel is even more likely to be Mount Carmel in the northwest, given the drought and confrontation with worshipers of the thunder-god Baal that happened there in the previous century (cf. 1 Kgs 17-18).

figurative clothing for the land in these two wild regions. When the vegetation dies or browns, it is like human mourners disrobing and wearing sackcloth to lament a loss. Uncultivated fields can be devastated with the most fertile of forests. No place or plant is safe from the effects of the disaster (cf. Amos 9:3).[45]

The next wild place in Amos is a "forest" in Amos 3. We know that forests are wild places from a number of biblical texts.[46] As we heard in Amos 3:4: "Does a lion roar in the forest when it has no torn prey? / Does a young lion project its voice from its lair if it has not captured (anything)?" Here the יער ("forest") is the lion's preferred hunting ground. However, we should not understand מענה (its "lair") to be a permanent cave or den. Lions roam in large areas and rarely spend the night in the same place twice in a row.[47] In Amos 3:4, then, it is best to understand "lair" as a generic term for any hiding spot or haunt for a lion in the dense forest or thicket of undergrowth away from urban centers.[48] The forest serves as a realistic and wild place of danger in this sequence of effect-and-cause reasoning.

In later chapters we see cultivated plants ruined by wild animals, disease, and military invasion (Amos 4:9; 7:2; 5:11, 17).[49] Amos 4:9 mentions שדפון ("scorching") and ירקון ("blight") on גן ("gardens") and כרם ("vineyards") along with a גזם ("locust horde") that consumed the תאנה ("fig trees") and זית ("olive trees") of the Israelites in the past.[50] These are used as examples of chastisements by God that Israel refused to heed. The very next verse speaks of an Egyptian-style דבר ("plague") that presumably affected people and animals alike (Amos 4:10). This plague may

---

45. Near the conclusion of the book, the Carmel Range features once more: "And if they hide at the top of the Carmel Range, from there I will search and take them" (Amos 9:3). Again, this could be the Carmel/carmel region of Judah, picturing a greater range of escape locations from east to west, or it could be the Carmel Range of Israel, picturing a greater range of height and depth, as I think is more likely. Directed against the northern kingdom, this vision would more likely mention a place within Israel as a potential escape location. The dense forests atop Israel's Carmel Range would also make a more logical hiding place than the exposed borders of Judah's wilderness would.

46. For the "forest" as a place for wild animals, see 2 Kgs 2:24; Pss. 50:10; 80:14; 104:20; Isa. 56:9; Jer. 5:16; 12:8; Ezek. 34:25; Hos. 2:14; Mic. 5:7. A forest is typically portrayed as a lush, non-cultivated area, and it is contrasted with urban areas (Josh. 17:15, 18; Isa. 10:18; 29:17; 32:15; Jer. 26:18; Ezek. 34:25; Hos. 2:14; Mic. 3:12).

47. Hope, "Problems," 203. Indeed, "anyone who knows anything about lions knows that they don't live in dens, except in zoos" (202). Hope adds, though, that lions "do have favourite places to which they return from time to time to rest" (203). Cf. Schaller, *Serengeti Lion*, 12–15, 119–25, 267–71; David J. A. Clines, "Misapprehensions, Ancient and Modern, about Lions (Nahum 2:13)," in *Poets, Prophets, and Texts in Play: Studies in Biblical Poetry and Prophecy in Honour of Francis Landy*, ed. Ehud Ben Zvi et al., LHBOTS 597 (New York: Bloomsbury T&T Clark, 2015), 58–76. Cf. Job 38:40; Song 4:8; Ps. 104:22.

48. Strawn, *What Is Stronger than a Lion*, 38; Strawn, "Material Culture," 100.

49. Sometimes cultivated plants or their products are not under threat. See Amos 7:14; 8:1-2; 9:14.

50. See also Amos 7:1-2 for locusts consuming vegetation. I am using the singular lexemes for ease of recognition, even though they are sometimes plural in the Hebrew text.

have been a pest infestation, a weather event, or a microscopic or fungal disease afflicting people or their livestock or crops.[51] Unlike Amos 1, the examples in Amos 4 have wild creatures like locusts as threats to places and plants closer to the homes of humans.

The only examples of the term מדבר ("wilderness") appear in passages that criticize Israel for their unfaithfulness despite Yahweh's faithfulness to them during the years in the wilderness after the exodus (Amos 2:10; 5:25). Noam Levin later in this volume describes the wilderness by way of its contrast with the "sown" land, meaning ground sown with agricultural crops. However, as Gene Tucker observes, "much of what is identified as wilderness was seasonal pasture land, and all of it, even the most barren and arid, supported life, including human life."[52] The wilderness and similar places like the ערבה ("Rift Valley, Arabah") of Amos 6:14 are not inherently negative in connotation, but they are often places of danger and scarcity, at the border of the domestic orbit controlled by humans.[53]

Another example of plant and place imagery that I would like to highlight is the most vivid of all. Two times the prophet accuses the powerful people in Israel of turning justice into "wormwood," once in Amos 5:7 and once more in Amos 6:12. Here is how Amos 6:12 accuses the powerful:

הירצון בסלע סוסים	6:12	Is it on the cliffside that horses run?
אם יחרוש בבקר ים		Or with oxen does one plow (the) sea?[54]
כי הפכתם לראש		But you have turned into poison hemlock
משפט		what was justice,
ופרי צדקה		and the fruit of righteousness
ללענה		(you have turned) into bitter wormwood.

51. This raises an interesting question: would ancient Israelites have considered microbial pathogens and fungal infections to be life forms at all, or were such plagues considered to come directly from God, with no living agents?

52. Tucker, "Rain on a Land," 10.

53. Scholars like William Cronon ("The Trouble with Wilderness: Or, Getting Back to the Wrong Nature," in *Uncommon Ground: Rethinking the Human Place in Nature*, ed. William Cronon [1995. Reprint, New York: W. W. Norton & Company, 1996], 69) argue that the concept of "wilderness" is still conceived of through cultural lenses, and that views can shift from idyllic to dangerous or adventurous (frontier) views depending on the society that is talking about the wild. Cf. Max Oelschlaeger, *The Idea of Wilderness: From Prehistory to the Age of Ecology* (New Haven: Yale University Press, 1991); Roderick Nash, *Wilderness and the American Mind*, 4th edn (New Haven: Yale University Press, 2001). A culture's or sub-culture's concept of wilderness can be largely a reflection or projection of its own hopes, fears, or dreams, according to Norman Wirzba, *From Nature to Creation: A Christian Vision for Understanding and Loving Our World*, The Church and Postmodern Culture (Grand Rapids: Baker Academic, 2015), 38–39. Nevertheless, the Hebrew texts of the Bible portray the wilderness as a sphere with less rainfall and a sphere at the border of human control.

54. The ancient versions differ, but all bring out the absurdity of something related to the actions or uses of animals. Symmachus (πέτρα) and the Aramaic ("Or is it plowed with the oxen?") took the object of plowing to be the "cliffside" (סלע) implied from the previous

The absurdity of horses galloping along or up a nearly vertical cliffside[55] or using oxen to plow the ocean shows the "cosmic nonsense" of the injustices before and after this verse.[56] The surrounding verses speak of consumeristic and militaristic tendencies that were having a deadly effect on the rest of the Israelite nation, including its poorer members. These activities are foolish, the prophet suggests, as

and parallel line, and they retain the plural "oxen" in the MT (so also Jeffrey J. Niehaus, "Amos," in *The Minor Prophets: An Exegetical and Expository Commentary*, ed. Thomas Edward McComiskey [1992. Reprint, Grand Rapids: Baker Academic, 2009], 445; Douglas K. Stuart, *Hosea–Jonah*, WBC 31 [Waco, TX: Word, 1987], 362; John H. Hayes, *Amos, the Eighth-Century Prophet: His Times and His Preaching* [Nashville: Abingdon, 1988], 191; Garrett, *Amos*, 199), but this gapping would be unprecedented for the rhetorical questions in Amos. A more serious objection to retaining the MT is that "oxen" is nearly always a (collective) singular in the Old Testament (i.e., 178 out of 180 times), per Spencer L. Allen, "Understanding Amos vi 12 in Light of His Other Rhetorical Questions," *VT* 58, no. 4–5 (2008): 442 n. 13. Cf. Andersen and Freedman, *Amos*, 578. Alan Cooper suggests what could be translated, "Or does in the valley a wild ox plow? (אם יחרוש בבקע רים)" ("The Absurdity of Amos 6:12," *JBL* 107, no. 4 [1988]: 725–27). This would imply a second negative answer and maintain structural and semantic parallelism, but there is no manuscript or translation evidence that the letter ע later dropped out. Cooper's reading of "valley" would be the only spelling without ה at the end of the word in the entire Hebrew Bible, and the preposition ב would no longer take its normal meaning ("with") when used with "plow." Elaborate emendations are thus not convincing. I prefer to emend to בַּבָּקָר יָם ("Does one plow the sea with oxen?"). This proposal is found in Hans Walter Wolff, *Joel and Amos: A Commentary on the Books of the Prophets Joel and Amos*, ed. S. Dean McBride Jr., trans. Waldemar Janzen, S. Dean McBride Jr., and Charles A. Muenchow, Hermeneia (Philadelphia: Fortress, 1977), 284; Paul, *Amos*, 218; Jörg Jeremias, *The Book of Amos: A Commentary*, trans. Douglas W. Stott, OTL (Louisville: Westminster John Knox, 1998), 109; Göran Eidevall, *Amos: A New Translation with Introduction and Commentary*, AYB 24G (New Haven: Yale University Press, 2017), 183, 187. It only requires a different word division and vocalization of the consonants (i.e., בַּבָּקָר יָם instead of בַּבְּקָרִים). The word division would have been condensed when a scribe was influenced by the parallel term "horses" (Wolff, *Joel and Amos*, 284).

55. The "cliffside" is not a small stone or level ground with exposed rock but a rocky surface, probably a cliff face navigable only by mountain goats. See R. Reed Lessing, *Amos*, Concordia Commentary (St. Louis: Concordia, 2009), 420. Alternatively, it could refer "to rocky ground that is badly broken with fissures, large stones, and sheer drops, such that a horse could not run on it without breaking his leg" (Garrett, *Amos*, 199).

56. John Barton, "Natural Law and Poetic Justice in the Old Testament," *Journal of Theological Studies* 30, no. 1 (1979): 7. Cf. Hilary Marlow, "The Other Prophet! The Voice of Earth in the Book of Amos," in *Exploring Ecological Hermeneutics*, ed. Norman C. Habel and Peter L. Trudinger, SBLSS 46 (Atlanta: SBL, 2008), 80.

foolish as expecting a horse to run down a sheer cliffside or using oxen to plow the wrong terrain (Amos 6:12).[57]

The prophet then accuses, "you have turned into poison hemlock what was justice, / and the fruit of righteousness (you have turned) into bitter wormwood" (Amos 6:12). The noun translated "poison hemlock" (ראש II) refers elsewhere to poisonous plants (Deut. 29:18; Hos. 10:4) or snake venom (Job 20:16), but in parallel with "wormwood" it is more likely a plant derivative, possibly from poison hemlock (*Conium maculatum*) found in this part of the world.[58] The term לענה ("bitter wormwood") also shows up in Amos 5:7.[59] The word denotes a type of plant with bitter, toxic juice (cf. Jer. 9:15; 23:15; Lam. 3:15).[60] Ironically, poison hemlock looks like a carrot plant,[61] and wormwood grows in the desert, making the reversal of justice and righteousness all the more appalling in Amos 6:12. In other words, the poisonous plants look deceptively like edible ones or are found in wilderness regions, the exact opposite of good-tasting, edible crops that can sustain human life (cf. Hos. 10:4). See Figure 1.3 for a sketch of these plants.

This is the imagery, but what does it mean in this context? The pair of terms "justice" and "righteousness" function in tandem to convey the idea of "social justice."[62] Does this mean legal justice and administrative justice in creating and

---

57. Marlow ("The Other Prophet," 80) explains the relationship between the halves of the verse: "It contrasts the natural wisdom of a horse whose hooves are unsuited to mountaineering with the foolishness (and danger) of setting justice aside, and compares the absurdity of an ox ploughing the sea with the stupidity of neglecting righteousness."

58. United Bible Societies, *Fauna and Flora of the Bible*, 2nd edn, Helps for Translators (New York: UBS, 1980), 167–68.

59. My translation: "They are the ones who turn into bitter wormwood what was justice, / and righteousness to the land they cast down" (Amos 5:7).

60. The species may have been *Artemisia judaica* or *alba*, according to United Bible Societies, *Fauna and Flora*, 198. Cf. Hayes, *Amos*, 160: "[It] is a bush-like plant of the *Artemisia* genus whose pulp has a sharply bitter taste (see [Amos 5:7;] 6:12). The plant yields a slightly aromatic dark green oil used in absinthe liqueur."

61. United Bible Societies, *Fauna and Flora*, 168.

62. See Moshe Weinfeld, "'Justice and Righteousness'—וצדקה משפט—The Expression and Its Meaning," in *Justice and Righteousness: Biblical Themes and Their Influence*, ed. Henning Graf Reventlow and Yair Hoffman, JSOTSup 137 (Sheffield: Sheffield Academic, 1992), 228–9; Moshe Weinfeld, *Social Justice in Ancient Israel and in the Ancient Near East* (Minneapolis: Fortress, 1995), 34. Pairings with "righteousness" (צדקה/צדק) in the Old Testament and similar pairings in ancient Near Eastern texts show concerns for proper order in society. Cf. Gen. 18:19; 2 Sam. 8:15; 1 Kgs 3:6; Pss. 9:9 (Eng. 8); 33:5; 58:2 (1); 72:1-2; 85:12 (11); 89:15 (14); 97:6; 98:9; 99:4; Prov. 8:20; Isa. 9:6; 11:4-5; 16:5; 33:15; 45:19; 59:4, 8-9; Jer. 9:23; 22:13, 15-16; Amos 5:7, 24; 6:12; Zech. 8:8.

Figure 1.3 Hemlock (*Conium maculatum*) above Wormwood (*Artemisia alba*). German Bible Society, "Hemlock and Wormwood." © Deutsche Bibelgesellschaft/German Bible Society. Used with permission.

enforcing fair laws? In Amos 5, at least, "justice" probably does mean that.[63] But here in Amos 6:12, the sense of justice is broader. The powerful are consuming more resources than the poor, and the military exploits of the nation require even more food to supply the military. In this effort to expand Israel's territory, not everyone was enjoying greater access to food and land. Some were going hungry and losing their land due to agricultural debt.[64] Instead of producing social justice, which would be like growing edible plants that sustain life (cf. Ps.

63. In Amos 5:7 "justice" probably refers to the administrative or legal responsibility of those with power to provide fair policies and decisions for the population, especially the poor or otherwise vulnerable in society. Weinfeld (*Social Justice*, 44) emphasizes the administrative responsibility of rulers to create and enforce laws for social justice, not primarily the judicial responsibility of judges to give fair rulings in disputes. However, many biblical traditions put this responsibility on the people and not just the king of Israel, as Walter Houston (*Contending for Justice: Ideologies and Theologies of Social Justice in the Old Testament*, rev. edn [New York: T&T Clark, 2008], 161) notes.

64. As Houston (*Contending for Justice*, 92) says, "the loss of justice for the poor means the loss of land, livelihood, freedom, or indeed life."

85:12 [Eng. 11]; Isa. 45:8; Hos. 10:12),[65] these influential Israelites are accused of producing poisonous "plants" from the soil of unjust social policies (Amos 6:12; cf. Isa. 5:7; Hos. 10:4, 13; Amos 5:7). Their lavish lifestyles and political expansions were bringing death rather than life to the weaker citizens of Israel. Amos critiques these leaders using wild plants and places to underscore that their injustices are foolish and deadly. These people will only cause harm if they try to go against the God-given, cosmic order of justice while pretending that everything is great.

הנה ימים באים נאם יהוה	9:13	"Look, days are coming (speech of Yahweh),
ונגש חורש בקצר		when one plowing will come near the one harvesting,
ודרך ענבים במשך הזרע		and one treading grapes (will meet) the one sowing the seed,
והטיפו ההרים עסיס		and the mountains will drip with sweet-wine,
וכל הגבעות תתמוגגנה		and all the hills will melt (with it),
ושבתי את שבות עמי ישראל	9:14	and I will turn back the captivity of my people Israel, and
ובנו ערים נשמות וישבו		they will rebuild desolate cities and reside (in them), and
ונטעו כרמים ושתו את יינם		plant vineyards and drink their wine, and make gardens
ועשו גנות ואכלו את פריהם		and eat their fruit,
ונטעתים על אדמתם	9:15	and I will plant them on their soil,
ולא ינתשו עוד מעל אדמתם		and they will not be uprooted anymore from their soil
אשר נתתי להם אמר יהוה אלהיך		which I gaven to them," Yahweh your God said.

Finally, the entire book of Amos ends with plant imagery, this time with cultivated plants rather than wild ones:

The book started out with liminal and fertile places turning to wilderness, drying up (Amos 1:2), but the book closes with the renewal and abundance of agriculture (Amos 9:13-14). Even the Israelites are portrayed as cultivated plants that will be planted securely by their divine gardener (Amos 9:15). It is a homecoming, from the wild to the peaceful, from the threat of wilderness to the promise of farming without scarcity.

Conclusion

To conclude, think of the "bewildering" number of ways that wild imagery is used in the rhetoric of Amos. First, in Amos 5:19 we saw three animals that are symbolic or representative of deadly threats (cf. Amos 9:3). Thus, animals can be used as examples of divine judgment in the past or the future (cf. Amos 4:9-10; 7:1-2), even if future judgment ultimately manifests as foreign armies and warfare. Second,

---

65. Conceptually, "righteousness" (צדקה) or the act of rulers maintaining righteous conditions could be associated with life-giving rain from God above (cf. Pss. 72:6; 85:12 [Eng. 11]; Isa. 45:8; Hos. 10:12; Joel 2:23; Matt 5:45), or with life-giving plants springing up from the ground below (cf. Ps. 72:7; Isa. 45:8; Hos. 10:12).

wild animals can illustrate cause and effect in the natural world to convince the audience that some other activity—prophecies of judgment—had an appropriate cause (Amos 3:3-8). The lion roaring is a pedagogical tool in that case. Third, wild animal imagery portrays violent enemies or even the Israelites as non-human in their brutality against the weak (Amos 1:11, 13; 2:7; 8:4). When portrayed as domestic animals, people are considered vulnerable (Amos 3:12; 4:1-3; 5:19). We even see that Yahweh himself is portrayed in non-human terms as a lion in two or three places (Amos 1:2; 3:8, 12). This makes the deity more transcendent and "other" in the religious imagination, such that he is not approachable when he acts like a lion rather than like a shepherd (Amos 3:12).

For wild places and plants, we see field and forest as wild places or borderline places away from urban centers. Even remote places and vegetation are not immune from divine judgment (Amos 1:2). All places suffer together for the evils of the human communities that reside there. More often, however, it is cultivated plants and places that are under threat from wild animals like locusts (Amos 4:9; 5:11, 17; 7:1-2; cf. Amos 8:1-2). Ironically, the "wilderness," the driest zone of all, is not directly mentioned as a future threat but rather as a place where Israel was unfaithful to Yahweh in the past, despite his faithful care for them (Amos 2:10; 5:25). A final example of wild plant and place imagery concerns social injustice comparable to out-of-place animals and poisonous plants (Amos 5:7; 6:12). Instead of giving life and safety, the greed and militarism of the powerful in Israel led to dangerous conditions for the poor, making them swallow a bitter pill.

But wild plants, places, and fearsome animals are not Yahweh's final word to Israel in the book. The book, rather, concludes with abundance, fertility, and harvests that are utopian (Amos 9:13-15). Israel's crops and people will be "planted" securely, not by their Lion King but by their Royal Gardener (Amos 9:15). Their God has become familiar to them again, anthropomorphic, and he promises a homecoming that joins the remnant of Judah and Israel together. From wild and dangerous to a life that is manageable and safe—that is the trajectory of Amos, but hope is only found on the other side of the painful uprooting for the northern kingdom. The severity of the wild things in the book speaks to how seriously Yahweh takes injustice and how closely the moral order and natural order were linked in the Israelite view of the cosmos. There is an ethos to the cosmos in Amos.[66]

Bibliography

Allen, Spencer L. "Understanding Amos vi 12 in Light of His Other Rhetorical Questions." *VT* 58, no. 4–5 (2008): 437–48.

Anderson, Bernhard W. "Creation and Ecology." In *Creation in the Old Testament*, edited by Bernhard W. Anderson, 135–51. Issues in Religions and Theology 6. 1983. Reprint, Philadelphia: Fortress, 1984.

---

66. Alexander Coe Stewart, "The Ethos of the Cosmos in Amos: Creation Rhetoric and Character Formation in Old Testament Ethics" (PhD diss., McMaster Divinity College, 2019).

Andersen, Francis I., and David Noel Freedman. *Amos: A New Translation with Introduction and Commentary.* AB 24A. New York: Doubleday, 1989.

Barton, John. "Natural Law and Poetic Justice in the Old Testament." *Journal of Theological Studies* 30, no. 1 (1979): 1–14.

Borowski, Oded. *Every Living Thing: Daily Use of Animals in Ancient Israel.* Walnut Creek, CA: AltaMira, 1999.

Clines, David J. A. "Misapprehensions, Ancient and Modern, about Lions (Nahum 2:13)." In *Poets, Prophets, and Texts in Play: Studies in Biblical Poetry and Prophecy in Honour of Francis Landy,* edited by Ehud Ben Zvi, Claudia V. Camp, David M. Gunn, and Aaron W. Hughes, 58–76. LHBOTS 597. New York: Bloomsbury T&T Clark, 2015.

Cooper, Alan. "The Absurdity of Amos 6:12." *JBL* 107, no. 4 (1988): 725–27.

Cronon, William. "The Trouble with Wilderness: Or, Getting Back to the Wrong Nature." In *Uncommon Ground: Rethinking the Human Place in Nature,* edited by William Cronon, 69–90. 1995. Reprint, New York: W. W. Norton & Company, 1996.

Eidevall, Göran. *Amos: A New Translation with Introduction and Commentary.* AYB. New Haven: Yale University Press, 2017.

Fretheim, Terence E. *God and World in the Old Testament: A Relational Theology of Creation.* Nashville: Abingdon, 2005.

Garrett, Duane A. *Amos: A Handbook on the Hebrew Text.* Baylor Handbook on the Hebrew Bible. Waco, TX: Baylor University Press, 2008.

German Bible Society. "Hemlock and Wormwood." In *1000 Bible Images.* Logos Research Edition (electronic). Stuttgart: German Bible Society, 2009.

Hagedorn, Anselm C. "Edom in the Book of Amos and Beyond." In *Aspects of Amos: Exegesis and Interpretation,* edited by Anselm C. Hagedorn and Andrew Mein, 41–57. LHBOTS 536. New York: T&T Clark, 2011.

Hayes, John H. *Amos, the Eighth-Century Prophet: His Times and His Preaching.* Nashville: Abingdon, 1988.

Hiebert, Theodore. *The Yahwist's Landscape: Nature and Religion in Early Israel.* New York: Oxford University Press, 1996.

Hope, Edward R. "Problems of Interpretation in Amos 3.4." *The Bible Translator* 42, no. 2 (1991): 201–205.

Houston, Walter J. *Contending for Justice: Ideologies and Theologies of Social Justice in the Old Testament.* Rev. edn. New York: T&T Clark, 2008.

Jeremias, Jörg. *The Book of Amos: A Commentary.* Translated by Douglas W. Stott. OTL. Louisville: Westminster John Knox, 1998.

Jobling, David, and Nathan Loewen. "Sketches for Earth Readings of the Book of Amos." In *Readings from the Perspective of Earth,* edited by Norman C. Habel, 72–85. The Earth Bible 1. Sheffield: Sheffield Academic, 2000.

King, Philip J. *Amos, Hosea, Micah: An Archaeological Commentary.* Philadelphia: Westminster, 1988.

Kochva, Elazar. "Venomous Snakes of Israel: Ecology and Snakebite." *Public Health Review* 26 (1998): 209–32.

Laato, Antti. "Yahweh Sabaoth and His Land in the Book of Amos." In *Enigmas and Images: Studies in Honor of Tryggve N. D. Mettinger,* edited by Göran Eidevall and Blaženka Scheuer, 115–29. ConBOT 58. Winona Lake, IN: Eisenbrauns, 2011.

Lessing, R. Reed. *Amos.* Concordia Commentary. St. Louis: Concordia, 2009.

Lewis, C. S. *The Lion, the Witch, and the Wardrobe.* New York: HarperCollins, 1950.

Lipscomb, Anthony I. "'And He Leans His Hand against the Wall': A Cognitive Grammar Approach to an Overlooked Clause in Amos 5:19." Paper presented at the Annual Meeting of the Midwest Region of the SBL, Bourbonnais, IL, February 8, 2015.

Marlow, Hilary. "The Other Prophet! The Voice of Earth in the Book of Amos." In *Exploring Ecological Hermeneutics*, edited by Norman C. Habel and Peter L. Trudinger, 75–83. SBLSS 46. Atlanta: SBL, 2008.

Moeller, Henry R. "Ambiguity at Amos 3:12." *The Bible Translator* 15, no. 1 (1964): 31–34.

Nahkola, Aulikki. "Amos Animalizing: Lion, Bear and Snake in Amos 5.19." In *Aspects of Amos: Exegesis and Interpretation*, edited by Anselm C. Hagedorn and Andrew Mein, 83–104. LHBOTS 536. New York: T&T Clark, 2011.

Nash, Roderick. *Wilderness and the American Mind*. 4th edn. New Haven: Yale University Press, 2001.

Niehaus, Jeffrey J. "Amos." In *The Minor Prophets: An Exegetical and Expository Commentary*, edited by Thomas Edward McComiskey, 315–494. 1992. Reprint, Grand Rapids: Baker Academic, 2009.

Oelschlaeger, Max. *The Idea of Wilderness: From Prehistory to the Age of Ecology*. New Haven: Yale University Press, 1991.

Paul, Shalom M. *Amos: A Commentary on the Book of Amos*. Edited by Frank Moore Cross. Hermeneia. Minneapolis: Fortress, 1991.

Pro Sound Effects. "Lions Feeding." In *Sounds of Animals: Lions, Tigers and Bears*. Pro Sound Effects Library, 2012. https://www.youtube.com/watch?v=3JxOc6STpTY (accessed September 15, 2023).

Pyper, Hugh S. "The Lion King: Yahweh as Sovereign Beast in Israel's Imaginary." In *The Bible and Posthumanism*, edited by Jennifer L. Koosed, 59–74. SBLSS 74. Atlanta: SBL, 2014.

Rabinowitz, Isaac. "The Crux at Amos III 12." *VT* 11, no. 2 (1961): 228–31.

Rogerson, John W. "The Old Testament View of Nature: Some Preliminary Questions." In *Instruction and Interpretation: Studies in Hebrew Language, Palestinian Archaeology and Biblical Exegesis. Papers Read at the Joint British-Dutch Old Testament Conference Held at Louvain, 1976*, by H. A. Brongers et al., 67–84. OTS 20. Leiden: Brill, 1977.

Schaller, George B. *The Serengeti Lion: A Study of Predator-Prey Relations*. Wildlife Behavior and Ecology Series. Chicago: University of Chicago Press, 1972.

Stewart, Alexander Coe. "The Ethos of the Cosmos in Amos: Creation Rhetoric and Character Formation in Old Testament Ethics." PhD diss., McMaster Divinity College, 2019.

Stith, D. Matthew. "Whose Lion Is It, Anyway? The Identity of the Lion in Amos 3:12." *Koinonia* 11, no. 1 (1999): 103–18.

Strawn, Brent A. "Material Culture, Iconography, and the Prophets." In *The Oxford Handbook of the Prophets*, edited by Carolyn J. Sharp, 87–116. New York: Oxford University Press, 2016.

Strawn, Brent A. *What Is Stronger than a Lion? Leonine Image and Metaphor in the Hebrew Bible and the Ancient Near East*. OBO 212. Göttingen: Vandenhoeck & Ruprecht, 2005.

Stuart, Douglas K. *Hosea-Jonah*. WBC 31. Waco, TX: Word, 1987.

Tucker, Gene M. "Rain on a Land Where No One Lives: The Hebrew Bible on the Environment." *JBL* 116, no. 1 (1997): 3–17.

United Bible Societies. *Fauna and Flora of the Bible*. 2nd edn. Helps for Translators. New York: UBS, 1980.

Van Hecke, Pierre. "'For I Will Be like a Lion to Ephraim': Leonine Metaphors in the Twelve Prophets." In *The Books of the Twelve Prophets: Minor Prophets—Major*

Theologies, edited by Heinz-Josef Fabry, 387–402. BETL 295. Bristol, CT: Peeters, 2018.

Weinfeld, Moshe. "'Justice and Righteousness'— משפט וצדקה —The Expression and Its Meaning." In *Justice and Righteousness: Biblical Themes and Their Influence*, edited by Henning Graf Reventlow and Yair Hoffman, 228–46. JSOTSup 137. Sheffield: Sheffield Academic, 1992.

Weinfeld, Moshe. *Social Justice in Ancient Israel and in the Ancient Near East*. Minneapolis: Fortress, 1995.

Weippert, Helga. "Amos: Seine Bilder und ihr Milieu." In *Beiträge zur prophetischen Bildsprache in Israel und Assyrien*, edited by Helga Weippert, Klaus Seybold, and Manfred Weippert, 1–29. OBO 64. Freiburg: Universitätsverlag Freiburg, 1985.

Whitekettle, Richard. "Where the Wild Things Are: Primary Level Taxa in Israelite Zoological Thought." *JSOT* 25, no. 93 (2001): 17–37.

Wirzba, Norman. *From Nature to Creation: A Christian Vision for Understanding and Loving Our World*. The Church and Postmodern Culture. Grand Rapids: Baker Academic, 2015.

Wolff, Hans Walter. *Joel and Amos: A Commentary on the Books of the Prophets Joel and Amos*. Edited by S. Dean Mcbride Jr. Translated by Waldemar Janzen, S. Dean Mcbride Jr., and Charles A. Muenchow. Hermeneia. Philadelphia: Fortress, 1977.

Chapter 2

OUTSIDE THE WALLS: THE PORTRAYAL OF WILD ANIMALS IN THE HEBREW BIBLE

Dorit Pomerantz

When people left the protection of their sheltered settlements, villages, or towns in ancient times, they were likely to encounter a variety of wild animals. Settlements were close to forests and deserts; both the number and diversity of wild mammals enabled more frequent encounters than in modern times. Ancient authors recorded their responses—from fear and excitement to awe and admiration—which are expressed in their literature. This article addresses the interaction between biblical authors and wild animals, and assesses whether they relied on firsthand knowledge of the fauna.

The first section examines the extent to which the writers were familiar with wild animals on the basis of their description of their habitat, appearance, and behavior. Taking the leopard as a case study, I analyze the occurrences in the Hebrew Bible where the animal appears, describe the context in which it is adduced, and discuss how its characteristics serve the biblical authors to portray dangerous and unexpected attackers. The second section explores human-animal relations in four spheres—hunting, "zoological gardens," war, and herding. Herein, I examine the metaphorical use of wild animals in these spheres and the way in which it enriches the biblical text.

Ancient Near Eastern literature in general and the Hebrew Bible in particular distinguish between two major types of territories: stable, built-up, populated areas within walls and the threatening, uninhabited wild.[1] The borders between the two were neither rigid nor permanent, as there was a transition from fertile lands giving way to grazing areas, these then yielding to the steppes and true wilderness.[2]

---

1. See מדבר (desert), ערבה (steppe), שממה (wasteland), ישימון (desert, desolation), ציה (arid place), יער (forest/thicket), חורש/ה (wood), שדה (field, steppe). For the desolate wilderness in the Bible, see 2 Sam. 18:6; Jer. 9:9-10, 12:8-9; Hos. 2:3; Joel 1:19-20; Lam. 5:18. For uninhabited land in ancient Near Eastern Literature, see, for example, *Epic of Gilgamesh* 1–3; *Aššur-bel-kala* 07, iv; *The Curse of Agade*.

2. Deut. 11:11-17; Isa. 32:14-15; cf. Isa. 6:11-12; Jer. 51:43; Zeph. 2:13; 2 Chron. 26:10.

The Hebrew Bible adduces human-wild animal relations in two principal literary forms:

1. Narrative, wherein the animal functions as a "character" in the story: "Thereupon, two she-bears came out of the woods and mangled forty-two of the children" (2 Kgs 2:24b).[3]
2. Symbolically and metaphorically, wherein a concept is widened and its meaning deepened through the image, simile, comparison of the animal: "For thus the LORD has said to me: As a lion—a great beast—growls over its prey and, when the shepherds gather in force against him … So the LORD of hosts will descend to make war against the mount and the hill of Zion" (Isa. 31:4). Figurative language is also employed to prompt an emotional response in the listener/reader: "My foes have snared me like a bird, without any cause" (Lam. 3:52). The metaphor is more than a comparison of two objects; rather it establishes a relationship between them, such as their qualities become interchanged. For example, the poet's thirst for God is like the deer's thirst for water, a basic sustaining element: "As a deer longs for flowing streams, so my soul longs for you, O God. My soul thirsts for God" (Ps. 42:1-2).[4]

All these uses indicate the extent of the shared imagination of authors and readers as well as the knowledge based on observation that the biblical authors possessed of animals—their habitat, appearance, and behavior.

Knowledge of the Wild

The Hebrew Bible refers to more than fourteen species of wild mammals, describing their habitat and interaction with their environment, such as the ibex that reside in the rocks ("The high mountains are for wild goats" [Ps. 104:18a], see Figure 2.1) and the deer that feed in pastures ("Her leaders were like stags that found no pasture; they could only walk feebly before the pursuer" [Lam. 1:6b], see Figure 2.2). The biblical authors also depict their physical features: "You raise my horn high like that of a wild-ox" (Ps. 92:11a); "Samson went and caught three hundred foxes. He took torches, and, turning [the foxes] tail to tail, he placed a torch between each pair of tails" (Judg. 15:4); "Hark! My beloved! There he comes, leaping over mountains, bounding over hills" (Cant. 2:8); "Asahel was swift of foot, like a gazelle in the open field" (2 Sam. 2:18b).

---

3. Unless otherwise noted, quotations from the Hebrew Bible follow the New Jewish Publication Society Bible.
4. Adele Berlin, "Introduction to Hebrew Poetry," in *The First Book of Maccabees; the Second Book of Maccabees; Introduction to Hebrew Poetry; the Book of Job; the Book of Psalms*, ed. Leander E. Keck, The New Interpreter's Bible 4 (Nashville, TN: Abingdon, 1999), 301–15.

Figure 2.1 "The high mountains are for wild goats" (Ps. 104:18a). Photo: Eitan Bino.

Figure 2.2 "Her leaders were like stags that found no pasture" (Lam. 1:6b). Photo: Eitan Bino.

These observations were the fruit of time and patience, many animal characteristics not being readily discernible.

The biblical authors' familiarity with faunal life is demonstrated in numerous texts. They are thus aware of the wild ass's behavior when it is thirsty: "stand on the bare heights, sniffing the air like jackals; their eyes pine, because there is no herbage" (Jer. 14:6 MT).⁵ They also know that the ibex delivers its young in hiding: "Do you know the season when the mountain goats give birth? Can you mark the time when the hinds calved?" (Job 39:1). They know the doe separates itself from the herd to care for her offspring: "Even the hind in the field forsakes her new-born fawn, because there is no grass" (Jer. 14:5).

Case Study: The Leopard

The ancients appear to have derived their knowledge of wild animals from two sources: their ideas and understanding of the wild could have developed through observation of the animals. However, biblical authors could have been exposed to literature from the Levant, Mesopotamia, and Egypt and adopt that perception of the wild via a cultural contact with other societies. This literary corpora could have generated common ideas as authors of ancient Near Eastern literature relating to the faunal world and human-animal relations.

The complexity of the biblical authors' knowledge may be illustrated here by a carnivore, whose natural residence is outside the walls: the leopard. For my present purposes, I am assuming the biblical leopard to be the same animal we know today.⁶ While the royal Assyrian inscriptions indicate that leopards were frequently hunted and ancient iconography depicts the way in which their skins were used as a garment, ancient Near Eastern literature—mythology, epics, proverbs, royal inscriptions—rarely notes their habitat, behavior, or characteristics.⁷ We may thus assume that the biblical authors developed their understanding of the leopard under little or no influence from foreign written traditions.⁸

The Hebrew Bible refers to the leopard (*Panthera pardus*) on seven occasions— five times in the prophets (Isa. 11:6; Jer. 5:6; 13:23; Hos. 13:7; Hab. 1:8), once in Canticles (4:8), and once in Daniel (7:6). The largest predator to survive in Israel, its yellow body with dark spots enables it to camouflage itself in light and shaded

---

5. MT Jer. 14:6 "וּפְרָאִים֙ עָמְד֣וּ עַל־שְׁפָיִ֔ם שָׁאֲפ֥וּ ר֖וּחַ כַּתַּנִּ֑ים כָּל֥וּ עֵינֵיהֶ֖ם כִּי־אֵ֥ין עֵֽשֶׂב" פראים refers to wild ass (פרא pl.). In contrast to MT, the Septuagint translates ὄνοι ἄγριοι ("wild ass") but avoids the comparison to jackals כַּתַּנִּים.

6. The names of the animals by which they are known today do not necessarily correspond to those employed in ancient times. I shall not address the issue of identification, however. See DNI Bible: https://dni.tau.ac.il/dictionary-entry/leopard-נמר-panthera-pa (accessed August 18, 2023).

7. See Aššur-bel-kala 07, iv 22; Ashurnasirpal II 002, 37; Shalmaneser III 016, 347; Nadine Nys and Joachim Bretscheider, "Research on the Iconography of the Leopard," *UF* 39 (2008): 555–615.

8. Cf. also the she-bear who is robbed of her young (Hos. 13:8), a behavior not noted in ancient Near Eastern literature—although royal inscriptions do differentiate between hunted male bear and female bear (Ashurnasirpal II 002, 35). See Dorit Pomerantz, "Outside the Walls: The Portrayal of Wild Animals in the Hebrew Bible and Ancient Near Eastern Literature" (MA thesis, Tel Aviv University, 2019) (Hebrew).

vegetation while ambushing its potential prey—a skill that offsets its inability to run rapidly over long distances.⁹

Isaiah 11 refers to the leopard and other wild carnivores alongside domesticated animals: "The wolf shall dwell with the lamb, the leopard lie down with the kid, the calf, the beast of prey, and the fatling together, with a little boy to herd them. The cow and the bear shall graze, their young shall lie down together; and the lion, like the ox, shall eat straw" (Isa. 11:6-7). Wild carnivores frequently represent Israel's enemies in the Hebrew Bible (cf. Isa. 5:29; Jer. 2:15); this prophecy appears to express the hope that the four largest wild predators will become non-violent domesticated herbivores in the future, symbolizing the disappearance of injustice, violence, and destruction.¹⁰

Jer. 5:6 treats the leopard as one of the enemies whom God will send to punish the houses of Israel and Judah: "The lion of the forest strikes them down, the wolf of the desert ravages them. A leopard lies in wait by their towns; whoever leaves them will be torn in pieces." The four short independent clauses in this verse evince the habitat and behavior of each of the predators. The lion, wolf, and leopard represent the threat posed by the wilderness: the lion comes from the forest, the wolf approaches from the steppe or desert, and the leopard lurks outside the city. All hope of deliverance is thus cut off. Whoever goes out will be devoured, with no one escaping punishment.¹¹ The root שקד reflects the leopard's practice of ambushing its prey outside walled settlements (see Figure 2.3).¹²

Hosea similarly notes how leopards prowl around cities and inhabited regions: "So I am become a lion to them, like a leopard I lurk on the way; like a bear robbed of her young ..." (13:7-8). Here, rather than sending a foreign army, God himself turns on his people. Having brought them out of Egypt and cared for them (vv. 4-6), they believed he would continue to protect them. Instead, God acts like an enraged predator. The lurking leopard lying in wait for its prey along the road emphasizes the element of surprise—of unexpected turn of events, the surprise facing the punished people of Israel (and Ephraim); God's decision to punish rather than extend grace to the Israelites. Since the leopard's anatomy prevents it from running fast and over long distances like the cheetah, it seeks to ambush its prey.¹³ Thus, when Habakkuk describes the enemy's fast steeds (1:8), he probably refers to the cheetah rather than the leopard: "Their horses are swifter than leopards, fleeter than wolves of the steppe."

---

9. Heinrich Mendelssohn and Yoram Yom-Tov, *Plants and Animals of the Land of Israel: An Illustrated Encyclopedia* (Tel Aviv: Ministry of Defense, 1987), 225; Menachem Dor, *Fauna in the Times of the Bible, Mishna and Talmud* (Tel Aviv: GraphOr-Deftel, 1997) (Hebrew).

10. See, for example, Yehuda Felix, *Nature and Land in the Bible: Chapters in Biblical Ecology* (Jerusalem: Ruben Mass, 1992), 167 (Hebrew); J. J. M. Roberts, *First Isaiah*, Hermeneia (Minneapolis: Fortress, 2015), 180.

11. William Holladay, *Jeremiah*, Hermeneia (Philadelphia: Fortress, 1986), 179.

12. For שקד as "lurking," see BDB, 1052.

13. Dor, *Fauna*, 63–65.

Figure 2.3 "The lion of the forest strikes them down, the wolf of the desert ravages them" (Jer. 5:6). Photo: Yosi Rubin.

Jeremiah's familiarity with the leopard's yellow fur and dark spots—"Can the Cushite change his skin, or the leopard his spots?" (Jer. 13:23)—led him to draw an analogy between it and the Jerusalemites (see Figure 2.4). Just as the leopard cannot change its spotted fur for a solid color nor the naturally dark-skinned person become lighter, so the Judahites cannot change their behavior for the better.[14] This rhetorical question in the service of the argument that a person habituated to sin cannot alter his or her conduct rests on good zoological grounds:

1. the leopard is not sexually dimorphic. Both male and female (unlike lion and lioness, deer and doe) bear the same markings;
2. its spots appear at birth and never fade—unlike lion cubs, whose leg spots vanish when they mature or wild boar, who lose their stripes at around four to five months;
3. its appearance does not change significantly with the seasons—in contrast to deer, for example, who lose their antlers.
4. every leopard has its own distinctive marking.[15]

14. No evidence exists that the melanistic leopard or black panther ever inhabited Israel, the reference being solely to the spotted species: see Andrew Brett Stein and Virginia Hayssen, "Panthera Pardus (Carnivora: Felidea)," *Mammalian Species* 45, no. 900 (2013): 30–48.

15. Ibid.; Dor, *Fauna*, 63.

Figure 2.4 "Can the Cushite change his skin, or the leopard his spots?" (Jer. 13:23). Photo: Yosi Rubin.

The leopard's physiology and characteristics, thus, well illustrate that the Jerusalemites will not change their ways and abandon their idol worship to walk in God's ways.

Daniel dreams of four animals arising from the depths:

> Four mighty beasts different from each other emerged from the sea. The first was like a lion … Then I saw a second, different beast, which was like a bear … After that, as I looked on, there was another one, like a leopard, and it had on its back four wings like those of a bird; the beast had four heads, and dominion was given to it. After that … there was a fourth beast … and it had ten horns.
>
> (Dan. 7:6-7)

These may represent enemy kingdoms from the past and present: the lion Babylon or Assyria, the bear the Medes, the leopard Persia, and the fourth creature the Greek or Seleucid Antiochus IV Epiphanes.[16]

Only in one text is the leopard not portrayed as a predator or an immediate threat. This nonetheless gradually narrows its focus onto the dangerous location whence the beloved comes: "From Lebanon … from Amana's peak, from the peak of Senir and Hermon, from the dens of lions, from the hills of leopards" (Cant. 4:8).[17] This reflects the author's familiarity with the fact that mountains are a favorite habitat of leopards.

---

16. According to Rapaport, the leopard's four heads may symbolize the four kings of Persia: Uriel Rappaport, *Bible World: Daniel, Ezra and Nehemiah*, 6th edn (Tel Aviv: Divre Hayamim Publishing, 2002), 68–72.

17. Yair Zakovitch, *The Song of Songs*, Mikra Leyisra'el (Tel Aviv: Am Oved; Jerusalem: Magnes, 1992), 91 (Hebrew). See also Ps. 76:5b.

While it cannot be categorically determined whether all the biblical authors had personal experience of leopards, they demonstrate an ecological and biological knowledge of their appearance and predatory nature.

Human-animal Interaction

Carnivores are portrayed in the Hebrew Bible as predators in their interaction with human beings in four realms—hunting, "zoological gardens," war, and herding flocks.

Hunting

Hunting provided the ancients with protein-rich food, clothing, and tools. Since it became unnecessary once animals were domesticated, its continued existence raises numerous questions. Did people engage in it in order to diversify their food sources, or was it a way of protecting themselves and their property? Did it grant prestige, honor, or social status?

The profession of hunter is first mentioned in Genesis (10:9; 25:27; 27:3). While several hunting scenes occur elsewhere in the biblical texts, only two laws indicate its practice—Lev. 17:13 and Deut. 12:22. Although biblical literature contains no direct parallels to the Mesopotamian kings' boasts of their prolific hunting tours, the biblical texts allude to the activity of hunting indirectly—albeit not in the service of royal ideology.[18] For example, in emphasizing David's physical prowess in the face of Goliath, 1 Sam. 17:34-36 states that David hunted in order to protect his father's flocks. Benaiah b. Jehoiada likewise proved his worthiness for a commission in David's army by killing a lion (2 Sam. 23:20).

Hunting involved following and chasing, observing animal behavior, and—once caught—physical contact with the prey. The prophets employ the metaphor of hunting in order to draw on their audience's familiarity with the powerlessness of the hunted and might of the hunter. Thus, they frequently describe Israel's enemies as predators in order to reproach leaders and people alike: "And after that I will send for many hunters, and they shall hunt them out of every mountain and out of every hill and out of the clefts of the rocks" (Jer. 16:16).

Biblical literature also cites the equipment used by hunters: nets (רשת) (cf. Ezek. 12:13a), snares/holes/pits (פח) (cf. Jer. 48:43-44; Hos. 5:1b), traps (פחת/מוקש) (cf. Isa. 24:18; Amos 3:5), and bows and arrows (קשת וחיצים) (cf. Isa. 7:24). These devices demonstrate knowledge of various techniques, heightening the verisimilitude of the hunting scenes. Thus, they enable their audience/readers to imagine and visualize the scenes described. For example, Isaiah's description of the Jerusalemites as wild animals chased through the narrow streets of the city until they fall exhausted in an enclosed space—"Your sons lie in a swoon at the corner of every street—like an antelope caught in a net" (Isa. 51:20)—may refer to the use of kites. Deer, gazelles, and oryx may similarly have been driven into a wide

---

18. Cf. Ashurnasirpal II 030, 110; Aššur-bel-kala 07, iv 1.

opening between two low (or hidden) walls that gradually became higher and more tightly spaced in a V shape in order to cut off their escape route.[19]

The use of metaphors of hunting and hunting tools evinces the biblical authors' exploitation of their audience's acquaintance with the art of hunting to demonstrate the polarization of power between predator and prey and the inevitability of punishment for sin.

Zoological Gardens

Ancient Near East royal inscriptions contain elaborate descriptions of wild animals captured alive.[20] These were occasionally brought into enclosed settlements or kept in proximity to the walls in "zoological gardens." This not only signaled the king's wealth and recreational opportunities but also control and domination over the wild as well as human subjects.[21] Wild animals and birds were given as gifts (e.g., 1 Kgs 10:22), paid as taxes, sacrificed in temples, used for their feathers and eggs—and possibly served as a method of punishment (e.g., Dan. 6:17).[22]

The Hebrew Bible does refer to royal gardens (e.g., 2 Kgs 25:4; Jer. 39:4; Neh. 3:15). These may have housed wild animals as a way of facilitating viewing and experiencing the wilderness—roaming gazelles and deer providing access to nature without the need to travel far. The king may also have used them to practice his hunting skills, taking advantage of enclosed spaces close to his palace.[23] The fact that the gardens were located within or near the walls enabled controlled contact with the tamed wilderness.[24]

Wars

Soldiers came into contact with wild animals in several ways. War not only pitted men against men but also cast them to the dogs, carnivores devouring the corpses of the dead before they could be buried: "I will give their carcasses as food to the birds of the sky and the beasts of the earth" (Jer. 19:7b). Animals also invaded

19. Guy Bar-Oz, Dani Nadel, Uzi Avner, and Dan Malkinson, "Mass Hunting Game Traps in the Southern Levant," *Near Eastern Archaeology* 74, no. 4 (2011): 208–15.

20. Tiglath-pileser I 01, vi 85; Sennacherib 8, 4.

21. Chikako E. Watanabe, *Animal Symbolism in Mesopotamia: A Contextual Approach* (Vienna: Institut für Orientalistik, Universität Wien, 2002); Benjamin R. Foster, "Animals in Mesopotamian Literature," in *A History of Animal World in the Ancient Near East*, ed. Billie Jean Collins, Handbuch der Orientalistik 64 (Leiden: Brill, 2002), 271–88.

22. Berthold Laufer, *Ostrich Egg-Shell Cups from Mesopotamia and the Ostrich in Ancient and Modern Times* (Chicago: Field Museum of Natural History, 1926). The Black Obelisk of Shalmaneser III (858–824 BCE) describes a tribute that included wild animals. For sacrifices, see Tiglath-pileser I 01, vi 85.

23. Felix, *Nature and Land in the Bible*, 40.

24. The Assyrian royal gardens were located close to the royal palaces at Nimrud, Khorsabad, and Nineveh: see Pauline Albenda, "Assyrian Royal Hunts: Antlered and Horned Animals from Distant Lands," *BASOR* 349 (2008): 61–78.

the ruins of settlements, making them their dwelling place: "Because of Mount Zion, which lies desolate; jackals prowl over it" (Lam. 5:18). This process started with the abandonment of villages or cities after a defeat (e.g., Jer. 5:17), leading to the growth of wild thorns (Isa. 34:13a). Herbivores, such as rodents, followed on their heels and in their wake small carnivores—jackals and foxes: "It shall be a home of jackals, an abode of ostriches" (Isa. 34:13b).

This metaphor of small wild animals taking over what once were human dwellings emphasizes the profound change from settlements to wilderness and the chaotic nature of the destruction. While war pitted men against men, the battlefield after defeat brought the dead into contact with wild animals. In the last stage—of abandoned cities—all human-animal interaction ceased in forsaken cities and settlements, spelling tragedy for the former inhabitants. Animals that normally would have kept their distance from settlements now came and made them their own, embodying the invasion of the wilderness, faunal domination, and human helplessness.

Herding

Herding prompted an undesirable but inescapable interaction between human beings, domesticated animals, and wild predators. Ancient shepherds took their flocks some distance from the walls in order to avoid conflict with nearby settlements or with farmers whose agricultural fields were in the vicinity. Domesticated animals passing through cultivated zones caused damage to crops:

> They would attack them, destroy the produce of the land all the way to Gaza, and leave no means of sustenance in Israel, not a sheep or an ox or an ass. For they would come up with their livestock and their tents, swarming as thick as locusts; they and their camels were innumerable. Thus they would invade the land and ravage it.
>
> (Judg. 6:4-5)

Areas designated for agriculture were, thus, clearly marked off from the wilderness: "He built towers in the wilderness and hewed out many cisterns, for he had much cattle, and farmers in the foot-hills and on the plain" (2 Chron. 26:10). As shepherds looked for pasture far away from fields, they encountered difficult conditions in the wilderness—lack of water and pasture (e.g., Jer. 14:3-4), exposure to the heat of the sun—causing them to look for caves and shade under rocks (e.g., Isa. 32:2b)—and attack by wild animals. Since sheep and goats move more slowly than wild herbivores, they are an easy prey for wild carnivores.

By night, the shepherds kept their sheep and goats in fenced enclosures, making it easier to protect them: "We will build here sheepfolds for our flocks ..." (Num. 32:16a). During the day, however, lions, leopards, wolves, and jackals were always lurking to pounce on sheep that wandered off from under the shepherd's watchful eye as the flocks spread over the grazing area (cf. Ezek. 34:4b-6).

The prophets were familiar with herding culture and the danger shepherds faced in the wilderness. Thus, they adduce these to describe God's relationship with his people. As owner of the flock, God is invested in protecting it and ensuring its well-being: "As a lion—a great beast—growls over its prey and, when the shepherds gather in force against him, is not dismayed by their cries nor cowed by their noise …" (Isa. 31:4). Although God "hired" shepherds to lead the flock, they often neglected their duties: "My flock is scattered all over the face of the earth, with none to take thought of them and none to seek them … my flock has been a spoil—My flock has been a prey for all the wild beasts, for want of anyone to tend them" (Ezek. 34:5, 8). As God instructs Zechariah to tend the sheep meant for slaughter, the shepherds wail as the fires consume the pastures, and the wild animals roar over their ravaged habitat (Zech. 11).

The prophets also portray God as a wild carnivore who attacks the flocks: "So I am become like a lion to them, like a leopard I lurk on the way. Like a bear robbed of her young I attack them and rip open the casing of their hearts; I will devour them there like a lion, the beasts of the field shall mangle them" (Hos. 13:7-8). The actions of these three predators highlight the threat the wilderness poses to human beings and their habitat.

Conclusion

Biblical authors employ metaphoric language based on knowledge of the wilderness. In general, they were familiar with wild animals, accurately describing their habitat, appearance, and behavior. While some written conventions and traditions relating to wild animals—lions and royal power, foxes and ruins, for example—may have existed, the biblical faunal imagery suggests personal experience of the wild. The case study of the leopard demonstrates that, without an apparent Mesopotamian tradition of the leopard to follow, the Hebrew Bible treats it as an enemy who attacks unexpectedly, its employment of the element of surprise serving as a metaphor for the enemies sent by God to punish Israel when they least expected to be assaulted.

The biblical authors represent the danger of interacting with leopards, lions, bears, and wolves—all of whom symbolize the menace posed by the wilderness. Smaller carnivores, in contrast, are more closely associated with ruins, where human habitation is replaced by foxes and jackals. Wild herbivores, such as gazelles, deer, and ibex, metaphorically symbolize the pursuit of individuals or the Israelites as a whole.

Knowledge of the wilderness from personal experience or information gained from others while trading in remote locations, hunting, visiting royal gardens, dealing with the aftermath of battle, and shepherding all lie behind the biblical authors' faunal imagery—in narrative accounts, or through similes and metaphors that impart a deeper meaning to the text and devices that elicit greater emotions in their readers. As a well-known phenomenon, human-animal interaction serves as a way of enriching the text and giving it a more profound significance.

Bibliography

Albenda, Pauline. "Assyrian Royal Hunts: Antlered and Horned Animals from Distant Lands." *BASOR* 349 (2008): 61–78.

Bar-Oz, Guy Bar-Oz, Dani Nadel, Uzi Avner, and Dan Malkinson. "Mass Hunting Game Traps in the Southern Levant." *Near Eastern Archaeology* 74, no. 4 (2011): 208–15.

Berlin, Adele. "Introduction to Hebrew Poetry." In *The First Book of Maccabees; the Second Book of Maccabees; Introduction to Hebrew Poetry; the Book of Job; the Book of Psalms*, edited by Leander E. Keck, 301–15. The New Interpreter's Bible 4. Nashville, TN: Abingdon, 1999.

Borowski, Oded. *Every Living Thing: Daily Use of Animals in Ancient Israel*. Walnut Creek, CA: AltaMira, 1998.

Brown Francis, Samuel R. Driver, and Charles A. Briggs. *A Hebrew and English Lexicon of the Old Testament*. Oxford: Clarendon, 1907 (BDB).

Dor, Menachem. *Fauna in the Times of the Bible, Mishna and Talmud*. Tel Aviv: GraphOr-Defte, 1997 (Hebrew).

Felix, Yehuda. *Nature and Land in the Bible: Chapters in Biblical Ecology*. Jerusalem: Ruben Mass, 1992 (Hebrew).

Forti, Tova. *Like a Lone Bird on a Roof: Animal Imagery and the Structure of Psalms*. Winona Lake, IN: Eisenbrauns, 2018.

Foster, Benjamin R. "Animals in Mesopotamian Literature." In *A History of Animal World in the Ancient Near East*, edited by Billie Jean Collins, 271–88. Handbuch der Orientalistik 64. Leiden: Brill, 2002.

Holladay, William. *Jeremiah*. Hermeneia. Philadelphia: Fortress, 1986.

Johnson, Mark and Georg Lakoff. *Metaphors We Live By*. Chicago: University of Chicago Press, 2003.

Laufer, Berthold. *Ostrich Egg-Shell Cups from Mesopotamia and the Ostrich in Ancient and Modern Times*. Chicago: Field Museum of Natural History, 1926.

Mendelssohn, Heinrich and Yoram Yom-Tov. *Fauna and Flora of the Land of Israel: Mammals*. Tel Aviv: Ministry of Defense, 1987 (Hebrew).

Nys, Nadine, and Joachim Bretscheider. "Research on the Iconography of the Leopard." *UF* 39 (2008): 555–615.

Patrick, D. P. "The Imperial Gardens of Mesopotamia: Landscapes of Power." MA thesis, University of Guelph, 2016.

Pomerantz, Dorit. "Outside the Walls: The Portrayal of Wild Animals in the Hebrew Bible and Ancient Near Eastern Literature." MA thesis, Tel Aviv University, 2018 (Hebrew).

Rappaport, Uriel. *Bible World: Daniel, Ezra and Nehemiah*. 6th edn. Tel Aviv: Divre Hayamim Publishing, 2002.

Roberts, J. J. M. *First Isaiah*. Hermeneia. Minneapolis: Fortress, 2015.

Stein, Andrew Brett, and Virginia Hayssen. "Panthera Pardus (Carnivora: Felidea)." *Mammalian Species* 45, no. 900 (2013): 30–48.

Watanabe, Chikako E., *Animal Symbolism in Mesopotamia: A Contextual Approach*. Vienna: Institut für Orientalistik, Universität Wien, 2002.

Zakovitch, Yair. *The Song of Songs*. Mikra Leyisraʾel. Tel Aviv: Am Oved; Jerusalem: Magnes, 1992 (Hebrew).

Chapter 3

FLORA AND FAUNA IN THE METAPHORICAL LANDSCAPES OF THE SONG OF SONGS

Martien A. Halvorson-Taylor

This volume considers "how 'wild' is defined" in ancient Israel, particularly in its interaction with the "domestic," a question I seek to answer in the context of the Song of Songs. This issue has been explored using a number of different methods, including critical spatial theory,[1] as well as other related approaches.[2] The findings have been illuminating, but there remain other possible approaches, such as how the syntax, metaphors, and genres contribute to the construction of the "wild" over and against the "domestic." Here, one can consider how the metaphors and poetic forms of the Song draw on and contribute to the representation of the wild; and, further, how the Song's redaction—the process by which poems were assembled, juxtaposed, and linked—depends upon and contributes to those representations. In the Song, "wild" is constructed through the tinge of metaphor, by the cross-pollination of lexical contiguity, and by the forms of poetry that it subsumes. Or, to

---

1. For example, see Yvonne Sophie Thöne, *Liebe zwischen Stadt und Feld: Raum and Geschlecht im Hohelied* (Berlin: Lit, 2012); Anselm C. Hagedorn, "Place and Space in the Song of Songs," *ZAW* 127 (2015): 207-23; and Christopher Meredith, *Journeys in the Songscape: Space and the Song of Songs* (Sheffield: Sheffield Phoenix, 2013).

2. Marcia Falk (*Love Lyrics from the Bible: A Translation and Literary Study of the Song of Songs* [Sheffield: Almond, 1982], 88-91) perceives a pattern in the various poems' "contexts," which she defines as "setting" and "ambiance"; isolating four settings—countryside, wild, interior environments, city streets—she finds a strong connection to ambiance, namely, how the setting is or is not conducive to love: The countryside supports love, the wild highlights the mysterious and elusive aspects of love, love is consummated in interior space, the city streets are dangerous, etc. But for each of these, there are notable exceptions that seriously broach the distinctions, as Falk herself notes. And, considering this approach diachronically, it is no wonder that there is variance given the Song's literary layers (and the multiple provenances of those layers); while it has strong thematic resonances, the Song's multiple contributors may not be expected to sustain a singular or resolved treatment of space.

put it more polemically, I am skeptical that the wild is "defined" since a definition has an air of finality for which the Song does not settle. The significance of the wild in the Song is its pluriform expression and manifestation; it is suggested, mooted, transformed, but never firmly defined. Accounting for this process has the advantage of not trying to harness the Song's diversity or systematize its language but, instead, to follow its course.

I will begin by observing several initial strategies by which the Song, in its current form, conveys the wild over and against the domestic or the domesticated, which include metaphor and the literary hybridity that results from a poem that one may argue was assembled over time but at the very least contains subunits with different genres and settings. Keeping these in mind, I will then consider, in greater detail, one of the longest sustained poems on the wild, the poem in 2:8-17 that features the lover approaching, leaping upon the mountains, bounding like a wild animal, a gazelle or a young stag. These strategies give us a view into the particular ways in which the poem navigates wild and domestic.[3] For one, the Song's resplendent metaphors, which draw on rich images of the wild, as well as key terms like קול, which apply to multiple species, serve to destabilize the distinctions between "wild" and "domestic." The Song, further, contains interweaving descriptions of the wild and the domestic, as well as interleaving poetic forms and genres; the Song's representation of the wild and the domestic comes about through the relationship between the two when they are laid side by side, so that the relationship between wild and domestic will be brought into sharper focus by noting the diversity of literary forms, the jostling between and juxtaposition of various different settings for its scenes. In the process, the representation of the wild will, in fact, elide the distinction between the wild and the domestic—as well as troubling suppositions about female and male space.[4] And, along the way, with our colleagues in environmental studies, the reader may recover the nonhuman actors, the other living and sometimes breathing forces—flora, fauna, eco-systems—within the text, to discover a fuller cast of beings in the Song, one that challenges in a whole new way the boundary between wild and domestic.

---

3. See also Elaine James (*Landscapes of the Song of Songs: Poetry and Place* [New York: Oxford University Press, 2017], 16–23) on how the poetry of the Song, and particularly 2:8-17, and its representation of "landscape" negotiates the relationship between the lovers and their environments.

4. Anselm C. Hagedorn ("Place and Space in the Song of Songs," 209) has considered the false separation of private and public space particularly as it applies to the Song. Not only was "an absolute separation of the spheres impossible to maintain" in the ancient world, the association between female and private space vs. male and public space does not map on to reality. While these categories are different from those considered in this chapter, Hagedorn's more general caution of the problems that strict distinctions of space—particularly binary oppositions—will inevitably encounter is worth keeping in mind.

As a general observation, the "wild" of the Song does not always resemble the wild, the wildness, or the wilderness in certain other biblical texts. Its view is distinctive in part because of the perspectives of its poets, which are relentlessly life-affirming, but also because it perceives a different "wild" than, say, those texts that associate terms like יער and שדה with danger, devastation, and wild animals.[5] The poets of the Song have in view something more like "nature" in surveying not only the cultivated vineyards and gardens but also the great out-of-doors that are its setting, rather than death-defying wilderness and desert.[6] That the poets do not find the "wilds of nature" threatening, then, says as much about what spaces are in their orbit as their perspective. But, also, their wild is selected, invoked, and described for a particular purpose: the context for the lovers, but also the fields and ranges for the metaphors by which they will describe each other. And, perhaps because of this, the range is limited to aspects of the wild that convey the lovers' perception of each other as beautiful and desirable. In this sense, the poets appropriate (perhaps even subdue) the wild for the purposes of their poetry—in a sense not far off from how the first humans are to "subdue" and "have dominion" over creation (Gen. 1:28).

5. In the Hebrew Bible, "wild" does not correspond to one term. Moreover, these terms have differing connotations and associations in different books and compositional layers. Focusing on terms that dominate in the Hebrew Bible and that also appear in the Song, one can see the multiple ways they figure across the collection: (1) יער, for example, which appears in Song 2:3, figures in Ps. 104:20–22 in relation to animals; the "animals of the forest (יער)" and the "young lions" are associated especially with the darkness (and dangers) of the night. And in 2 Sam. 18:8, the dangers of the "forest" (again, יער) are laid with a different nuance in David's early battle against the Israelites at the forest of Ephraim: וירב היער לאכל בעם מאשר אכלה החרב ביום ההוא "the forest consumed more of the people on that day than did the sword." There is also (2) שדה to consider, which appears in Song 2:7; 3:5; 7:12 (Eng v. 11): in certain texts, שדה, appears to be a cultivated field (Prov. 23:10; 24:27)—although, even if it is a cultivated field, it may still be associated with danger (the murder of Abel may be an example, Gen. 4:8); in other settings, it appears to refer to the space outside the protection of the city ("the open country" in Mic. 4:10; and again, in contrast to the city, Deut. 22:25–27) and in others it refers to animals "of the field," more specifically "wild" animals (so, the serpent of Gen. 3:1; cf. the refrain of Song 2:7; 3:5 באילות השדה, in which the noun is a modifier to mean "wild" or at least "undomesticated"). There is also (3) "the wilderness," המדבר, which appears twice in the Song, 3:6 and 8:5, echoes of a refrain that either have been reworked into a new context (in the first case) or that stand alone (the second)—in either case, not particularly disclosive of the meaning of the term. See further the chapter in this volume by Dalit Rom-Shiloni.

6. There are also other references to "untamed" or wilder topographies within the Song. For example, in the very poem that is central to our focus, 2:8-17, there is the reference to the lover, like a wild gazelle or young stag, "bounding over mountains, leaping over hills" (vv. 8-9) and the dove "in the clefts of the rock, in the covert of a cliff" (v. 14a; see חגוי הסלע also in Jer. 49:16 and Obad. 3, where it refers to a high, inaccessible place).

Metaphor and Juxtaposition

In the Song's opening chapters, there are several literary strategies—involving simile, metaphor, and also simple juxtaposition—by which the poems both negotiate and transgress the boundaries between wild and domestic.[7] The first is how the lovers represent themselves and each other, eventually becoming, in fits and starts, the living things to which they liken themselves. Early in the Song, already by the end of the first chapter, the lovers begin to cast themselves as the flora and fauna of the natural world around them. The first moves are tentative, through comparison: לססתי ברכבי פרעה דמיתיך רעיתי, 1:9; "to the mare, of a Pharaoh's chariot, / I compare you, my friend." And these are marked by subjective perspective: צרור המר דודי לי ... אשכל הכפר דודי לי; *to her*, he is a bundle of myrrh, to *her*, he is a cluster of Henna (1:13-14). Very quickly, however, their qualifications recede, as he announces that her eyes *are* doves (עיניך יונים, v. 15) and she announces, "I *am* a narcissus of the plain, a lotus of the valley" (אני חבצלת השרון שושנת העמקים, 2:1). "Like a lotus (כשושנה) among brambles, / so is my friend among women!" he says, to which she responds, "like an apricot tree (כתפוח) among the trees of the thicket, / so is my beloved among men"—"In his shade, I delight to remain ..." (2:2-3, בצלו חמדתי וישבתי).

Having described themselves not only by, but as the trees and flowers of their landscape, the lovers dress their set, which will further blur the boundary between "wild" and "domestic" in imagining their spaces. In her description in 1:16b-17, the woman likens their natural setting to a house—"our home"—an image she extends through the references to "our couch," "beams," and "rafters": "... אף ערשנו רעננה קרות בתינו ארזים רחיטנו (ק: רהיטנו) ברותים, [indeed] our couch is luxuriously verdant;/the beams of our house are cedars; our rafters, cypresses." She imagines the natural surroundings through the metaphor of a built environment, transforming the trees and the green bower into its frame and couch and claiming it as "their" space.[8] Michael V. Fox maintains that the woman regards this abode more specifically "as a house of royal luxury,"[9] perhaps under the influence of the royal imagery at the start of the poem (esp. 1:9, 12). It may be, too, that the substance of the building materials—the cedar and the cypresses—also evoke

---

7. For a fuller exploration of the metaphors of the Song, see Brian P. Gault, *Body as Landscape, Love as Intoxication: Conceptual Metaphors in the Song of Songs*, Ancient Israel and Its Literature 36 (Atlanta: SBL, 2019).

8. It may be that a couple that cannot meet in their respective homes instead are left to imagine within the wilds of the forest a common home that they build and furnish together—free from the gaze of the Women of Jerusalem and the night guards. This would be a vivid example of George Lakoff and Mark Johnson's (*Metaphors We Live By* [Chicago: University of Chicago Press, 1980], 157) assertion that metaphors "have the power to define reality."

9. Michael Fox, *The Song of Songs and the Ancient Egyptian Love Songs* (Madison: University of Wisconsin Press, 1985), 104.

the Jerusalem palace and Temple;[10] in this reading, she is, then, projecting this royal vision onto the cedars and cypresses that loom above the lovers. Though cedar and cypresses stand in for actual building materials in 2 Sam. 7 and 1 Kgs 6, here the references appear metaphorically. The particle אף with its additive sense of "how much more so!" provides a tip off that she continues to spin subjective description; the reference to the luxuriant greenery[11] will tilt the poem toward a fuller network in which natural features are pressed into service, in a flight of fancy, to create "their home." Most commentators view the language of their house as a metaphor for their intimate natural surroundings.[12] Her language may gesture to the majesty of a royal building, it may claim the private space of a humbler abode, but it more certainly celebrates the lofty trees and verdant bowers which provide the setting in which the lovers luxuriate in their intimacy.

Here we might consider how both target and source bring something to the metaphor—in our case, the semantic range of a domestic structure and the semantic range of natural growth, flora, and trees. And, in this case, meaning may not simply be "transferred" from one term to another, from source to target (despite the implication in the Greek that lies behind the term "metaphor"); source and target create meaning by joining their systems of association and, the source, like the target, here undergoes a degree of revision because of the interaction.[13] To recognize metaphor's "interanimative" capacities means to recognize that, through metaphor, target and source can be mutually illuminating if not destabilized; Shakespeare's "all the world's a stage" is not far from imagining the stage as a world—by which the source and target have been revised. This does not happen with all metaphors, and our field's strong turn toward Conceptual Metaphor Theory, in particular, has turned against presuming this exchange. But, in this

10. For example, 2 Sam. 7:2, 7; 1 Kgs 6:9, 10, 15.

11. Unlike ארזים and ברותים, which can be both the actual tree and also its material, רעננה refers to the greenery of trees and not to building materials.

12. For example, Roland Murphy, *The Song of Songs*, Hermeneia: A Critical & Historical Commentary on the Bible (Minneapolis: Fortress, 1990), 135–6; Fox, *The Song of Songs*, 104; Michael Fishbane, *The Song of Songs*, Jewish Publication Society Bible Commentary (Philadelphia: Jewish Publication Society, 2015), 51–53. Othmar Keel (*The Song of Songs*, Continental Commentary Series [Minneapolis: Fortress, 1994], 68, 73) argues that "one can properly read the three nominal clauses [of 1:16b-17] as wishes rather than statements" and that while both a literal and figurative meaning is possible, the latter is probable.

13. As Janet Soskice (*Metaphor and Religious Language* [London: Oxford University Press, 1985]) has reminded us in her "interanimative" theory of metaphor, the target (or tenor, as she calls it) is immersed in the system of associations that surrounds the source domain (or vehicle), but so is the source immersed in that of the target. One of the ways that metaphors create meaning is by joining the systems of associations or domains of target and source; both target and source are transformed in the process. The source, in our case, the metaphor of the home, undergoes change through its contact with the target, the natural world. See, too, Paul Rocœur, *Interpretation Theory: Discourse and the Surplus of Meaning* (Fort Worth: Texas Christian University, 1976), 63–68.

particular case, it is fruitful to consider how, when the language of the domestic is used to describe the natural world, its potential meaning, a glimmer of thought, runs along the other direction. The consideration is further warranted because of the lack of general markers—or "salient features"—for where the lovers are at any given moment; there is precious little to stand in the way of this kind of exchange.

Reading the interaction between source and target as interanimative transforms the lovers' depiction of—if not their understanding of—their reality. So that, as the woman likens the natural setting to a built environment, the comparison hints at the reverse. It may be that her (domestic) bed is reanimated into a leafy bank; or it may be that the actual rafters of her house, made of cypress or cedar, become, in her imagination, *living* cypress and cedar. The house, if it is one at all, lives and breathes. It is a natural collaborator with the lovers; these are living trees and leafy beds. In this way, a tree is not a resource, not material, not lumber, but rather an actor, a nonhuman actor, but a collaborator nonetheless, in the lovers' scene; it is the beam of the lovers' house and it is the beloved himself at one point (2:3). The lovers are *as* entangled with these nonhuman actors as they are with one another. Their story is a collaboration with the natural world.[14] The lovers, as elements of the wild themselves, infuse any structure they inhabit with verdant life. Their expressions of love and their admiration for one another breathe life into structures of wood, rendering them living beings.

The ambiguity of the leafy bed is but one example of the Song's many moves from wild to domestic and back again, which has the effect of blurring easy distinctions between the two. This is accomplished through the inversions that can be an implicit part of some metaphors. But further, within discrete poems and from one poem to the next, the Song skips from location to location with the prerogative of poetry, defying narrative's concern for chronology and plot. Either by redaction or by authorial intent, or both, these sudden shifts in scene are a literary means by which the wild and the domestic are also juxtaposed and the borders between them are made porous, transgressed, analogous to the workings of metaphor. Already between the first poem (1:2-4) and the second (vv. 5-6), the Song has travelled to, and then from, the royal bed chambers (v. 4) on to Qedar[15] and perhaps Salmah[16] (1:5) back to the local vineyard (v. 6) and then, by the

---

14. See also Hos. 2, esp. vv. 16-25 (Eng. vv. 14-23), and also 14:5-9 (Eng. 14:4-8), passages that have been compared to the Song, in which YHWH returns to Israel in love and the wilderness blooms. Love, and specifically sexual love, awakens the natural environment.

15. קדר may designate the tribe of Qedar (Gen. 25:13), though it may also evoke the related verbal form, קדר, "to be dark," thus also functioning as a synonym for שחורה, "black," in the previous line.

16. MT points this as, "Solomon," which is also how it is rendered in LXX. But some (e.g., Marvin Pope, *Song of Songs: A New Translation with Introduction and Commentary*, AYB [Garden City, NY: Doubleday, 1977]) prefer to repoint this as *Salmah*, another nomadic Arabian tribe, to make the phrase parallel to the tribe of Qedar; this is not necessary, even if it may be in the background. At least by the time of the shaping of the MT, the word is meant to evoke Solomonic splendor.

third poem, to the shepherds' camp of her lover (another kind of domestic area that is not settled or urban, v. 8). This kind of rapid change in setting produces a juxtaposition not unlike the juxtaposition of target and source, whereby domestic spaces are leafy green and crawl with life and the out-of-doors and natural world are domesticated into intimate spaces, the chambers of the beloved.

Poem 2:8-17

All of these literary features—the possible inversions of metaphor, the fluidity of target and source, the geographic flights between poems—are at play in one of the Song's more sustained units about the natural world, the composition that now runs from 2:8-17.[17] In diachronic perspective, the composition is wrought from a poem in which the female lover heralds the male lover's advance and departure (vv. 8-9, 16-17), his putative song about the felicitousness of the season (vv. 10b-13), lines that woo his "dove" to reveal herself (v. 14), and a sing-song adage about little foxes in the vineyard (v. 15).[18] Over the course of multiple subunits (and subgenres), the lovers again use natural images to describe each other—she now likens him to a gazelle or a young stag (vv. 9, 17), and he her to a dove (v. 14)—that evoke their "wild" selves. Through both metaphorical reciprocity and literary hybridity, the

---

17. The boundaries of the poems that make up the Song are always a matter for debate. While clearly developed from smaller units (see below), the poem now extends from 2:8-17, bound as a unit by the repetition of themes and catchwords, as noted above. Thus, Murphy, *The Song*, 138–42; Renita Weems, "The Song of Songs: Introduction, Commentary, and Reflections," in *New Interpreters Bible Proverbs-Sirach*, vol. 5, ed. Leander E. Keck and Richard J. Clifford (Nashville: Abingdon, 1997), 392–95; and Fox, *Song of Songs*, 11–16. Cf. others who treat it as separate poems, including Keel (*Song*, 95–118) who regards this as five discrete units while acknowledging their literary relationship to one another; Fishbane (*Song of Songs*, 67–81), who views vv. 8-13 as one episode in two parts (vv. 8-9, 10-13), followed by an entreaty in v. 14, and the final unit of vv. 15-17.

The poem's opening is decisive, since the preceding verse, 2:7, is the adjuration refrain that closes the first unit of the Song as a whole. The extent of the poem is less clear, since its ending is porous, though certainly the nighttime scene of 3:1-5 appears as a new turn. Nonetheless, Cheryl Exum (*Song of Songs: A Commentary*, OTL [Louisville: Westminster John Knox, 2005], 119–38) treats this poem, 3:1-5, as part of the unit, which she calls "the Woman's First Long Speech"; this has the advantage of extending the poem until the second adjuration refrain in 3:5.

18. Again, the poem of 2:8-17 has been wrought from individual units, and there are clear differences in setting with each; the poem begins with 2:8-9, the opening frame, followed by vv. 10b-13 (with 10a as a redactional transition), v. 14; v. 15, which is something like an interlude, positioned here because of its reference to "vineyards in blossom" (cf. v. 13a); vv. 16-17, which are redacted to provide the bottom frame, resuming the themes, voice, and perhaps setting of vv. 8-9.

poem explores and dissolves the boundary between the wild and the domestic; this is evident both in the lovers' use of animal images for each other, and further through the spaces in which they function across the composition as a whole.

The poem in 2:8-17 is framed by the woman's description of her lover's approach at the start (v. 8) and will end with his retreat (v. 17) in a verbal play that will go beyond simple simile and metaphor. In both the top and the bottom of the frame, she likens him to a gazelle or a young stag, evoking his animal presence in multiple senses.[19] The woman then makes a formal comparison: "My beloved is like (דומה) a gazelle or a young stag" (v. 9a). Earlier, the lovers had tended to compare each other by simple juxtaposition or with the particle—כ, "like" (aside from 1:9). Moreover, at the end of the poem in the concluding frame, she will urge him to again "be like" (דמה לך) a gazelle or a young stag (v. 17b). This is literary artistry that makes a show of its literary artistry, signaling her powers to evoke the natural world and to summon up her lover within it; it frames the perceptions that follow as hers, even when other voices are speaking.

Her "likening" and asking him "to be like" is a further way to play with the boundary between the species, which are inherent to metaphor. Is her lover *like* a gazelle or young stag or are those animals like the one whom she loves? While the former is usually supposed, the metaphor (and the way that metaphors work) allows for the latter. This play is deepened by the double meaning of קול as both "sound" and "voice,"[20] a term which will thread through the poem to liken her words and his to the sounds of the animal species that they invoke. In the first instance, she hears the sound of her beloved approaching, as a gazelle (קול דודי, 2:8), a reference that is ambiguous: does she hear the sound of his approaching or a (vocal) sound that he makes? Are these, moreover, the speech of a human or the sounds of a stag? Then, in the body of the poem, she purports to convey his speech, "My lover spoke and said to me ..." (v. 10a)—though this again may not be actual (human) speech, but the import of his "sounds," her translation of the sounds of the animal world. Or this could even suggest her "likening" the gazelle's sounds to human speech. This sound, as she conveys and interprets it, is his song for the season (vv. 10b-13). Within this seasonal song itself, he notes that "the voice [again, קול] of the turtledove is heard" (v. 12b), and he will also, in wooing her, ask her, as his dove, "let me hear your voice for your voice [both קול] is sweet" (v. 14). In this image, she too now has assumed the voice of the animals of the wild.

One may translate קול as "voice," "song," or "sound," depending on the being that is making the sound or giving voice, but the Hebrew noun runs, unchanged, across the poem to bind its parts; it threads across the different subunits of the

---

19. At the opening, she notes his arrival by sounds and sight—"leaping upon the mountains/bounding upon the hills" (v. 8b)—and thus implicitly by a third sense, scent: "leaping" and "bounding" over the dense thicket of plants, the natural vegetation that grow on these hills, releases the sweet-smelling etheric oils to herald his arrival. She—and the audience—would have understood the trio of senses working together in this image.

20. The same double meaning is at play in Gen. 3:8 when the couple hear the "voice/sound" (קול) of YHWH walking in the garden.

poem, linking them, even if the noun itself has different nuances according to each subunit. Its repetition in diverse contexts (and with multiple subjects or agents) makes a subtler connection, one that undergirds the poem. To follow the tracks of the term קול, she alerts us to his sounds as a gazelle, then gives voice to his words, in which he is giving voice to the turtledove and is asking that she, as a dove, sing.[21] The resulting indirection—she speaks, she says what he says, she says what he says about her sounds—makes clear that this is all perception; it is, moreover, her perception that frames the whole. More to the point, the capacity to "give voice"[22] serves as a bridge between the image of her lover as a gazelle and her lover as a singer of the song of the rainy season and back again to the beloved as a dove of sweet voice. It is not simply a word that binds the poem's units, then, it is an activity that crosses species.

One may be tempted to imagine the gazelle as poet and the dove as singer of human songs, as some sort of fantastical, if anthropomorphized, image. This, however, is to see these beings in human terms, and, as the anthropologist Eduardo Kohn, who urges us to set aside anthropocentric approaches to social sciences, has written, "Such encounters with other kinds of beings force us to recognize the fact that seeing, representing, and perhaps knowing, even thinking, are not exclusively human affairs."[23] Each—lover, beloved, gazelle, dove—has a voice and all give voice to this poem. In the same way, the season of which the man sings is not simply "their" season—his and her season—in which the blossoms and figs are invoked as metaphors for the ripening of their love; it is also the season of the blossoms and the fig tree and the turtledove; it is the season of a wide cast of characters, human and otherwise, including gazelles, stags, doves, and foxes, as Kohn has alerted us. It is a song of the season that is also "sung" (or sounded) in a different fashion by "the fig tree forming its fruit and the vines in blossom giving off their fragrance" (התאנה חנטה פגיה והגפנים סמדר נתנו ריח, v. 13a).[24]

21. See also F. W. Dobbs-Allsopp, *On Biblical Poetry* (New York: Oxford University Press, 2015), 157–60.

22. The repeated references to קול also bring the reader into the lovers' world where they reside in separate spaces listening for the other's much-anticipated approach.

23. Eduardo Kohn, *How Forests Think: Toward an Anthropology Beyond the Human* (Berkeley: University of California Press, 2013), 1.

24. Cyrus Gordon ("New Directions," *The Bulletin of the American Society of Papyrologists* 15 [1978], 59–60) drew attention to the felicitous use of זמיר, which can mean both "pruning" and "music," and provides a multi-directional linking to the opening and closing lines of the verse, a Janus parallelism. עת הזמיר can mean "pruning season" (Lev. 25:3; Isa. 5:6), paralleling the preceding phrase, "the blossoms have appeared in the land" (12a), but in its second sense, "a time of music" (Isa. 24:16; 25:5; Pss. 95:2; 119:54), it also anticipates a parallelism with the following phrase, "the voice of the turtledove is heard in our land" (12b). These phrases that precede and follow "the time of pruning/singing has come" are in themselves parallel, but the intervening polysemous reference to the "pruning/singing season" serves to link their two semantic ranges, and both would have been heard by the original audiences for the Song.

קוֹל serves as a key term that is sustained across the multiple units that now comprise 2:8-17; as much as the term binds the poem together, it also binds the various species within it. In the same way, the variety of natural spaces that are invoked by these subunits are threaded together by virtue of now presenting them as a fuller composition. Just as distinctions between animal and human were disturbed by tracing the making of sound through the poem, a sense of "wild vs. domestic" is troubled by the invocation of multiple spaces. Through this diverse composition, in which even different forms of poetry are laid side by side, the Song moves from the hills, over which the lover bounds, to a vineyard on the brink of bloom, to the clefts of a rock and the covert of the cliff, and back again to a vineyard. But even within subunits, there is variety; the opening vv. 8-9 extend from mountains to "our wall," for example. As the poem has become "of a piece," absorbing multiple forms, so, too, have its diverse locational indicators assembled into a whole without clear demarcation or distinction. The diversity of the spaces may be due to what source critics call the redaction of units but what a poet might call literary artistry. The artistry comes in invoking all of these spaces as the lovers' context. In the process, the poem not only elides firm distinctions between wild and human, then, but distinctions between wild, natural, and domestic, as poems in one setting seep into another and return again. Again, this landscape is the landscape of the lovers' imaginations and defies easy characterization or distinction.

The fluidity of setting should caution us against the commonplace that the woman of the Song is confined to the home while her lover is out in the world. Verse 9 has been taken to support this reading since it suggests that he is out-of-doors, a gazelle on the hills and then standing by the wall, and she appears on the other side of the wall, through a window.[25] Closer attention to the language of the verse reveals the problems with this reading. For one, to place the woman firmly in the domestic sphere is to ignore that it is her literary command of the natural world that places him there and that, indeed, launches the poem: he would not be on the thicket, bounding like a gazelle, were she not summoning (or imagining) him there and beckoning him closer. As it stands, the poem as a whole is her perception and retelling. It also ignores the image of her as a dove in the cliffs (v. 14). Furthermore, a closer reading of v. 9 itself may not in fact support this notion—or at least it makes it ambiguous. The woman describes her lover as standing behind a wall and gazing in, which in turn suggests that she is gazing out from within. The use of the preposition—מִן emphasizes most of all that this is her perspective on his perspective, consonant with the poem's progression. The verse highlights perspective, rather than location, their stance toward one another rather than their place. And these perspectives need not be dependent on different settings.

The lovers' different settings, however, have been construed from the reference to the wall through which they peer at each other. It is true that the perspectives of the lovers are not the same, but the significance of this has been overdrawn as an

---

25. This, indeed, is taken to be another dimension of her comparison to him as a gazelle or a young stag: he has the capacity to roam and she does not. Thus, it is presumed that she is of the domestic realm and he of the wild.

indicator of their different spheres, geographies, and even different modes of living rather than positional stance or differing perspective. From this wall, interpreters have constructed a domestic space for the woman, taking the wall as a synecdoche for the domicile. Keel, more particularly, suggests that her reference to "our wall"— "now he stands behind *our* wall" (הנה זה עומד אחר כתלנו, v. 9b)—probably means the wall of her mother's house. (This seeks to harmonize with references to her mother's house that appear later in the Song, after our poem, 3:4 and 8:2.)[26] There are, however, several indicators that contravene the assumption that this is the wall to her house, an important intervention, too, for understanding how the wild is defined over and against the domestic. First, the common possessive "our" in "our wall" more likely refers to her and him than it does to her and the house of her mother or her natal family unit.[27] The house that she had imagined just before, in 1:16-17, she called "our house," and this "our" referred to her and her lover (see, too, "our couch," v. 16, and "our rafters," v. 17). The possessive in each of these examples is a form of intimacy, something they share, rather than something that they own or that is material enough to own.[28] He will echo this but with an even broader gesture that includes the animals in their common possessive pronoun, when he says "the voice of the turtledove is heard in *our* land" (וקול התור נשמע בארצנו, 2:12) —this "our" includes her and him, and gazelles, and now blossom and turtle doves. This common possessive emphasizes, at minimum, the lovers as a unit, but it also begins to dismantle the distinction between spaces.

Second, the house that was theirs—"our house" in 1:16-17—already had a startling naturalness to it, with a leafy "couch" and cedar and cypress trees as framing its imaginary space. This may also be true of "our wall" in the poem at hand, 2:8-17. The Song is always and ever speaking through metaphor, and the wall may be yet another metaphorical reference to their meeting place, a place in the natural world and, in any case, may not be "domestic space" at all; as human perception is shot through with metaphor, this is the landscape of the lovers' imagination. It may be no more than a garden or boundary wall, if that. It is described as having a window and an "opening"; חרכי is a hapax and is often translated as "lattice," under the influence of its parallel term, "window," but it may mean simply "opening" or "gap." And, as an image, all this fragment of a wall or this metaphor of a wall does is provide the mechanism through which they can view each other, have perspective on one another a perspective that may be rendered by metaphor and not by an actual building. Images that use built environments as sources—the image of the house in 1:16-17 and perhaps walls in 2:9—are nestled

26. Keel, *Song of Songs*, 96.

27. For more on the significance of her mother's house, see Cindy Chapman, *The House of the Mother: The Societal Roles of Maternal Kin in Biblical Hebrew Narrative and Poetry* (New Haven: Yale University Press, 2016).

28. Ariel Bloch and Chana Bloch (*The Song of Songs: A New Translation with an Introduction and Commentary* [New York: Random House, 1995], 153, 147) point out that "our" may also be a particle of their shared intimacy rather than an indication of formal ownership; indeed, the man will refer to "our land" in v. 12, which suggests this same intimacy without ownership.

between poems in which she more literally appears to be indoors (for example, in the subsequent poem of 3:1-5 in which she lies at home on her bed at night dreaming of her beloved). These more literal domestic settings should not make the domicile metaphors of other poems disappear, flattening into reality.

All of this is to suggest that she, too, could be in a natural setting and, thus, there may not be a reason to resort to the supposition that the Song, as Cheryl Exum puts it, "presents a somewhat conventional picture of gender relations" in which the man roams "freely" and the "woman is inside the house."[29] For one, it is not clear that this would have been convention. Though there is a timelessness to the danger that she meets at the hands of the night watchmen "who roam the city" in the second night dream scene of 5:2-8, that danger may not be relevant to the woman's setting in 2:8-9, particularly since it is daytime. The perception that a woman must remain home may ignore the process by which the Song grew to include, along the way, poems that are located both in urban and more rural settings, and that may have included a range of social conventions; within 2:8-17 there are a range of more rural settings, including references to hills (v. 8), perhaps a vineyard or equivalent orchard (v. 13), the rougher terrain of rocks and cliffs (v. 14), and clear reference to a vineyard (v. 15).

If some of the references to the built environment are instead recognized for the metaphors (and fantasies) that they are, then the force of the metaphor is simply to convey that the lovers have perspective on each other, that they gaze at each other. This is the inevitable apartness that is always a part of togetherness, a tension that is in keeping with the Song's more consistent theme of longing: that there is always and ever the tension of separation even when they are together due to their different perspectives as individuals, the simple fact that they stand outside one another and can gaze upon each other. It is this separation that she seeks to overcome as she beckons his approach and to which he refers when he begs to catch sight of her, his dove, in the clefts of the rock. On the one hand, the dove's capacity for flight and the gazelle's capacity to leap also allow the lovers to imagine themselves having the same freedom of mobility to transgress any boundaries; on the other hand, these images also express the distance between the lovers, she out of reach, he bounding away at the end of the poem. The metaphors of space—of a wall or a house over and against the natural world—further animate this principle: that they are ever desiring to be together in an intimate space, an imagined house, and yet also always separated, as if by a wall. In this way, the references to the wild and the domestic are lyric expressions of the erotic agony and ecstasy of the Song. As such, the natural world more properly reflects their innermost thoughts; where one begins and the other ends is not defined.

The lovers cast themselves and each other as elements of the natural world, and revel in their natural surroundings, freely imaging their house as a forest and a forest as their house. This kind of verbal and imaginative play between species and settings not only draws on imagery from their world, but produces their imagined landscape, one that elides easy distinctions between wild and domestic. This

---

29. Exum, *Song of Songs*, 125.

landscape is rendered by metaphor and literary diversity and takes full advantage of its poetic forms as heightened expression. The resulting poems are an exercise in erotic imagination, an imagination fueled by the beauty of the land but also tinged by unfulfilled desire—the kind of desire that cannot be quenched. Rather than focusing on making sense of the poems, domesticating it into a linear plot, taming its metaphors so that they point in one direction, the reader remembers that the Song produces its meaning mostly—most vividly, most charmingly—through the full flourishing of metaphor, to convey a depth of meaning, and a deep desire, that cannot be otherwise conveyed.

Bibliography

Bloch, Ariel, and Chana Bloch. *The Song of Songs: A New Translation with an Introduction and Commentary*. New York: Random House, 1995.

Chapman, Cindy. *The House of the Mother: The Societal Roles of Maternal Kin in Biblical Hebrew Narrative and Poetry*. New Haven: Yale University Press, 2016.

Dobbs-Allsopp, F. W. *On Biblical Poetry*. New York: Oxford University Press, 2015.

Exum, J. Cheryl. *The Song of Songs: A Commentary*. OTL. Louisville: Westminster John Knox, 2005.

Falk, Marcia. *Love Lyrics from the Bible: A Translation and Literary Study of the Song of Songs*. Bible and Literature Series. Sheffield: Almond, 1982.

Fishbane, Michael. *The Song of Songs*. JPS Bible Commentary. Philadelphia: Jewish Publication Society, 2015.

Fox, Michael. *The Song of Songs and the Ancient Egyptian Love Songs*. Madison: University of Wisconsin Press, 1985.

Gault, Brian P. *Body as Landscape, Love as Intoxication: Conceptual Metaphors in the Song of Songs*. Ancient Israel and Its Literature 36. Atlanta: SBL Press, 2019.

Gordon, Cyrus. "New Directions." *The Bulletin of the American Society of Papyrologists* 15 (1978): 59–66.

Hagedorn, Anselm. "Place and Space in the Song of Songs." *ZAW* 127 (2015): 207–23.

James, Elaine T. *Landscapes of the Song of Songs: Poetry and Place*. New York: Oxford University Press, 2017.

Keel, Othmar. *The Song of Songs*. Continental Commentary Series. Minneapolis: Fortress, 1994.

Kohn, Eduardo. *How Forests Think: Toward an Anthropology Beyond the Human*. Berkeley: University of California Press, 2013.

Lakoff, George, and Mark Johnson. *Metaphors We Live By*. Chicago: University of Chicago Press, 1980.

Murphy, Roland. *The Song of Songs*. Hermeneia. Minneapolis: Fortress, 1990.

Pope, Marvin. *Song of Songs: A New Translation with Introduction and Commentary*. The AYB. Garden City, NY: Doubleday, 1977.

Ricœur, Paul. *Interpretation Theory: Discourse and the Surplus of Meaning*. Fort Worth: Texas Christian University, 1976.

Soskice, Janet. *Metaphor and Religious Language*. London: Oxford University Press, 1985.

Weems, Renita. "The Song of Songs: Introduction, Commentary, and Reflections." In *New Interpreters Bible Proverbs–Sirach*, vol. 5, edited by Leander E. Keck and Richard J. Clifford, 361–434. Nashville: Abingdon, 1997.

Chapter 4

WILDSCAPES, LANDSCAPES, AND SPECIALIZED LAND MANAGEMENT: THE IMPACT OF THE ASSYRIAN RULE OVER LAND EXPLOITATION IN THE KINGDOM OF JUDAH

Dafna Langgut and Yuval Gadot

Introduction

The transformation of the natural wildscape into a landscape sculpted by humans is a hotly debated subject.[1] It is clear that changes took place gradually.[2] It is also apparent that the intensity and scale of human involvement was dependent on, among other things, the size and complexity of human society. While hunter gatherers and tribal bodies adapted to their surroundings, more complex societies

---

1. Karl W. Butzer, "Climatic Change in Arid Regions since the Pliocene," in *A History of Land Use in Arid Regions*, ed. Laurence Dudley Stamp, Arid Zone Research 17 (Paris: UNESCO, 1961), 31–56; Simcha Lev-Yadun, "Flora and Climate in Southern Samaria: Past and Present," in *Highlands of Many Cultures, Vol. 1*, ed. Israel Finkelstein, Zvi Lederman, and Shlomo Bunimovitz, Monograph Series of the Institute of Archaeology of Tel Aviv University (Tel Aviv: Tel Aviv University, 1997), 85–102; John Bintliff, "Time, Process and Catastrophism in the Study of Mediterranean Alluvial History: A Review Source," *World Archaeology* 33 (2002): 417–35; Shimon Gibson, "From Wildscape to Landscape: Landscape Archaeology in the Southern Levant—Methods and Practice," in *The Rural Landscape of Ancient Israel*, ed. Aren M. Maeir, Shimon Dar, and Ze'ev Safrai, BAR International Series 1121 (Oxford: Archaeopress, 2003), 1–15; Simone Riehl, "Archaeobotanical Evidence for the Interrelationship of Agricultural Decision-Making and Climate Change in the Ancient Near East," *Quaternary International* 197 (2009): 93–114; Erika Weiberg et al., "Mediterranean Land Use Systems from Prehistory to Antiquity: A Case Study from Peloponnese (Greece)," *Journal of Land Use Science* 14 (2019): 1–20.

2. E.g., Lev-Yadun, "Flora."

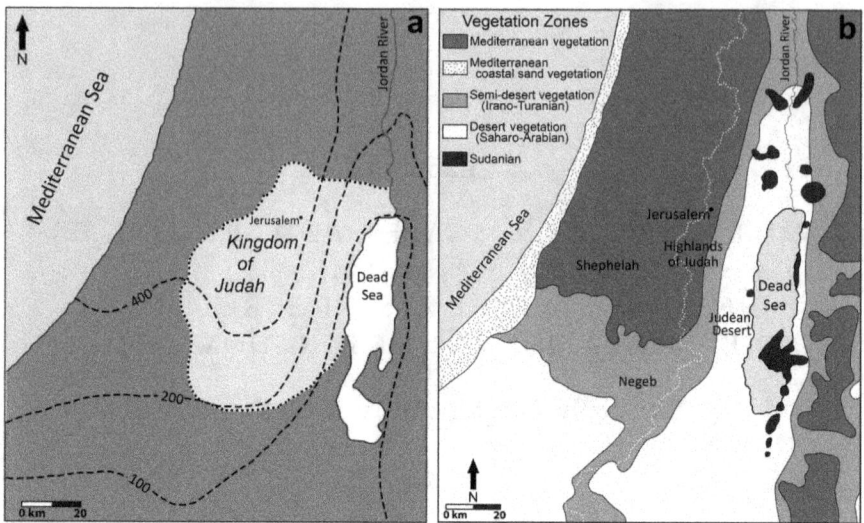

Figure 4.1 (a) The Kingdom of Judah in the eighth to seventh centuries BCE, together with rainfall isohyets.[3] (b) Vegetation zones of the southern Levant.[4] The watershed is represented by the white dashed line.

were able to execute massive projects that completely altered the landscape.[5] In this chapter we highlight how the assumption of hegemony in the southern Levant by the Assyrian empire during the eighth–seventh centuries BCE, the first massive empire formation recorded in history, constituted a marked change in the degree and scope of human exploitation of the natural environment. This research focuses on the Judean Highlands and the hills to their west (the Shephelah; Figure 4.1), regions that came under the Assyrian yoke by the end of the eighth century BCE.[6] Though these regions were exploited by hunter-gatherer

---

3. Haim Srebro and Tamar Soffer, *The New Atlas of Israel: The National Atlas, Survey of Israel* (Jerusalem: The Hebrew University of Jerusalem, 2011).

4. Michael Zohary, *Plant Life of Palestine: Israel and Jordan* (New York: Ronald, 1962).

5. Paul Rainbird, "A Message for Our Future? The Rapa Nui (Easter Island) Ecodisaster and Pacific Island Environments," *World Archaeology* 33 (2002): 436–51; Oren Ackermann et al., "The Paleo-Anthropocene and the Genesis of the Current Landscape of Israel," *Journal of Landscape Ecology* 10 (2017): 109–40.

6. Angelika Berlejung, "The Assyrians in the West: Assyrianization, Colonialism, Indifference, or Development Policy," in *Congress Volume Helsinki 2010*, ed. Martti Nissinen, VTSup 148 (Leiden; Boston: Brill, 2012), 21–60; Oded Lipschits, *Age of Empires: The History and Administration of Judah in the 8th–2nd Centuries BCE in Light of the Storage-Jar Stamp Impressions*, Monograph Series of the Institute of Archaeology of Tel Aviv University (Winona Lake, IN: Eisenbrauns, 2021).

groups throughout the Pleistocene Epoch, only since the early Holocene, with the beginning of the Neolithic revolution (c. 9000 BCE), was a more profound human influence on the natural environment documented.[7] During the Chalcolithic period (c. 5000–3900 BCE), with the domestication of fruit trees, this phenomenon probably intensified.[8] Subsequently, in the Early Bronze Age (beginning c. 3700/3600 BCE), evidence shows that human exploitation of the landscape strengthened with the transformation to urbanization.[9] During this period, fruit-tree horticulture was already abundant in the Judean Highlands and the Shephelah and grapes and olives were an important supplement to grain crops throughout the Levant.[10] These horticultural activities were placed near

---

7. Zev Naveh and Joel Dan, "The Human Degradation of Mediterranean Landscapes in Israel," in *Mediterranean Type Ecosystems*, ed. Francesco di Castri and Harold A. Mooney (Berlin; Heidelberg: Springer, 1973), 373–90; Omry Barzilai, Nuha Aga, and Onn Crouvi, "Prehistoric Artifacts from Emeq Rephaim (Area C)," in *New Studies in the Archaeology of Jerusalem and Its Region: Collected Papers Vol. IV*, ed. David Amit, Guy D. Steibel, and Orit Peleg-Barkat (Jerusalem: Israel Antiquities Authority, 2010), 31–39; Hamoudi Khalaily and Jacob Vardi, "The New Excavations at Motza: An Architectural Perspective on a Neolithic 'Megasite' in the Judean Hills," in *The Mega Project at Motza (Moza): The Neolithic and Later Occupations up to the 20th Century, New Studies in the Archaeology of Jerusalem and Its Region, Supplementary Volume*, ed. Hamoudi Khalaily et al. (Jerusalem: Israel Antiquities Authority, 2020), 60–100.

8. Daniel Zohary and Pinhas Spiegel-Roy, "Beginnings of Fruit Growing in the Old World," *Science* 187 (1975): 319–27; Daniel Zohary, Maria Hopf, and Ehud Weiss, *Domestication of Plants in the Old World*, 4th edn (Oxford: Oxford University Press, 2012); Dafna Langgut and Yosef Garfinkel, "7000-year-old evidence of fruit tree cultivation in the Jordan Valley, Israel," *Scientific Reports* 12.1 (2022): 7463.

9. Arlene Miller Rosen, *Civilizing Climate: Social Responses to Climate Change in the Ancient Near East* (Lanham: Rowman Altamira, 2007); Oren Ackerman et al., "The Environmental and Paleogeographical History of Tell Es-Safi/Gath During the Last Eight Millennia," in *Tell Es-Safi/Gath I: The 1996–2005 Seasons*, ed. Aren M. Maeir, Ägypten und Altes Testament 69 (Wiesbaden: Harrassowitz, 2012), 531–56; Dafna Langgut, Matthew J. Adams, and Israel Finkelstein, "Climate, Settlement Patterns and Olive Horticulture in the Southern Levant During the Early Bronze and Intermediate Bronze Ages (c. 3600–1950 BCE)," *Levant* 48 (2016): 117–34; Yitzhak Paz, Oren Ackermann, et al., "The Earliest Compost Pit? An Early Bronze Age Fertilized Agricultural Plot Discovered near Tel Yarmouth, Ramat Bet Shemesh, Israel," *Journal of Archaeological Science: Reports* 15 (2017): 226–34.

10. Riehl, "Archaeobotanical Evidence"; Zohary, Hopf, and Weiss, *Domestication*; E. Weiss, "'Beginnings of Fruit Growing in the Old World'—Two Generations Later," *Israel Journal of Plant Sciences* 62 (2015): 75–85; Langgut, Adams, and Finkelstein, "Climate, Settlement"; Mordechay Benzaquen, Israel Finkelstein, and Dafna Langgut, "Vegetation History and Human Impact on the Environs of Tel Megiddo in the Bronze and Iron Ages (c. 3,500–500 BCE): A Dendroarchaeological Analysis," *Tel Aviv* 46 (2019): 42–61.

the vicinity of the settlements as olive oil was traded internationally and its value helped local rulers gain political power.[11] Although the region under discussion was densely settled during the Intermediate, Middle and late Bronze Age, as well as the early Iron Age, we suggest that the next marked change in the dimensions of the exploitation of the land occurred as the region came into the Assyrian sphere of dominance, close to the second segment of the Iron Age II, in the eighth and seventh centuries BCE.[12] We contend that during this period, human impact on the natural environment seems to have become more specialized as large-scale regional economic strategies suppressed local variations and policies that were based on risk management.

As the basis of our argument, we will explore the impact that the Assyrian imperial system had on the natural landscape around the most important urban centers of Judah: Jerusalem and Lachish.[13] We present data from our own field work conducted in the agricultural areas surrounding ancient Jerusalem in addition to presenting all available data from previous archaeological studies performed in the Highlands and in the Shephelah regarding agricultural activities. We also correlate between the archaeological finds and regional environmental information, such as fossil pollen data.

11. E.g., Simcha Lev-Yadun and Ram Gophna, "Exportation of Plant Products from Canaan to Egypt in the Early Bronze Age I: A Rejoinder to William A. Ward," *BASOR* 287 (1992): 89–90; Israel Finkelstein and Ram Gophna, "Settlement, Demographic, and Economic Patterns in the Highlands of Palestine in the Chalcolithic and Early Bronze Periods and the Beginning of Urbanism," *BASOR* 289 (1993): 1–22; Oren Ackermann et al., "Palaeoenvironment and Anthropogenic Activity in the Southeastern Mediterranean Since the Mid-Holocene: The Case of Tell Es-Safi/Gath, Israel," *Quaternary International* 328–9 (2014): 226–43; Langgut, Adams, and Finkelstein, "Climate, Settlement"; Benzaquen, Finkelstein, and Langgut, "Vegetation History"; Paz et al., "The Earliest Compost Pit?"

12. Stephanie Dalley, "Recent Evidence from Assyrian Sources for Judaean History from Uzziah to Manasseh," *JSOT* 28 (2004): 387–401; Oded Lipschits, "The Changing Faces of Kingship in Judah under Assyrian Rule," in *Changing Faces of Kingship in Syria-Palestine 1500–500 BCE*, ed. Agustinus Gianto and Peter Dubovský, AOAT 459 (Münster: Ugarit-Verlag, 2018), 115–38.

13. The Negev, especially the Beer-sheba and Arad Valleys, was also an integral part of the kingdom (Israel Finkelstein, "The Archaeology of the Days of Manasseh," in *Scripture and Other Artifacts: Essays on the Bible and Archaeology in Honor of Philip J. King*, ed. Michael D. Coogan, J. Cheryl Exum, and Lawrence E. Stager [Louisville, KY: Westminster John Knox Press, 1994], 169–87). As we do not have enough information regarding agricultural activities outside of the main trading centers and forts, this region will not be discussed here.

Reconstructing the Ancient Landscape

Distinguishing between natural (mainly climate changes) and human impact on the evolution of the landscape is not an easy task. The Holocene climate of the Mediterranean southern Levant is reconstructed based on several proxies: palynology,[14] Soreq Cave isotope analysis,[15] and the reconstruction of the Dead Sea levels.[16] In order to trace evidence of human influence on the environment in a specific area, interdisciplinary research is required. This combines relevant archaeological findings and information derived from sources such as ancient documents, archaeobotany, and palynology. This study is an attempt to implement an interdisciplinary research project of such a nature for the Judean Highlands and the Shephelah during the eighth to seventh centuries BCE, based on the proxies detailed in the section below.

Archaeology

The identification of agricultural activities around settlements is a highly problematic task for archaeologists. With no written record, we are restricted to nonperishable materials and recorded installations that have been etched into rock and that have left a permanent mark. New technologies have improved this difficult situation. Bee keeping is an example of an agricultural industry that once left few marks.[17] Recently, however, with the use of Residue Analysis, we can begin to appreciate the

---

14. Thomas Litt et al., "Holocene Climate Variability in the Levant from the Dead Sea Pollen Record," *Quaternary Science Reviews* 49 (2012): 95–105; Dafna Langgut et al., "Vegetation and Climate Changes During the Bronze and Iron Ages (3600–600 BCE) in the Southern Levant Based on Palynological Records," *Radiocarbon* 57 (2015): 217–35.

15. Miryam Bar-Matthews and Avner Ayalon, "Speleothems as Palaeoclimate Indicators, a Case Study from Soreq Cave Located in the Eastern Mediterranean Region, Israel," in *Past Climate Variability through Europe and Africa*, ed. Richard W. Battarbee, Françoise Gasse, and Catherine E. Stickley, vol. 6 of *Developments in Paleoenvironmental Research* (Dordrecht: Springer, 2004), 363–91; Miryam Bar-Matthews and Avner Ayalon, "Mid-Holocene Climate Variations Revealed by High-Resolution Speleothem Records from Soreq Cave, Israel and Their Correlation with Cultural Changes," *The Holocene* 21 (2011): 163–71; Ben Laugomer, "High Resolution Climate Reconstruction During the Bronze and Iron Ages from Soreq Cave Speleothems" (MA thesis, Tel Aviv University, 2017).

16. Claudia Migowski et al., "Holocene Climate Variability and Cultural Evolution in the Near East from the Dead Sea Sedimentary Record," *Quaternary Research* 66 (2006): 421–31; Elisa Joy Kagan et al., "Chronology of Dead Sea Levels During the Bronze-Iron Ages," *Radiocarbon* 57 (2015): 237–52.

17. Amihai Mazar et al., "Iron Age Beehives at Tel Rehov in the Jordan Valley," *Antiquity* 82 (2008): 629–39; Guy Bloch et al., "Industrial Apiculture in the Jordan Valley During Biblical Times with Anatolian Honeybees," *Proceedings of the National Academy of Sciences of the United States of America* 107 (2010): 11240–44.

Figure 4.2 Iron Age wine press in the Jerusalem highlands characterized by the presence of two small niches that were usually etched in the vertical rock wall at the back of the treading surface. The niches may have been used to install a wooden beam that was employed for secondary pressing of the crushed grapes.

scale of bee-keeping activities in Iron Age Israel and Judah.[18] A second challenge is that of dating. Landscapes are essentially palimpsests, meaning each generation incorporates earlier modifications of the surroundings into its current usage of the landscape. Thus, identifying initial operations and accurately differentiating them from later cycles of construction constitutes a challenging task for the archaeologists. A recent breakthrough in landscape studies is the use of OSL (Optically Stimulated Luminescence) dating. This method dates the soil and is able to identify and date episodes of soil movement by humans. The construction of terrace walls, for example, includes the placing of soil behind a built wall which can be dated by OSL.[19]

18. Ayala Amir et al., "Heated Beeswax Usage in Mortuary Practices: The Case of Ḥorvat Tevet (Jezreel Valley, Israel) c. 1000 BCE," *Journal of Archaeological Science: Reports* 36 (2021): 102904; Dvory Namdar et al., "Organic Content of YHWD-Stamped Storage Jars," in *Ramat Raḥel VI: The Babylonian-Persian Pit: Pottery Assemblage and Stamp Impressions*, ed. Oded Lipschits, Liora Freud, Yuval Gadot, and Manfred Oeming, Monograph Series of the Institute of Archaeology of Tel Aviv University (Winona Lake, IN: Eisenbrauns, 2021), 121–30.

19. Uri Davidovich et al., "Archaeological Investigations and OSL Dating of Terraces at Ramat Raḥel, Israel," *Journal of Field Archaeology* 37 (2012): 192–208; Naomi Porat et al., "Using OSL Measurements to Decipher Soil History in Archaeological Terraces, Judean Highlands, Israel: Using OSL to Decipher Soil History in Archaeological Terraces," *Land Degradation & Development* 29 (2018): 643–50.

Archaeological fingerprints for agricultural activities include mainly wine presses: rock-cut installations for treading grapes. These installations include a flattened rock surface where the treading took place and a collecting vat. Iron Age wine presses in the highlands of Jerusalem also include one or two niches that were cut in the vertical rock wall at the back of the treading surface (Figure 4.2).[20] These niches may have been used to install a wooden beam that was used for secondary pressing of the crushed grapes. A second type of installation is the olive press. During the early Iron Age in the Mediterranean southern Levant, olive oil was produced using installations constructed from a large flat stone surrounded by smaller fieldstones. These stone-built presses were often rounded.[21] In the Iron Age IIA, this type was replaced by a freestanding monolithic press. Bunimovitz and Lederman report that the Iron Age IIB (late eighth century BCE) stone presses at Beth-Shemesh were without rounded corners.[22] These carved monolithic crushing and pressing basins of the Iron Age IIB (and IIA, at Gath) were typical of sites in the entire region, at both Philistia and Judah.[23]

While terrace walls were the most common agricultural installation in the landscape, archaeological exploration conducted in the last decade has shown that terracing for dry farming became a widespread economic strategy only during the Hellenistic period.[24] Earlier agricultural activity included mainly the exploitation of soil pockets in between rock outcrops for horticultural activities. Extensive stone clearance was needed in order to turn more soil pockets available for cultivation. The high number of such piles in the landscape is sometimes the only indication that a certain plot was exploited in the past.[25]

20. David Amit and Irit Yezerski, "An Iron Age II Cemetery and Wine Presses at An-Nabi Danyal," *IEJ* 51 (2001): 171–93. See further below.

21. Ron Beeri, "Round Oil Presses of the 13th–10th Centuries BCE in Palestine and Their Implications: Chronology, Function and Geographical Distribution," *PEQ* 140 (2008): 159–67; Takuzo Onozuka, "Keeping Up with the Demand for Oil? Reconsidering the Unique Oil Presses from Late Bronze Age IIB to Iron Age IIA in the Southern Levant," *Orient* 47 (2012): 67–90.

22. Shlomo Bunimovitz and Zvi Lederman, *Tel Beth-Shemesh: A Border Community in Judah. Renewed Excavations 1990-2000: The Iron Age*, Tel Aviv University Sonia and Marco Nadler Institute of Archaeology Monograph Series 34 (Tel Aviv: Emery and Claire Yass Publications in Archaeology, 2016), 464–65.

23. Aren M. Maeir et al., "Technological Insights on Philistine Culture: Perspectives from Tell Es-Safi/Gath," *Journal of Eastern Mediterranean Archaeology & Heritage Studies* 7 (2019): 76; Aren M. Maeir, Eric L. Welch, and Maria Eniukhina, "A Note on Olive Oil Production in Iron Age Philistia: Pressing the Consensus," 153 (2021): 129–44.

24. Yelena Elgart-Sharon, Naomi Porat, and Yuval Gadot, "Land Management and the Construction of Terraces for Dry Farming: The Case of the Soreq Catchment, Israel," *Oxford Journal of Archaeology* 39 (2020): 274–89.

25. Davidovich et al., "Archaeological Investigations"; Yuval Gadot et al., "What Kind of Village Is This? Buildings and Agro-Economic Activities North-West of Jerusalem during the Iron IIB-C Period," in *The Last Century in the History of Judah: The 7th Century BCE in Archaeological, Historical and Biblical Perspectives*, ed. Filip Čapek and Oded Lipschits (Atlanta: Society of Biblical Literature, 2019), 89–118. See further below.

Generally, there was a higher degree of environmental manipulation near permanent water sources, mainly springs. Subterranean tunnels were cut in order to increase the efficiency of the spring and the water was collected into a pool. From there, above-ground channels distributed the water into small terraced plots that were dedicated to cultivation that required permanent watering.[26] The dating of these sophisticated systems was disputed, but a recent find at the spring of Ain Joweizeh shows that the earliest use of this system dates to the late Iron Age (eighth–seventh centuries BCE).[27]

Archaeobotany

The identifiable macro-botanical remains of plants include seeds, wood, and charcoal. In the Mediterranean vegetation zone, where our study area is located, most of the macro-botanical material is found in its charred form. Anatomical and morphological identification of seed and charcoal assemblages is considered to be a powerful tool in the southern Levant in the reconstruction of ancient diet, past natural vegetation, and environmental conditions.[28] Identification of macro-botanical remains (chiefly charcoals) also has the ability to illuminate human influence on past vegetation such as horticultural activities and deforestation.[29] It is based on the principal assumption that timber for everyday use (e.g., construction, fuel) was usually collected from areas close to the sites. Therefore, charcoal remains found in certain archaeological contexts often reflect the natural and cultivated

---

26. Daniel Ein-Mor and Zvi Ron, "Ain Joweizeh: An Iron Age Royal Rock-Cut Spring System in the Naḥal Refa'im Valley, near Jerusalem," *Tel Aviv* 43 (2016): 127–46; Azriel Yechezkel and Amos Frumkin, "Spring Tunnels in Ancient Israel and the Jerusalem Hills: Physical, Geographical and Human Aspects," *Horizons in Geography* 96 (2019): 154–80 (Hebrew); Azriel Yechezkel, Amos Frumkin, and Shaul Tzionit, "Ancient Spring Tunnels of Jerusalem, Israel: Physical, Spatial, and Human Aspects," *Environmental Archaeology* 21 (2022): 323–41.
27. Ein-Mor and Ron, "Ain Joweizeh."
28. E.g., Ehud Weiss and Mordechai E. Kislev, "Plant Remains as Indicators for Economic Activity: A Case Study from Iron Age Ashkelon," *Journal of Archaeological Science* 31 (2004): 1–13; Simcha Lev-Yadun, "Wood Remains from Archaeological Excavations: A Review with a Near Eastern Perspective," *Israel Journal of Earth Sciences* 56 (2007): 139–62; Nili Liphschitz, *Timber in Ancient Israel: Dendroarchaeology and Dendrochronology*, Monograph Series of the Institute of Archaeology of Tel Aviv University 26 (Tel Aviv: Tel Aviv University, 2007).
29. E.g., Benzaquen, Finkelstein, and Langgut, "Vegetation History"; Helena Roth, Yuval Gadot, and Dafna Langgut, "Wood Economy in Early Roman Period Jerusalem," *BASOR* 382 (2019): 71–87.

arboreal environment.³⁰ Only rarely was precious wood imported from afar and it was mainly used for the construction of prestige buildings or the manufacture of delicately crafted objects.³¹ It is therefore suggested that most of the charred remains that are found in the rural areas of Jerusalem reflect the immediate natural and cultural environment of the city. The problem is that most of the macro-botanical remains that have been identified thus far derive from the city itself. Archaeobotanical information from the hinterland sites of Jerusalem is relatively rare, or appears in insufficient amounts, while a slightly more detailed picture is available for the Shephelah.³² Another obstacle relates to selective preservation. Some species within the archaeological record are less durable than others. For example, *Vitis* (grape) is under-represented in wood-charcoal assemblages since it possesses a low density of 0.40 g/cm³ and therefore the weak constitution of lianas deteriorates easily.³³

Palynology

Palynology is considered one of the best proxies for a regional reconstruction of vegetation and climate.³⁴ Fossil pollen grains, the fingerprints of plants, tend to preserve well in anaerobic environments such as ancient lake deposits. In Israel, relatively long consecutive palynological records have been studied mainly from the Dead Sea Rift water bodies.³⁵ In this study, we chose to use the well-dated high-resolution palynological record of the Ze'elim Dead Sea.³⁶ The pollen grains of Mediterranean trees, both natural (e.g., oaks, terebinth) and cultivated

---

30. E.g., Katleen Deckers et al., "Characteristics and Changes in Archaeology-Related Environmental Data During the Third Millennium BC in Upper Mesopotamia, Collective Comments to the Data Discussed During the Symposium," *Publications de l'Institut Français d'Études Anatoliennes* 19 (2007): 573–80.

31. E.g., Roth, Gadot and Langgut, "Wood Economy."

32. Charcoals—Liphschitz, *Timber*; seeds—Suembikya Frumin et al., "Studying Ancient Anthropogenic Impacts on Current Floral Biodiversity in the Southern Levant as Reflected by the Philistine Migration," *Scientific Reports* 5 (2015); Suembikya Frumin, "Invasion Biology Analysis in Archaeobotany: Philistine Culture at Tell Es-Sâfi/Gath as a Case Study" (PhD diss., Bar-Ilan University, 2017).

33. Alan Crivellaro and Fritz Hans Schweingruber, *Atlas of Wood, Bark and Pith Anatomy of Eastern Mediterranean Trees and Shrubs* (Heidelberg: Springer, 2013), 569.

34. E.g., Vaughn M. Bryant, "Pollen: Nature's Fingerprints of Plants," in *Yearbook of Science and the Future* (Chicago: Encyclopedia Britannica, 1990), 92–111.

35. Aharon Horowitz, *The Jordan Rift Valley* (Boca Raton, FL: CRC, 2001); Langgut et al., "Vegetation and Climate Changes."

36. Dafna Langgut et al., "Dead Sea Pollen Record and History of Human Activity in the Judean Highlands (Israel) from the Intermediate Bronze into the Iron Ages (2500–500 BCE)," *Palynology* 38 (2014): 280–302.

(mainly olives) which were embedded at the Dead Sea originated from the eastern Judean Highlands (located on the eastern side of the watershed) (Figure 4.1b).[37] It seems that pollen grains from trees on the western side of the watershed are not represented; this means that most of the pollen that originated from the coastal plain, the Shephelah and the section of the western Judean Highlands is not reflected in the Dead Sea pollen records.

The simplified palynological diagram presented in Figure 4.4 is comprised of the group of natural Mediterranean trees (pinkish curve) and cultivated olive trees (green curve), together representing the relative frequencies of the total arboreal (versus non-arboreal) pollen for the Bronze and Iron Ages. Within this group, only trees common to the Mediterranean vegetation zone were included; the majority among them are wind-pollinated. The most dominant are evergreen and deciduous oaks (*Quercus calliprinos* and *Quercus ithaburensis*, respectively). Pollen of other airborne Mediterranean trees appear in lower percentages

---

37. Uri Baruch, "The Palynology of Late Quaternary Sediments of the Dead Sea" (PhD diss, Hebrew University of Jerusalem, 1993); Litt et al., "Holocene Climate Variability"; Langgut et al., "Dead Sea Pollen." Tracing the origin of pollen grains deposited in a waterbody environment might be sometimes complicated. Therefore, in order to shed more light on the sources of the Ze'elim fossil pollen sequence, a previous systematic study of recent pollen patterns, which calculates the ratios of the extant vegetation in the Dead Sea area and the composition of present-day pollen rain of a given taxon, was used (Baruch, "The Palynology"). This study is based on thirty-five soil surface samples that were collected from thirty-four vegetation stations along three transects stretching from the western foot of the Judean Highlands to the western shore of the Dead Sea, covering three basic vegetation zones (Figure 4.3): Mediterranean, Irano-Turanian (steppic), and Saharo-Arabian (desert and the Dead Sea shore). In each station one recent pollen sample was collected and the vegetation was mapped (the vegetation was recorded during several consecutive years). This enables the calculation of the Pollen Rain Index: the ratio between the share of a taxon in the actual vegetation and its share in the pollen rain. The main observations from Baruch are that the pollen grains were embedded in the Dead Sea by both wind and fluvial transportation from different vegetation zones. The study shows that the Mediterranean territory is characterized by a high percentage of arboreal pollen grains with a dominance of evergreen oaks and pines. The leading plant taxa in the Irano-Turanian part are the Brassicaceae (crucifers), grasses, *Artemisia* (wormwood), Caryophyllaceae (pink family), and *Sarcopoterium spinosum* (prickly burnet). This semi-shrub was rare during the periods under discussion and has become more common since the Hellenistic period. The dominant taxa of the desert territory are characterized by high percentages of Brassicaceae and Asteraceae (aster) pollen, while along the Dead Sea shore the leading types in the pollen rain and in the vegetation cover belong to the Chenopodiaceae (beets).

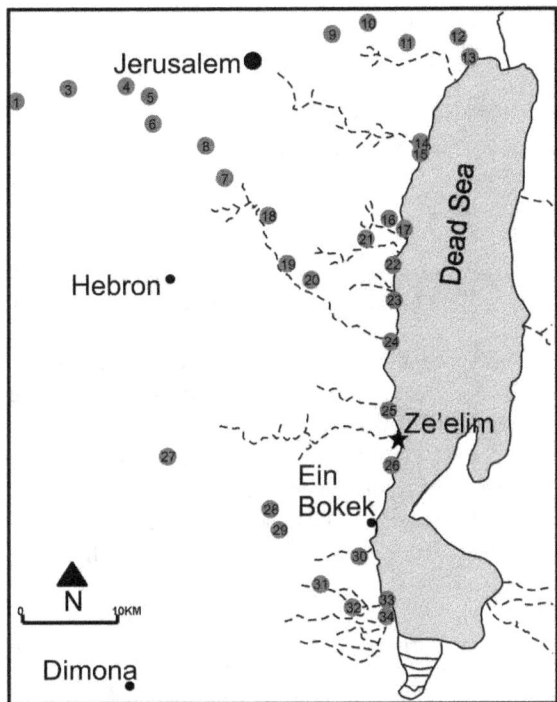

Figure 4.3 The locations of surface samples collected from the thirty-four vegetation stations from the Baruch study.[38] Samples were collected along three transects stretching from the western foot of the Judean Highlands to the western shore of the Dead Sea, covering the following vegetation zones: Mediterranean (Stations 1–8), Irano-Turanian (Stations 9–10, 18–19, 27–28) and Saharo-Arabian (Stations 11–17, 20–26, 29–34). In each station one recent pollen sample was collected and the vegetation was mapped. The vegetation was recorded during several consecutive years. This enables the calculation of the Pollen Rain Index: the ratio between the share of a taxon in the actual vegetation and their share in the pollen rain.[39]

(e.g., *Phillyrea*, *Pistacia* [pistachios], and *Pinus halepensis* [Aleppo pine]).[40] Pollen grains of some taxa such as grape (*Vitis*) are usually under-represented in the palynological spectrum due to very low pollen dispersal efficiency, and, therefore, can hardly be traced in the Ze'elim pollen record.[41] In Figure 4.4 the olive trees were combined with the other Mediterranean trees since they occupy almost the same ecological niches. This method was used in previous

38. Baruch, "The Palynology."
39. Modified after Baruch, "The Palynology."
40. For a detailed pollen diagram of the Ze'elim Dead Sea, see Langgut et al., "Dead Sea Pollen."
41. Langgut et al., "Dead Sea Pollen."

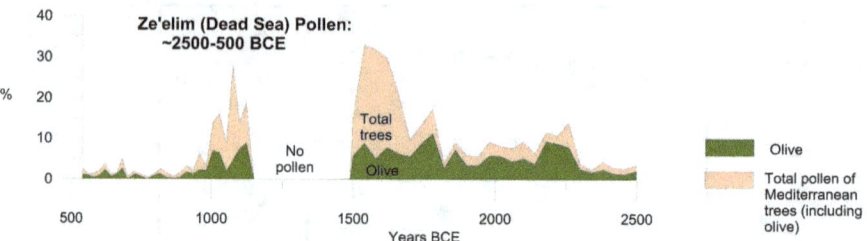

Figure 4.4 Simplified pollen diagrams of the Dead Sea (Ze'elim) record presenting paleo-environmental reconstruction for the *c.* 2500–500 years BCE time interval.[44]

palynological studies from the region.[42] Olive trees, like other Mediterranean trees, require at least 400 mm of annual rainfall in order to thrive.[43] In antiquity, areas of Mediterranean forest/maquis had already been replaced by olive orchards through human agency. The combined arboreal pollen curve is used in this study to trace changes in humidity: high arboreal pollen percentages represent humid climate conditions and vice versa. The olive pollen curve is used in order to trace changes in the extent of olive orchards in the Judean Highlands.

The Jerusalem Highlands

The site of ancient Jerusalem is located east of the central highland watershed on the fringe of the Judean Desert (Figures 4.1b and 4.5).[45] Today, the immediate surroundings of the city (one to three kilometers away from the Old City) are characterized by inhospitable, rocky terrain, and it seems that similar conditions typified the region in the past, as very few archaeological sites of any kind or from any period have been uncovered in this area.[46] By contrast, the area to the northwest, west, and southwest of Jerusalem is dominated by two major valleys

---

42. Aharon Horowitz, *The Quaternary of Israel* (New York: Academic, 1979), 193; Uri Baruch, "The Late Holocene Vegetational History of Lake Kinneret (Sea of Galilee), Israel," *Paléorient* 12 (1986): 37–48.

43. Israel Finkelstein and Dafna Langgut, "Climate, Settlement History, and Olive Cultivation in the Iron Age Southern Levant," *BASOR* 379 (2018): 153–69.

44. Finkelstein and Langgut, "Climate," fig. 2b.

45. The Old City of Jerusalem is adjacent to the watershed on its eastern side (Figure 4.5). Gehenna (literally translated as "Valley of Hinnom"), a small stream of Nahal Kidron, separates the Old City and the watershed. The watershed line surrounds the city from the north and the west: Mount Scopus, Bar-Ilan Street, Jaffa Street, Nachlaot Neighborhood, King George Street, Keren Hayesod Street, and Hebron Road. The circle that the watershed line established around the Old City is responsible for shaping Jerusalem's hilly landscape, as mentioned in Psalms (125:2): As the mountains surround Jerusalem.

46. Yuval Gadot, "In the Valley of the King: Jerusalem's Rural Hinterland in the 8th–4th Centuries BCE," *Tel Aviv* 42 (2015): 3–28.

4. Wildscapes, Landscapes, and Specialized Land Management

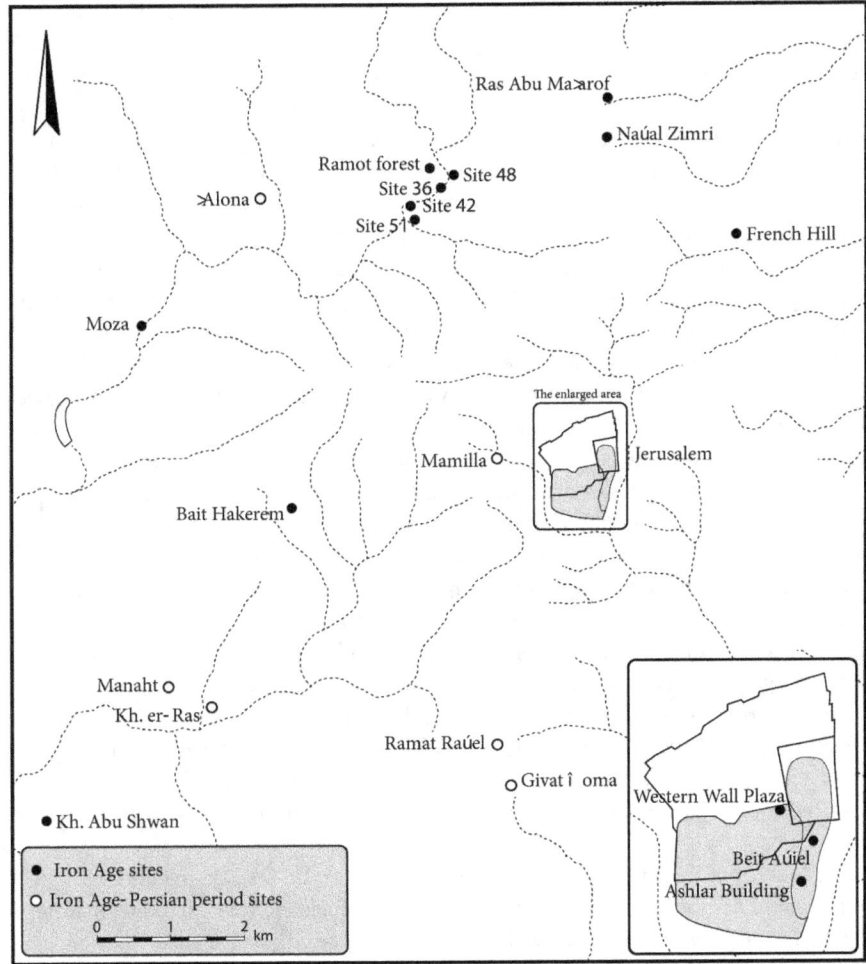

Figure 4.5 The location of the Repha'im and Soreq Valleys and their tributaries, the watershed, Jerusalem as well as other sites mentioned in the text.

(= wadi beds) that merge about ten kilometers to the southwest of the city—the Soreq and the Repha'im Valleys (Figure 4.5). Together with their tributaries, these valleys served as the "food basket" of ancient Jerusalem.[47] Their wadi beds hold rich alluvial soil suitable for dry farming, and small springs located along these valleys could have been used for watering crops requiring intensive irrigation. The hills located immediately to the east of the city could have been utilized primarily for herding.

47. Gershon Edelstein and Shimon Gibson, "Ancient Jerusalem's Rural Food Basket," *BAR* 8 (1982): 46–54.

The Iron Age IIB–C (late eighth to early sixth centuries BCE) marks an extraordinary intensification of rural activities all around Jerusalem and especially in the Soreq and Repha'im Valleys (Figure 4.5).[48] Sixty-five sites were counted in previous publications and there are a few more that have been excavated since then, some of them of extraordinary importance for understanding early seventh-century BCE Jerusalem.[49] The accumulated knowledge from these excavated sites allows us to truly recognize the unique function of some of the sites and the hierarchy among them. It seems that outside of Jerusalem itself we can recognize four tiers of sites: (i) isolated agricultural production sites such as wine presses, (ii) isolated buildings and farmsteads, (iii) villages, and finally, (iv) sites that carry with them monumental grandeur.[50] In the case of Jerusalem, the highest tier includes two centers that are located in the immediate vicinity of the city, each serving a different purpose: Tel Moza and Ramat Raḥel. At Moza there are thirty-seven large granaries that were probably a means to store vast quantities of cereals that were grown in the fertile land of the Soreq Valley further to the east (Figure 4.5).[51] The site's animal economy is that of a production site.[52] The very small number of handles stamped with *lmlk* stamp impressions or other later types indicate that storing wine was not an important component of the site's economy. Ramat Raḥel was above all a palatial center built with grandeur, using architectural elements such as decorated stone capitals, window balustrades, and more, in order to communicate messages of might and control. It served for ceremonies and political gatherings. While not even a single silo was found and the animal economy was typical of a consumer site, the high number of stamped *lmlk* handles at Ramat Raḥel is a clear indication of the site's role as a collection center for taxes such as wine and possibly other beverages.[53]

At a lower tier were the villages such as Kh. el-Burj and 'Alona to the north and Kh. Er-Ras to the southwest. These were composed of large dwellings that were

48. Gadot, "In the Valley of the King"; Yuval Gadot et al., "OSL Dating of Pre-Terraced and Terraced Landscape: Land Transformation in Jerusalem's Rural Hinterland," *Journal of Archaeological Science: Reports* 21 (2018): 575–83; Gadot et al., "What Kind."

49. Benyamin Storchan, "Jerusalem, 'Emeq Lavan," *Hadashot Arkheologiyot* 127 (2015); Benyamin Storchan, "Jerusalem, Ramat Shelomo," *Hadashot Arkheologiyot* 129 (2017); Ya'akov Billig, Liora Freud, and Efrat Bocher, "A Luxurious Royal Estate from the First Temple Period in Armon ha-Natziv, Jerusalem," *Tel Aviv* 49.1 (2022): 8–31; Neria Sapir, Nathan Ben-Ari, Liora Freud and Oded Lipschits, "History, Economy and Administration in Late Iron Age Judah in Light of the Excavations at Mordot Arnona, Jerusalem," *Tel Aviv* 49.1 (2022): 32–53.

50. It should be noted that, even within these four categories, it is possible to recognize variation in the nature and function of specific sites.

51. Zvi Greenhut, Alon De-Groot, and Eldad Barzilay, *Salvage Excavations at Tel Moza: The Bronze and Iron Age Settlements and Later Occupations* (Jerusalem: Israel Antiquities Authority, 2009).

52. Lidar Sapir-Hen, Yuval Gadot, and Israel Finkelstein, "Animal Economy in a Temple City and Its Countryside: Iron Age Jerusalem as a Case Study," *BASOR* 375 (2016): 103–18.

53. Oded Lipschits et al., *What Are the Stones Whispering: 3000 Years of Forgotten History at Ramat Raḥel* (Winona Lake, IN: Eisenbrauns, 2017).

either built one next to the other or at some distance from each other.[54] In either case the dwellings were surrounded by rock-cut agricultural installations, mainly wine presses. These sites seemed to be a continuation of an earlier local agrarian tradition that began long before Judah came under Assyrian domination.

Thirty-three sites may be recognized as single farmsteads or even single small buildings. These buildings are not uniform in their ground plan and vary between those built to fit the surrounding topography and those that had a more pre-planned design.[55] A number of the excavated sites should be understood as intermediate collecting hubs and, as such, pointed toward the way the landscape was administrated. One example of such a place is the "Storeroom Building," located on the slopes of the Soreq, part of a "Building Cluster" that was built along the upper Soreq stream.[56] The building is unique in its size and the number of its rooms. Other examples of buildings with a semi-public nature are the ones built with a large frontal courtyard surrounded by two or three wings. This design, termed "Open Courtyard Building," was introduced to Judah with the coming of the Assyrians, after it was already adapted in the former territory of Israel.[57] The best example of an "Open-Courtyard Building" was found in Mamilla, just west of the Old City of Jerusalem and outside the boundary of the city during the Iron Age II.[58] It includes a large, isolated building measuring 20 × 20 m with two wings, one to the south and one to the west, and each is further divided into rooms. Three such buildings were found at Kh. Er-Ras and one at the "Building Cluster." It seems that the common denominator in all these buildings is the uniqueness of the courtyard and its relation to other components of the building. It is much larger than the inner courtyards that typify other types of buildings and it is positioned in front of the two wings. These features turn the courtyards into an area that can serve an administrative, public function. Finally, it should be noted that the many single building sites as well as farmsteads are not an indication of demographic growth. Their distribution along the tributaries of the Repha'im and Soreq Valleys points towards their connection with farming activities (Figure 4.5).

The main agro-production installation documented along the slopes of the Repha'im and the Soreq Rivers and their many tributaries are the rock-cut wine presses which are found inside and outside of the settlements. In a 2003 publication,

54. E.g. Gadot, "In the Valley of the King," fig. 2; S. Weksler-Bdolah, "Alona," *Excavations and Surveys in Israel* 19 (1997): 68–70.

55. Yuval Gadot and Efrat Bocher, "The Introduction of the 'Open-Courtyard Building' to the Jerusalem Landscape and Judean-Assyrian Interaction," in *Archaeology and History of Eight-Century Judah*, ed. Zev I. Farber and L. Jacob Wright (Atlanta: Society of Biblical Literature, 2018), 205–28.

56. Gadot et al., "What Kind."

57. Ruth B. K. Amiran and Immanuel Dunayevsky, "The Assyrian Open-Court Building and Its Palestinian Derivatives," *BASOR* 149 (1958): 25–32; Gadot and Bocher, "The Introduction."

58. David Amit, "First and Second Temple Period Discoveries Near the Mamilla Pool in Jerusalem," *Qadmoniot* 44 (2011): 29–34.

Table 4.1 The fifty-seven excavated and surveyed wine presses along the Repha'im and Soreq Catchments dating to the late Iron Age

Name of site	No. of presses	Region	Reference and comments
Rogem Gannim	8	Repha'im Catchment	Raphael Greenberg and Gilad Cinamon, "Stamped and Incised Jar Handles"
Giv'at Massuah	5	Repha'im Catchment	Gilad Ovadia, "Jerusalem, Giv'at Massu'a," *Excavations and Surveys in Israel* 12 (1993): 71–6
Beit Safafa	4	Repha'im Catchment	Nurit Feig, "Excavations at Beit Safafa: Iron Age II and Byzantine Agricultural Installations South of Jerusalem," *'Atiqot* 44 (2003): 191–238
Manhat	16	Repha'im Catchment	Raphael Greenberg and Gilad Cinamon, "Stamped and Incised Jar Handles"
Kh. Er. Eas	2	Repha'im Catchment	Gadot, "In the Valley of the King"
'Emeq Lavan	3	Repha'im Catchment	Storchan, "Jerusalem, 'Emeq Lavan"
'En Lavan	1	Repha'im Catchment	Yuval Baruch, "A Farmstead from the End of the Iron Age and Installations at the Foot of Khirbat Abu Shawan," *Atiqot* 56 (2007): 25–55 (Hebrew with English summary)
Nahal Draga	3	Kidron Catchment	Brzaily, pers. comm.
Har Homa	1	Kidron Catchment	Gideon Solimany, "Jerusalem, Har Homa," *Hadashot Arkheologiyot* 124 (2012); Internet Edition: www.hadashot-esi.org.il/report_detail_eng.aspx?id=2020&mag_id=119 (accessed August 21, 2023)
Pisgat Ze'ev	1	Nahal Zimri Catchment	Yitzhak Maitlis, "Jerusalem, Wadi Zimra," *Excavations and Surveys in Israel* 10 (1991): 125–7
Tel el-Ful	1	Soreq Catchment	Annette Nagar, "Jerusalem, Tell el-Ful," *Hadashot Arkheologiyot* 126 (2014); Internet Edition: www.hadashot-esi.org.il/Report_Detail_Eng.aspx?id=10615&mag_id=121 (accessed August 21, 2023)
Ramot Sholomo	1	Soreq Catchment	Storchan, "Jerusalem, Ramat Shelomo"
Ramot forest	3	Soreq Catchment	Uri Davidovich, et al, "Salvage Excavation at Ramot Forest and Ramat Bet-Hakerem: New Data Regarding Jerusalem's Periphery during the First and Second Temple Periods," *New Studies on Jerusalem* 11 (2006): 35–112 (Hebrew): Site 14/26
Nahal Shemuel	5	Soreq Catchment	See below
'Alona	2	Soreq Catchment	Weksler-Bdolah, "Alona"
Wadi 'Ein Karem	1	Soreq Cathment	Gadot, pers. comm.

Greenberg and Cinamon gathered published and unpublished archaeological data from the Repha'im Catchment and counted thirty-five wine presses.[59] Table 4.1 below is an updated count that includes similarly dated wine presses found along the Soreq Catchment as well as newly published ones from the Repha'im Catchment. All in all, the number stands now at fifty-seven such installations (Table 4.1 and Figure 4.5).

As was noted above, most of the wine presses dated to the late Iron Age have one or two niches carved into the back wall of the treading surface. D. Amit and I. Yezerski were the first to suggest that this technological feature, which allowed a second squeezing event by a beam, is indicative of an Iron Age wine press, although their dating was indirect.[60] Excavations conducted by one of the authors (Gadot) at Kh. Er-Ras seem to have unearthed more direct evidence for the proposed dating. Two wine presses were found at the site, both of them in association with structures built during the late Iron Age. Especially apparent was the connection between Wine press I and Building II where the western external wall of the southern wing of the building also served as a wall for the wine press, proving that the two features were planned and built together. A collection of at least twenty-three holemouth jars of different sizes were found in a pile inside the room just east of the wine press. These jars are conclusively dated to the last part of the Iron Age and are probably connected to the storage of products manufactured at the wine press (Figure 4.6).

An illuminating example for the nature of the specialized wine industry around Jerusalem is being excavated by the authors along the slopes of Nahal Shemuel. This short tributary of the Soreq, located northwest of the city, is a mosaic of different slope angles, soil types and thickness, vegetation, and, finally, agricultural activities; all are the result of a series of faults that have led to the exposure of different formations at varying levels.[61] Consequently, the slopes of Nahal Shemuel were only sporadically terraced. Instead, it seems that intensive stone clearance activities created small and shallow soil pockets in between the outcrops of Aminadav and Weradim rock formations. More than fifty stone heaps in various shapes and sizes were documented in a survey of the site and they serve as silent testimony for these activities. One of the stone heaps was sampled using OSL dating techniques. The test showed that the soil at the base of the heap had last been exposed to sunlight approximately 2,400 years ago (±160 years), a date that allows a possible connection to the act of clearing the stones to the end of the Iron Age or the Persian period. That said, it is clear that the act of stone clearing was not limited to the Iron Age. An ongoing study has excavated several more such stone heaps and taken samples for OSL dating. When the results are in, it will be possible to differentiate dates acquired from soil samples below the heaps from those acquired from soil samples inside the heaps, and thus narrow the margin of error regarding the dates the samples give.

59. Raphael Greenberg and Gilad Cinamon, "Stamped and Incised Jar Handles from Rogem Ganim and Their Implications for the Political Economy of Jerusalem, Late 8th–Early 7th Centuries BCE," *Tel Aviv* 33 (2006): table 2.

60. Amit and Yezerski, "An Iron Age II Cemetery and Wine Presses at An-Nabi Danyal."

61. Gadot et al., "OSL Dating."

Figure 4.6 Wine press I and the southwest room of Building II at Kh. Er-Ras.

Located in between the many stone piles (Figure 4.7) are the remains of at least four stone-built structures. We excavated one such structure made of large undressed stones and located about mid-way up the slope (Figure 4.8). It is a rectangular platform approximately 4.5 by 6.5 meters. The excavation found no clear "floor horizon" or any inner partition wall in the inner part of the structure. This is different from the single buildings found in nearby areas and discussed above. The structure's size and nature as well as its location in the middle of the slope indicates it was likely used as a watchtower. The pottery found in the fill of the structure was dated to the Iron Age IIC (mid-seventh to early sixth centuries BCE).

Another prominent feature of the slope was five stone-cut wine presses, with rectangular niches fitted into the press's carved back wall (Figure 4.2). The wine presses were not dated independently by us. We base their dating on the rock-cut niches and on their association with the well-dated stone piles and towers.

Taken together, the Nahal Shemuel eastern slope was adapted during the late Iron Age for growing grapes for wine production. The grapes were probably planted in soil pockets located in between the rock outcrops. We assume that the grapes were not trellised but were cultivated along the ground. This cultivation method is more common in traditional agriculture when growing grapes for wine (rather than for eating) since contact with the ground promotes fruit ripening due to the heat. Small stone towers served as watchtowers and possibly temporary

4. *Wildscapes, Landscapes, and Specialized Land Management* 75

Figure 4.7 A stone pile at Nahal Shemuel. Photo taken by Dafna Langgut.

Figure 4.8 Remains of a structure at Nahal Shemuel. Based on its size as well as its location in the middle of the slope, it is assumed that it was used as a watchtower. Photo taken by Dafna Langgut.

shelters for people, equipment, and possibly even the products. An interesting parallel to this reconstruction of an agricultural activity can be found in Isa. 5:1-2:

1 The Song of the Vineyard:
I will sing for the one I love
  a song about his vineyard:
My loved one had a vineyard
  on a fertile hillside.

2 He dug it up and cleared it of stones
  and planted it with the choicest vines.
He built a watchtower in it
  and cut out a wine press as well.

This text is debatably dated to between the eighth to fifth centuries BCE.[62] It describes the common viticulture elements and activities. These elements are wonderfully mirrored in our finds, and in our understanding and reconstruction of the agricultural activity during the Iron Age in this area: clearing stones, building towers, and producing wine (Figure 4.9).

The dedication of the slopes of Nahal Shemuel for vines was part of a larger system. Deep jar-shaped cellars were found in clusters in many Iron Age sites located on the Benjamin plateau north of Jerusalem. The largest concentration of such an installation was published from Gibeon with as many as sixty-three rock-cut cellars.[63] Pritchard has interpreted these cellars as large underground storage facilities for ageing wine and termed them a "Winery." Twenty-four such wineries were found at the site of el-Burj located on a high hill overlooking the Shemuel Stream and two kilometers away from the wine press described above.[64] It seems that the site of el-Burj was the collection center for wine grown along the slopes of Nahal Shemuel and probably other tributaries as well.

Contrary to the high number of wine presses found all around Jerusalem, the number of olive press installations is small. One such installation was found in the City of David ridge within a rock-cut room that was possibly used for

---

62. Marvin L. Chaney, "Whose Sour Grapes? The Addressees of Isaiah 5: 1–7 in the Light of Political Economy," *Semeia* 87 (1999): 106; Hugh G. M. Williamson, *Isaiah 1–5: A Critical and Exegetical Commentary* (London; New York: T&T Clark, 2006); Mark Chikuni, "A Critical Analysis of the Genre and the Message of Isaiah 5:1–7," *DARE: Holy Trinity College Journal* 11 (2019): 131–45.

63. James B. Pritchard, *Winery, Defenses, and Soundings at Gibeon* (Philadelphia: Penn Press, 1964), 1–8.

64. Alon De-Groot and Michal Weinberg-Stern, "Wine, Oil and Gibeonites: Iron II–III at Kh. El-Burj Northern Jerusalem," *New Studies on Jerusalem* 19 (2013): 95–102 (Hebrew with an English summary).

4. Wildscapes, Landscapes, and Specialized Land Management 77

Figure 4.9 Harvesting of grapes growing along the ground in soil pockets in the Hebron Mountains. Grapes grown on the ground ripen early, at the beginning of the summer. In the background to the left, a watchtower located at mid-slope and a stone pile can be seen. Undated (1900s–1930s), American Colony Photo, Department photographers, Roggel Collection, Rehovot, IL; courtesy of Bitmuna.

cult activities, and three other installations were found in villages surrounding the city.[65]

Finally, other kinds of agricultural activities dating to the late Iron Age should also be noted, as they were also conducted as part of a large-scale network typical

---

65. For the City of David, see Nahshon Szanton, "The Rock-Cut Rooms and Cave 1: Evidence for Cultic Activity along the City of David's Eastern Slope in the Iron Age II," *New Studies on Jerusalem and Its Region* 19 (2013): 58–67 (Hebrew); for el-Burj, see De-Groot and Weinberg-Stern, "Wine, Oil and Gibeonites: Iron II–III at Kh. El-Burj Northern Jerusalem"; for Abu Shawan, see Yuval Baruch, "A Farmstead from the End of the Iron Age and Installations at the Foot of Khirbat Abū Shawān," *'Atiqot* 56 (2007): 71–74 (Hebrew); for 'Alona, see Weksler-Bdolah, "'Alona."

of an estate. The center at Tel Moza seems to have been devoted to storing grain.[66] Several small buildings and one storage center were documented in salvage excavations that were conducted along the slopes of the upper Soreq Stream some four kilometers east of Tel Moza.[67] These buildings are located a short distance from each other and were termed a "Building Cluster." The lack of incised and imprinted storage jar handles shows that the system to which the building cluster belonged was not part of the estates that brought their produce in lmlk stamped jars. It seems therefore that the small buildings are an indication of the presence of laborers who worked on the plots of land in the stream itself; most probably grains were then collected and stored in the silos of Moza. Evidence for a second estate was found at the spring of 'Ain Joweizeh (along N. Repha'im) where a typical eighth-century BCE decorated, carved stone capital was found.[68] The spring's waters were collected via a long, rock-cut tunnel into a collecting pool. From there the waters were channeled and used for artificial irrigation of fields and gardens located on small terraces below. The location of the capital dates the establishment of the site to the late eighth/early seventh centuries BCE and indicates that it was part of a public enterprise, possibly a location of an Assyrian style "Bitanu."[69]

The Shephelah

While the archaeological and palynological evidence point to the expansion of viticulture in the Judean Highlands rather than olive culture during the late Iron Age, an opposite picture emerges for the Shephelah. Unfortunately, pollen grains which originated in the Shephelah olive orchards cannot be detected by the Dead Sea pollen records because of the barrier created by the massive block of the Judean Highlands.[70] Mid- to late Holocene palynological records west of the watershed are not available.[71] Yet, large-scale olive horticulture during the late Iron Age in the

---

66. Greenhut, De-Groot, and Barzilay, *Salvage Excavations at Tel Moza*; Israel Finkelstein and Yuval Gadot, "Mozah, Nephtoah and Royal Estates in the Jerusalem Highlands," *Semitica et Classica* 8 (2015): 227–34.

67. Gadot et al., "What Kind."

68. Daniel Ein-Mor, "Walajeh ('Ain Joweizeh): Preliminary Report," *Hadashot Arkheologiyot: Excavations and Surveys in Israel* 125 (2013).

69. Ali Asadpour, "Phenomenology of Garden in Assyrian Documents and Reliefs: Concepts and Types," *Bagh-e Nazar* 15, no. 60 (2018): 55–66.

70. Finkelstein and Langgut, "Climate."

71. Other proxies such as the identification of charcoal assemblages from sites located in the Shephelah can also be used only in a very limited way since, at most assemblages, Iron Age strata were grouped together and, therefore, cannot be used to trace changes in the extent of olive groves along that period (Liphschitz, *Timber*; Nili Liphschitz, "Reconstruction of the Arboreal Vegetation of Judea and Samaria Mountains," in *The Hill Country and the Shephelah and in the Arabah*, ed. Shay Bar [Chicago: Ariel, 2008], 48–55).

Shephelah is clearly evident by the widespread occurrence of olive oil installations found in the region. Olive oil presses are usually located near the vicinity of the orchards in order to save the need for transporting the raw material and since the oil extraction should take place no more than forty-eight hours from harvest, in order to avoid bitterness of the fruits.

To date, the earliest evidence of intensive olive oil production was published from the Philistine Tel es-Safi/Gath.[72] One such installation dates to the late Iron I/ early Iron IIA period and several other such installations are dated to the late Iron Age IIA period (ninth century BCE). These installations were found in the upper and lower city and indicate that much of this part of the city was dedicated to the production of olive oil well before the arrival of the Assyrian empire. It seems, however, that the taking over of Philistine royal cities by the Assyrians accelerated the region's specialization in olive oil. An unprecedented and intense olive oil production dated to Iron Age IIB–IIC (probably early seventh century BCE) was identified at Tel Miqne-Ekron. It is described as the largest olive oil industry in antiquity with over 115 installations characterized by scores of uniformly made olive presses found throughout the site.[73] Additional evidence for olive oil production in the region during the Iron Age IIB–IIC (probably early seventh century BCE) was documented at Tel Batash, where excavations revealed several olive press installations similar to those found at Tel Miqne-Ekron.[74]

Evidence for specialized olive oil production is also found at Judahite sites that date to the late eighth century BCE, a period when Judah was already under the yoke of the Assyrian empire. At Tell Beit Mirsim and Tel Beth-Shemesh, late eighth-century BCE olive oil presses were also reported.[75] The large number of *lmlk* storage jars which were retrieved from Stratum III at Lachish may also be related

---

72. Maeir, Welch, and Eniukhina, "A Note."

73. Seymour Gitin, "Ekron of the Philistines, Part II: Olive-Oil Suppliers to the World," *Biblical Archaeology Review* 16 (1990): 32; Seymour Gitin, "The Neo-Assyrian Empire and Its Western Periphery: The Levant, with a Focus on Philistine Ekron," in *Assyria 1995: Proceedings of the 10th Anniversary Symposium of the Neo-Assyrian Text Corpus Project, Helsinki, September 7–11*, ed. Simo Parpola and Robert Whiting, Neo-Assyrian Text Corpus Project (Helsinki: University of Helsinki, 1997), 77–103; Seymour Gitin, "Neo-Assyrian and Egyptian Hegemony over Ekron in the Seventh Century: A Response to Lawrence E. Stager," *Eretz Israel* 27 (2003): 55–61; David Eitam, "The Olive Oil Industry at Tel Miqne-Ekron During the Late Iron Age," in *Olive Oil in Antiquity: Israel and Neighbouring Countries from the Neolithic to the Early Arab Period*, ed. David Eitam and Mikha'el Heltzer, History of the Ancient Near East 8 (Padova: Sargon, 1996), 167–98.

74. Amihai Mazar, *Timnah (Tel Batash) I: Stratigraphy and Architecture, Vol. 2: Text*, Qedem 37 (Jerusalem: Institute of Archaeology, Hebrew University of Jerusalem, 1997), 262–3.

75. David Eitam, "Olive Presses of the Israelite Period," *Tel Aviv* 6 (1979): 146–55; Shlomo Bunimovitz, Zvi Lederman, and W. Manor Dale, "The Archaeology of Border Communities: Renewed Excavations at Tel Beth-Shemesh, Part 1: The Iron Age," *Near Eastern Archaeology* 72, no. 3 (2009): 114–42.

to the extensive olive oil production characterizing Judahite controlled areas in the Shephelah during the late Iron Age,[76] suggesting royal control over olive oil distribution. The Lachish reliefs may also be used as evidence of the reality of the cultural landscape of the Shephelah during the late Iron Age, indicating a vast occurrence of olive tree orchards in the region.[77]

Recent salvage excavations that were conducted in the eastern parts of Tel Beth-Shemesh revealed new and stimulating information regarding the history of the site after 701 BCE. Apparently, the site continued to flourish during the seventh century BCE.[78] Extensive olive oil production at the site is evident based on the presence of fourteen olive presses of the type well known at other contemporary sites.[79] The salvage excavation revealed that the seventh-century BCE olive oil presses were situated on the lower part of the tell, probably part of an industrial area at the periphery of the settlement.[80] This is a marked change from the previous occupation phase during which the presses were located inside the city.[81] It is supposed that during times of centralized administration, olive oil production would have been concentrated at industrial areas near the settlements. Apparently, not only did the settlement continue at Beth-Shemesh after 701 BCE, but there was also reorganization and intensification in olive oil production at the site.

All of the above survey of evidence demonstrates that the production of olive oil, which was known from the region during the Iron Age I and Iron Age IIA, intensified during the Iron Age IIB–IIC under the Assyrian hegemony. Since no climate change was detected during the Iron Age in the southern Levant,[82] the shift to large-scale olive horticulture in the Shephelah during the late Iron Age seems to be related to political, rather than to environmental, influences. In terms of habitat requirements, olives are suitable for cultivation in the Judean Highlands as well as in the Shephelah.[83]

76. Oded Lipschits, Omer Sergi, and Ido Koch, "Judahite Stamped and Incised Jar Handles: A Tool for Studying the History of Late Monarchic Judah," *Tel Aviv* 38 (2011): 10.

77. Zohar Amar, "Agricultural Produces in the Lachish Relief," *Beth Mikra* 159 (1999): 350–56 (Hebrew).

78. Eli Haddad, Nathan Ben-Ari, and Alon De Groot, "A Century Old Enigma: The Seventh-Century BCE Settlement at Tel Beit Shemesh," *IEJ* 70 (2020): 173–89.

79. Zvi Lederman, pers. comm.; Maeir, Welch, and Eniukhina, "A Note"; Boaz Gross, "The Other Side of Beth Shemesh: Salvage Archaeology Exposes Deep History of Famed Biblical Site," *Bible History Daily (May 28, 2021)* https://www.biblicalarchaeology.org/daily/the-other-side-of-beth-shemesh/ (accessed October 16, 2023).

80. Four olive oil presses dated to the late Iron Age II were found at the salvage excavation of Tel Beit Shemesh (East) and ten other contemporaneous olive oil installations were uncovered at the neighboring salvage excavation to the south. See further, Gross, "The Other Side."

81. Zvi Lederman, pers. comm.

82. The reconstructed climate conditions during the Iron Age II were similar to those prevalent today in the region (Langgut et al., "Vegetation and Climate Changes"; Laugomer, "High Resolution").

83. The success of the olive (*Olea europaea*), i.e., fruit yield, depends mainly on the amount of precipitation and/or moisture available in the soil. An olive tree can survive in environments with less than 200 mm of annual rainfall; however, to be profitable, it

Discussion

All of the evidence above points to an intensification in land exploitation that took place during the later part of the Iron Age, when the kingdoms of Judah, Ekron, and Ashkelon were integrated into the Assyrian political and economic system. While some scholars tend to contest the Assyrian impact theory,[84] it seems that our analysis supports the view that the interest of the Assyrian empire was both political and economic, for which they crafted a political order that allowed interregional connections.[85] Their policies impacted all parts of life from privately owned objects,

---

requires at least 400–450 mm of annual rainfall. Modern orchards that receive 300–400 mm of rain are not profitable, while orchards that receive 200–300 mm rain annually yield fruit only every three to four years (Avraham Zinger, *Olive Cultivation* [Tel-Aviv: Ministry of Agriculture, 1985], 27–28). The olive thrives best in light, aerated soils; it can succeed in a relatively large variety of soil types, as long as the soil is well drained. An olive tree often thrives in a climate characterized by great differences in summer and winter temperatures. Hot conditions during the summer are needed for oil accumulation and fruit ripening, while relatively low winter temperatures (but not sub-zero) are required for bud differentiation to take place. Flowering occurs on branches that developed in the previous year; therefore, the young growth has to survive both low temperatures in winter and water shortage in summer in order to produce a good crop. Olive trees grow well in regions characterized by low air humidity, where they are less vulnerable to diseases and pests. As a result of the above conditions, in the Mediterranean Levantine region, olives are most successful in the hill country and its margins, usually below 600 m above sea level, as freezing temperatures in the winter can destroy the yield. In the highlands, olive trees can succeed in patches of rich soil where other crops are unprofitable due to limited space (Zinger, *Olive Cultivation*, 29–30). The Shephelah, with its relatively well-drained soils, can also successfully accommodate olive orchards, as can the coastal plains of the Mediterranean areas (Zinger, *Olive Cultivation*, 29–30). Yet, the latter have usually been devoted to grain cultivation.

84. Lawrence E. Stager, "Ashkelon and the Archaeology of Destruction: Kislev 604 BCE," *Eretz-Israel: Archaeological, Historical and Geographical Studies* 25 (1996): 61–74; Avraham Faust and Ehud Weiss, "Judah, Philistia, and the Mediterranean World: Reconstructing the Economic System of the Seventh Century B.C.E.," *BASOR* 338 (2005): 71–92; Avraham Faust, "The Interests of the Assyrian Empire in the West: Olive Oil Production as a Test-Case," *Journal of the Economic and Social History of the Orient* 54 (2011): 62–86; Avraham Faust, "The Assyrian Century in the Southern Levant: An Overview of the Reality on the Ground," in *The Southern Levant under Assyrian Domination*, ed. Shawn Zelig Aster and Avraham Faust (University Park, PA: Eisenbrauns, 2018), 20–55; Avraham Faust, *The Neo-Assyrian Empire in the Southwest: Imperial Domination and Its Consequences* (Oxford: Oxford University Press, 2021); Daniel M. Master, "Economy and Exchange in the Iron Age Kingdoms of the Southern Levant," *BASOR* 372 (2014): 81–97.

85. Nadav Na'aman, "'The House-of-No-Shade Shall Take Away Its Tax from You' (Micah I 11)," *VT* 45, no. 4 (1995): 516–27; Seymour Gitin, "Tel Miqne-Ekron in the 7th Century BCE: The Impact of Economic Innovation and Foreign Cultural Influences on a Neo-Assyrian Vassal City-State," in *Recent Excavations in Israel: A View to the West*, ed.

such as seals,[86] through architecture,[87] and up to the creation of unified regional economies.[88] When it came to horticulture, the intensification and specialization of agricultural activities in the highlands meant exploitation of inhospitable rock terrain that was previously uncultivated. The agricultural lands were most probably managed by estates that may have belonged to the political or religious elite. Such activities required the deployment of manpower and other long-term investments. Most of the plots were dedicated for the production of one product: grapes/wine. On the lower hills to the west, olive oil production was centralized and an ever-growing number of cities became hubs of olive oil production. All of these characteristics are not typical of household-based cultivation which is usually based on a mixed economy (reducing risks),[89] cultivating small-sized plots and avoiding exploitation of micro-environments that demand a great deal of investment before they become cultivable.

Seymour Gitin (Dubuque, IA: Kendall Hunt Publishing, 1995), 61–79; Ephraim Stern, *Archaeology of the Land of the Bible: Vol. II: The Assyrian, Babylonian and Persian Periods. 732–332 BCE* (New York: Doubleday, 2001); Israel Finkelstein and Nadav Na'aman, "The Judahite Shephelah in the Late 8th and Early 7th Centuries BCE," *Tel Aviv* 31, no. 1 (2004): 60–79; Yifat Thareani, "In the Service of the Empire: Local Elites and 'Pax Assyriaca' in the Negev," *Eretz-Israel* 29 (2009): 184–91; Yifat Thareani, "The Empire and the 'Upper Sea': Assyrian Control Strategies along the Southern Levantine Coast," *BASOR* 375 (2016): 77–102; Lipschits, Sergi, and Koch, "Judahite Stamped and Incised Jar Handles"; K. Lawson Younger, "The Assyrian Impact on the Southern Levant in Light of Recent Study," *IEJ* 65 (2014): 179–204; Ido Koch, "Introductory Framework for Assyrian-Levantine Colonial Encounters," *Semitica* 60 (2018): 367–96.

86. Ariel Winderbaum, "Assur in Jerusalem: New Glyptic Evidence of the Assyrian Influence on Jerusalem," *New Studies in the Archaeology of Jerusalem and Its Region* 6 (2012): 83–104 (Hebrew).

87. D. Ussishkin, "The Water Systems of Jerusalem During Hezekiah's Reign," in *Meilenstein: Festgabe für Herbert Donner zum 16. Februar 1995*, ed. Stefan Timm and Manfred Weippert, Ägypten und Altes Testament 30 (Wiesbaden: Harrassowitz, 1995), 298–307; Gadot and Bocher, "The Introduction."

88. Gitin, "Tel Miqne-Ekron"; Lidar Sapir-Hen, Yuval Gadot, and Israel Finkelstein, "Environmental and Historical Impacts on Long Term Animal Economy: The Southern Levant in the Late Bronze and Iron Ages," *Journal of Economic and Social History of the Orient* 57 (2014): 703–44; Lidar Sapir-Hen, "Pax Assyriaca and the Animal Economy in the Southern Levant: Regional and Local-Scale Imperial Contacts," in *Rethinking Israel: Studies in the History and Archaeology of Ancient Israel, in Honor of Israel Finkelstein*, ed. Oded Lipschits, Yuval Gadot, and Matthew J. Adams (University Park, PA: Eisenbrauns, 2017), 341–53.

89. In historical periods, small-scale mixed Mediterranean farming usually combined intensively managed gardens with small fields for growing cereals/legumes and limited fruit tree horticulture as well as animal husbandry. Agricultural land use systems concentrated on localized, risk-buffering strategies, where food sources were carefully managed, and the risk of one resource failing could be compensated by another (e.g., Weiberg et al., "Mediterranean Land Use Systems").

4. Wildscapes, Landscapes, and Specialized Land Management

This picture of specialized horticulture under Assyrian influence emerges from several lines of evidence: archaeological findings of industrial installations (olive and wine presses) as well as findings related to centralized storage and distribution of agricultural products, changes in the settlement pattern (mainly in the highlands) and also based on fossil pollen data. The palynological evidence of the Dead Sea Ze'elim record demonstrates a shift in the economic strategy of the Judean Highlands based on a significant reduction in olive pollen ratios during the late Iron Age (Figure 4.4). The decreasing olive pollen percentages point to the shrinkage of olive orchards in the region (at least in the eastern sections of the Judean Highlands), in comparison to the intense olive horticulture which took place during the Iron Age I in the area.[90] Interestingly, grape (*Vitis*) pollen, which is usually under-represented in palynological spectra, begins to appear at the Ein Gedi Holocene diagram at the later stage of the eighth century BCE, after a total absence for thousands of years.[91] Low arboreal values in the Dead Sea pollen records (Ze'elim and Ein Gedi) during the Iron Age II do not reflect diminishing precipitation, as sediments along the sampling location were embedded in high lake levels.[92] Rather, this may reflect the peak of settlement activity, and hence deforestation, in the Judean Highlands in the Iron Age IIB–IIC.[93] It seems that under Assyrian domination, some of the settlement processes were dictated by geopolitical conditions, and it also seems that climate played no role in the shift to a specialized economy.[94]

Summary

Humans in the Levant have exploited landscapes for foraging and hunting throughout their history and, with growing extent and intensity over the last c. 11,000 years, for agriculture and animal production. Because of its long history and widespread spatial extent, land use represents the first major influence that humans had on the wild landscape of the region. Specific land uses are, thus,

---

90. Finkelstein and Langgut, "Climate."

91. Litt et al., "Holocene Climate Variability." Based on its sedimentology and lithology, the Ein Gedi sediment core that covers the Holocene was extracted from a high lake levels environment (versus shallow lake or shore environment). That means that local contribution of pollen from the Ein Gedi Oasis was very limited (Baruch, "The Palynology"; Litt et al., "Holocene Climate Variability").

92. Langgut et al., "Dead Sea Pollen"; Kagan et al., "Chronology."

93. Avi Ofer, "'All the Hill Country of Judah': From a Settlement Fringe to a Prosperous Monarchy," in *From Nomadism to Monarchy: Archaeological and Historical Aspects of Early Israel*, ed. Israel Finkelstein and Nadav Na'aman (Jerusalem: Yad Izhak Ben-Zvi, 1994), 92–121; Israel Finkelstein and Neil Asher Silberman, "Temple and Dynasty: Hezekiah, the Remaking of Judah and the Rise of the Pan-Israelite Ideology," *JSOT* 30 (2006): 259–85.

94. Langgut et al., "Vegetation and Climate Changes"; Laugomer, "High Resolution"; Finkelstein and Langgut, "Climate."

typically associated with certain environmental conditions. However, the physical environment alone does not determine the cultural landscape. The transformation of the natural wildscape into a landscape sculpted by humans is a function of the sociocultural characteristics of the people who live in the region: their diet, technology, land management practices, social organization, and changes in population density. This chapter presents a special case study in the history of the cultural landscape of the southern Levant, when political circumstances served as a critical factor that influenced land uses and shaped the landscape. Our case study demonstrates the massive influence of the Assyrian empire in the southern Levant, and by the intensive trade in the eastern Mediterranean basin, on a previously unknown scale, during the Iron Age IIB–IIC (late eighth to seventh centuries BCE). The southern Levant, on the periphery of the empire, was directly ruled by the imperial powers that imposed their military and economic interests on the region. This study illuminates the magnitude and the effects of this imperial intervention on horticultural activities in the area.

We claim that under Assyrian rule, the regional economy shifted from a typical mixed Mediterranean agriculture to a specialized one. In the Judean Highlands, the intensification and specialization of agricultural activities meant exploitation of inhospitable rock terrain that was previously uncultivated, management of land by estates (probably belonging to the political or religious elite), and the dedication of most of the plots for the production of one product: wine. On the lower hills to the west (the Shephelah), olive oil production was centralized, and a greater number of settlements became hubs of olive oil production during the seventh century BCE. Our study paints a clear picture of the integration of several lines of evidence: archaeological findings of industrial installations (olive and wine presses); findings related to centralized storage and distribution of agricultural products; changes in settlement patterns and within the location of the agricultural installations at the sites. This picture is also corroborated by fossil pollen data which point to a dramatic decrease in olive (*Olea*) pollen percentages and an increase in grape (*Vitis*) pollen ratios at the Judean Highlands during the late Iron Age. This integrated picture indicates that, under Assyrian influence, viticulture flourished in the Judean Highlands and oleaculture intensified in the Shephelah.

Acknowledgments

We gratefully thank Nitzan Ben-Melech for her help in co-directing the excavation at Nahal Shemuel. We are also grateful to the many volunteers who participated in the dig. Our appreciation goes to Israel Finkelstein, Naomi Porat, and Yoav Avni for the exchange of thoughts and ideas. Finally, we would like to thank Dalit Rom-Shiloni for her kind invitation to participate in the session, "Nature Imagery and Conceptions of Nature in the Bible" (San Diego, November 2019, Society of Biblical Literature). This chapter is based on the study that was presented at this conference.

Bibliography

Ackerman, Oren, Noam Greenbaum, Hendrik J. Bruins, Miryam Bar-Matthews, Avner Ayalon, Ahuva Almogi-Labin, Bettina Schilman, Michael Davis, and Aren M. Maier. "The Environmental and Paleogeographical History of Tell Es-Safi/Gath During the Last Eight Millennia." In *Tell Es-Safi/Gath I: The 1996–2005 Seasons*, edited by Aren M. Maeir, 531–56. Ägypten und Altes Testament 69. Wiesbaden: Harrassowitz, 2012.

Ackermann, Oren, Noam Greenbaum, Hendrik Bruins, Naomi Porat, Mira Bar-Matthews, Ahuva Almogi-Labin, Bettina Schilman, Avner Ayalon, Liora Kolska Horwitz, et al. "Palaeoenvironment and Anthropogenic Activity in the Southeastern Mediterranean Since the Mid-Holocene: The Case of Tell Es-Safi/Gath, Israel." *Quaternary International* 328–9 (2014): 226–43.

Ackermann, Oren, Aren M. Maeir, Suembikya Frumin, Tal Svoray, Ehud Weiss, Helena M. Zhevelev, and Liora Kolska Horwitz. "The Paleo-Anthropocene and the Genesis of the Current Landscape of Israel." *Journal of Landscape Ecology* 10 (2017): 109–40.

Amar, Zohar. "Agricultural Produces in the Lachish Relief." *Beth Mikra* 159 (1999): 350–56 (Hebrew).

Amir, Ayala, Yuval Gadot, Jordan Weitzel, Israel Finkelstein, Ronny Neumann, Hannes Bezzel, Karen Covello-Paran, and Omer Sergi. "Heated Beeswax Usage in Mortuary Practices: The Case of Ḥorvat Tevet (Jezreel Valley, Israel) c. 1000 BCE." *Journal of Archaeological Science: Reports* 36 (2021): article 102904.

Amiran, Ruth B. K., and Immanuel Dunayevsky. "The Assyrian Open-Court Building and Its Palestinian Derivatives." *BASOR* 149 (1958): 25–32.

Amit, David. "First and Second Temple Period Discoveries Near the Mamilla Pool in Jerusalem." *Qadmoniot* 44 (2011): 29–34.

Amit, David, and Irit Yezerski. "An Iron Age II Cemetery and Wine Presses at An-Nabi Danyal." *IEJ* 51 (2001): 171–93.

Asadpour, Ali. "Phenomenology of Garden in Assyrian Documents and Reliefs: Concepts and Types." *Bagh-e Nazar* 15, no. 60 (2018): 55–66.

Ayalon, Eitan. *Images from the Land of the Bible: People, Life and Landscapes, 1898–1946*. Tel Aviv: Eretz Israel Museum, 2012.

Bar-Matthews, Miryam, and Avner Ayalon. "Mid-Holocene Climate Variations Revealed by High- Resolution Speleothem Records from Soreq Cave, Israel and Their Correlation with Cultural Changes." *The Holocene* 21 (2011): 163–71.

Bar-Matthews, Miryam, and Avner Ayalon. "Speleothems as Palaeoclimate Indicators, a Case Study from Soreq Cave Located in the Eastern Mediterranean Region, Israel." In *Past Climate Variability through Europe and Africa*, edited by Richard W. Battarbee, Françoise Gasse, and Catherine E. Stickley, 363–91. Vol. 6 of *Developments in Paleoenvironmental Research*. Dordrecht: Springer, 2004.

Baruch, Uri. "The Late Holocene Vegetational History of Lake Kinneret (Sea of Galilee), Israel." *Paléorient* 12 (1986): 37–48.

Baruch, Uri. "The Palynology of Late Quaternary Sediments of the Dead Sea." PhD diss., Hebrew University of Jerusalem, 1993.

Baruch, Yuval. "A Farmstead from the End of the Iron Age and Installations at the Foot of Khirbat Abū Shawān." *'Atiqot* 56 (2007): 25–55 (Hebrew with English summary).

Barzilai, Omry, Nuha Aga, and Onn Crouvi. "Prehistoric Artifacts from Emeq Rephaim (Area C)." In *New Studies in the Archaeology of Jerusalem and Its Region: Collected*

Papers Vol. IV, edited by David Amit, Guy D. Steibel, and Orit Peleg-Barkat, 31–39. Jerusalem: Israel Antiquities Authority, 2010.

Beeri, Ron. "Round Oil Presses of the 13th–10th Centuries BCE in Palestine and Their Implications: Chronology, Function and Geographical Distribution." *PEQ* 140 (2008): 159–67.

Benzaquen, Mordechay, Israel Finkelstein, and Dafna Langgut. "Vegetation History and Human Impact on the Environs of Tel Megiddo in the Bronze and Iron Ages (*c*. 3,500–500 BCE): A Dendroarchaeological Analysis." *Tel Aviv* 46 (2019): 42–64.

Berlejung, Angelika. "The Assyrians in the West: Assyrianization, Colonialism, Indifference, or Development Policy." In *Congress Volume Helsinki 2010*, edited by Martti Nissinen, 21–60. VTSup 148. Leiden; Boston: Brill, 2012.

Bintliff, John. "Time, Process and Catastrophism in the Study of Mediterranean Alluvial History: A Review Source." *World Archaeology* 33 (2002): 417–35.

Billig, Ya'akov, Liora Freud, and Efrat Bocher. "A Luxurious Royal Estate from the First Temple Period in Armon ha-Natziv, Jerusalem." *Tel Aviv* 49.1 (2022): 8–31.

Bloch, Guy, M. Francoy Tiago, Ido Wachtel, Nava Panitz-Cohen, Stefan Fuchs, Amihai Mazar, and Bruce Smith. "Industrial Apiculture in the Jordan Valley During Biblical Times with Anatolian Honeybees." *Proceedings of the National Academy of Sciences of the United States of America* 107 (2010): 11240–44.

Bryant, Vaughn M. "Pollen: Nature's Fingerprints of Plants." In *Yearbook of Science and the Future*, edited by K. S. Suslick, 92–111. Chicago: Encyclopedia Britannica, 1990.

Bunimovitz, Shlomo, and Zvi Lederman. *Tel Beth-Shemesh: A Border Community in Judah. Renewed Excavations 1990–2000: The Iron Age*. Tel Aviv University Sonia and Marco Nadler Institute of Archaeology Monograph Series 34. Tel Aviv: Emery and Claire Yass Publications in Archaeology, 2016.

Bunimovitz, Shlomo, Zvi Lederman, and W. Manor Dale. "The Archaeology of Border Communities: Renewed Excavations at Tel Beth-Shemesh, Part 1: The Iron Age." *Near Eastern Archaeology* 72, no. 3 (2009): 114–42.

Butzer, Karl W. "Climatic Change in Arid Regions since the Pliocene." In *A History of Land Use in Arid Regions*, edited by Laurence Dudley Stamp, 31–56. Arid Zone Research 17. Paris: UNESCO, 1961.

Chaney, Marvin L. "Whose Sour Grapes? The Addressees of Isaiah 5:1–7 in the Light of Political Economy." *Semeia* 87 (1999): 105–22.

Chikuni, Mark "A Critical Analysis of the Genre and the Message of Isaiah 5:1–7." *DARE: Holy Trinity College Journal* 11 (2019): 131–45.

Crivellaro, Alan, and Fritz Hans Schweingruber. *Atlas of Wood, Bark and Pith Anatomy of Eastern Mediterranean Trees and Shrubs*. Heidelberg: Springer, 2013.

Dalley, Stephanie. "Recent Evidence from Assyrian Sources for Judaean History from Uzziah to Manasseh." *JSOT* 28 (2004): 387–401.

Davidovich, Uri. et al. "Salvage Excavation at Ramot Forest and Ramat Bet-Hakerem: New Data Regarding Jerusalem's Periphery during the First and Second Temple Periods." *New Studies on Jerusalem* 11 (2006): 35–112 (Hebrew).

Davidovich, Uri, Naomi Porat, Yuval Gadot, Yoav Avni, and Oded Lipschits. "Archaeological Investigations and OSL Dating of Terraces at Ramat Raḥel, Israel." *Journal of Field Archaeology* 37 (2012): 192–208.

Deckers, Katleen, Linda Herveux, Catherine Kuzucuoğlu, Joy McCorriston, Hugues Pessin, Simone Riehl, and Emmanuelle Vila. "Characteristics and Changes in Archaeology-Related Environmental Data During the Third Millennium BC in Upper

Mesopotamia, Collective Comments to the Data Discussed During the Symposium." *Publications de l'Institut Français d'Études Anatoliennes* 19 (2007): 573–80.

De-Groot, Alon, and Michal Weinberg-Stern. "Wine, Oil and Gibeonites: Iron II–III at Kh. El-Burj Northern Jerusalem." *New Studies on Jerusalem* 19 (2013): 95–102 (Hebrew with an English summary).

Edelstein, Gershon, and Shimon Gibson. "Ancient Jerusalem's Rural Food Basket." *BARev* 8 (1982): 46–54.

Ein-Mor, Daniel. "Walajeh ('Ain Joweizeh): Preliminary Report." *Hadashot Arkheologiyot: Excavations and Surveys in Israel* 125 (2013).

Ein-Mor, Daniel, and Zvi Ron. "Ain Joweizeh: An Iron Age Royal Rock-Cut Spring System in the Naḥal Refa'im Valley, near Jerusalem." *Tel Aviv* 43 (2016): 127–46.

Eitam, David. "Olive Presses of the Israelite Period." *Tel Aviv* 6 (1979): 146–55.

Eitam, David. "The Olive Oil Industry at Tel Miqne-Ekron During the Late Iron Age." In *Olive Oil in Antiquity: Israel and Neighbouring Countries from the Neolithic to the Early Arab Period*, edited by David Eitam and Mikha'el Heltzer, 167–98. History of the Ancient Near East 8. Padova: Sargon, 1996.

Elgart-Sharon, Yelena, Naomi Porat, and Yuval Gadot. "Land Management and the Construction of Terraces for Dry Farming: The Case of the Soreq Catchment, Israel." *Oxford Journal of Archaeology* 39 (2020): 274–89.

Faust, Avraham. "The Assyrian Century in the Southern Levant: An Overview of the Reality on the Ground." In *The Southern Levant under Assyrian Domination*, edited by Shawn Zelig Aster and Avraham Faust, 20–55. University Park, PA: Eisenbrauns, 2018.

Faust, Avraham. *The Neo-Assyrian Empire in the Southwest: Imperial Domination and Its Consequences*. Oxford: Oxford University Press, 2021.

Faust, Avraham, and Ehud Weiss. "Judah, Philistia, and the Mediterranean World: Reconstructing the Economic System of the Seventh Century B.C.E." *BASOR* 338 (2005): 71–92.

Faust, Avraham. "The Interests of the Assyrian Empire in the West: Olive Oil Production as a Test-Case." *Journal of the Economic and Social History of the Orient* 54 (2011): 62–86.

Feig, Nurit. "Excavations at Beit Safafa: Iron Age II and Byzantine Agricultural Installations South of Jerusalem." *'Atiqot* 44 (2003): 191–238.

Finkelstein, Israel. "The Archaeology of the Days of Manasseh." In *Scripture and Other Artifacts: Essays on the Bible and Archaeology in Honor of Philip J. King*, edited by M. D. Coogan, J. Cheryl Exum, and Lawrence E. Stager, 169–87. Louisville, KY: Westminster John Knox Press, 1994.

Finkelstein, Israel, and Yuval Gadot. "Mozah, Nephtoah and Royal Estates in the Jerusalem Highlands." *Semitica et Classica* 8 (2015): 227–34.

Finkelstein, Israel, and Ram Gophna. "Settlement, Demographic, and Economic Patterns in the Highlands of Palestine in the Chalcolithic and Early Bronze Periods and the Beginning of Urbanism." *BASOR* 289 (1993): 1–22.

Finkelstein, Israel, and Dafna Langgut. "Climate, Settlement History, and Olive Cultivation in the Iron Age Southern Levant." *BASOR* 379 (2018): 153–69.

Finkelstein, Israel, and Nadav Na'aman. "The Judahite Shephelah in the Late 8th and Early 7th Centuries BCE." *Tel Aviv* 31, no. 1 (2004): 60–79.

Finkelstein, Israel, and Neil Asher Silberman. "Temple and Dynasty: Hezekiah, the Remaking of Judah and the Rise of the Pan-Israelite Ideology." *JSOT* 30 (2006): 259–85.

Frumin, Suembikya. "Invasion Biology Analysis in Archaeobotany: Philistine Culture at Tell Es-Sāfi/Gath as a Case Study." PhD diss, Bar-Ilan University, 2017.

Frumin, Suembikya, Aren M. Maeir, Liora Kolska Horwitz, and Ehud Weiss. "Studying Ancient Anthropogenic Impacts on Current Floral Biodiversity in the Southern Levant as Reflected by the Philistine Migration." *Scientific Reports* 5 (2015): article 13308.

Gadot, Yuval. "In the Valley of the King: Jerusalem's Rural Hinterland in the 8th–4th Centuries BCE." *Tel Aviv* 42 (2015): 3–28.

Gadot, Yuval, and Efrat Bocher. "The Introduction of the 'Open-Courtyard Building' to the Jerusalem Landscape and Judean-Assyrian Interaction." In *Archaeology and History of Eight-Century Judah*, edited by Zev I. Farber and L. Jacob Wright, 205–28. Atlanta, GA: Society of Biblical Literature, 2018.

Gadot, Yuval, Sivan Mizrahi, Liora Freud, and David Gellman. "What Kind of Village Is This? Buildings and Agro-Economic Activities North-West of Jerusalem During the Iron IIB–C Period." In *The Last Century in the History of Judah: The 7th Century BCE in Archaeological, Historical and Biblical Perspectives*, edited by Filip Čapek and Oded Lipschits, 89–118. Atlanta: Society of Biblical Literature, 2019.

Gadot, Yuval, Yelena Elgart-Sharon, Nitsan Ben-Melech, Uri Davidovich, Gideon Avni, Yoav Avni, and Naomi Porat. "OSL Dating of Pre-Terraced and Terraced Landscape: Land Transformation in Jerusalem's Rural Hinterland." *Journal of Archaeological Science: Reports* 21 (2018): 575–83.

Gibson, Shimon. "From Wildscape to Landscape: Landscape Archaeology in the Southern Levant—Methods and Practice." In *The Rural Landscape of Ancient Israel*, edited by Aren M. Maeir, Shimon Dar, and Ze'ev Safrai, 1–15. BAR International Series 1121. Oxford: Archaeopress, 2003.

Gitin, Seymour. "Ekron of the Philistines, Part II: Olive-Oil Suppliers to the World." *BARev* 16 (1990): 32.

Gitin, Seymour. "Neo-Assyrian and Egyptian Hegemony over Ekron in the Seventh Century: A Response to Lawrence E. Stager." *Eretz Israel* 27 (2003): 55–61.

Gitin, Seymour. "Tel Miqne-Ekron in the 7th Century BCE: The Impact of Economic Innovation and Foreign Cultural Influences on a Neo-Assyrian Vassal City-State." In *Recent Excavations in Israel: A View to the West*, edited by Seymour Gitin, 61–79. Colloquia and conference papers. Dubuque, IA: Kendall Hunt Publishing, 1995.

Gitin, Seymour. "The Neo-Assyrian Empire and Its Western Periphery: The Levant, with a Focus on Philistine Ekron." In *Assyria 1995: Proceedings of the 10th Anniversary Symposium of the Neo-Assyrian Text Corpus Project, Helsinki, September 7–11*, edited by Simo Parpola and Robert Whiting, 77–103. Neo-Assyrian Text Corpus Project. Helsinki: University of Helsinki, 1997.

Greenberg, Raphael, and Gilad Cinamon. "Stamped and Incised Jar Handles from Rogem Ganim and Their Implications for the Political Economy of Jerusalem, Late 8th–Early 7th Centuries BCE." *Tel Aviv* 33 (2006): 227–43.

Greenhut, Zvi, Alon De-Groot, and Eldad Barzilay. *Salvage Excavations at Tel Moza: The Bronze and Iron Age Settlements and Later Occupations*. Jerusalem: Israel Antiquities Authority, 2009.

Gross, Boaz. "The Other Side of Beth Shemesh: Salvage Archaeology Exposes Deep History of Famed Biblical Site." *Bible History Daily* (May 28, 2021) https://www.biblicalarchaeology.org/daily/the-other-side-of-beth-shemesh/ (accessed October 16, 2023).

Haddad, Elie, Nathan Ben-Ari, and Alon De Groot. "A Century Old Enigma: The Seventh-Century BCE Settlement at Tel Beit Shemesh." *IEJ* 70 (2020): 173–89.

Horowitz, Aharon. *The Jordan Rift Valley*. Boca Raton, FL: CRC, 2001.

Horowitz, Aharon. *The Quaternary of Israel*. New York: Academic, 1979.

Kagan, Elisa Joy, Dafna Langgut, Elisabetta Boaretto, Frank Herald Neumann, and Mordechai Stein. "Chronology of Dead Sea Levels During the Bronze–Iron Ages." *Radiocarbon* 57 (2015): 237–52.

Khalaily, Hamoudi, and Jacob Vardi. "The New Excavations at Motza: An Architectural Perspective on a Neolithic 'Megasite' in the Judean Hills." In *The Mega Project at Motza (Moza): The Neolithic and Later Occupations up to the 20th Century, New Studies in the Archaeology of Jerusalem and Its Region, Supplementary Volume*, edited by Hamoudi Khalaily, Amit Re'em, Jacob Vardi, and Ianir Milevski, 60–100. Jerusalem: Israel Antiquities Authority, 2020.

Koch, Ido. "Introductory Framework for Assyrian-Levantine Colonial Encounters." *Semitica* 60 (2018): 367–96.

Langgut, Dafna, Matthew J. Adams, and Israel Finkelstein. "Climate, Settlement Patterns and Olive Horticulture in the Southern Levant During the Early Bronze and Intermediate Bronze Ages (c. 3600–1950 BCE)." *Levant* 48 (2016): 117–34.

Langgut, Dafna, Israel Finkelstein, Thomas Litt, Frank Harald Neumann, and Mordechai Stein. "Vegetation and Climate Changes During the Bronze and Iron Ages (3600–600 BCE) in the Southern Levant Based on Palynological Records." *Radiocarbon* 57 (2015): 217–35.

Langgut, Dafna, and Yosef Garfinkel. "7000-Year-Old Evidence of Fruit Tree Cultivation in the Jordan Valley, Israel." *Scientific Reports* 12, no. 1 (2022): 7463.

Langgut, Dafna, Frank Harald Neumann, Mordechai Stein, Allon Wagner, Elisa Joy Kagan, Elisabetta Boaretto, and Israel Finkelstein. "Dead Sea Pollen Record and History of Human Activity in the Judean Highlands (Israel) from the Intermediate Bronze into the Iron Ages (2500–500 BCE)." *Palynology* 38 (2014): 280–302.

Laugomer, Ben. "High Resolution Climate Reconstruction During the Bronze and Iron Ages from Soreq Cave Speleothems." MA thesis, Tel Aviv University, 2017.

Lev-Yadun, Simcha. "Flora and Climate in Southern Samaria: Past and Present." In *Highlands of Many Cultures, Vol. 1*, edited by Israel Finkelstein, Zvi Lederman, and Shlomo Bunimovitz, 85–102. Monograph Series of the Institute of Archaeology of Tel Aviv University. Tel Aviv: Tel Aviv University, 1997.

Lev-Yadun, Simcha. "Wood Remains from Archaeological Excavations: A Review with a Near Eastern Perspective." *Israel Journal of Earth Sciences* 56 (2007): 139–62.

Lev-Yadun, Simcha, and Ram Gophna. "Exportation of Plant Products from Canaan to Egypt in the Early Bronze Age I: A Rejoinder to William A. Ward." *BASOR* 287 (1992): 89–90.

Liphschitz, Nili. "Reconstruction of the Arboreal Vegetation of Judea and Samaria Mountains." In *The Hill Country and the Shephelah and in the Arabah*, edited by S. Bar, 48–55. Chicago: Ariel, 2008.

Liphschitz, Nili. *Timber in Ancient Israel: Dendroarchaeology and Dendrochronology*. Monograph Series of the Institute of Archaeology of Tel Aviv University 26. Tel Aviv: Tel Aviv University, 2007.

Lipschits, Oded. *Age of Empires: The History and Administration of Judah in the 8th–2nd Centuries BCE in Light of the Storage-Jar Stamp Impressions*. Monograph Series of the Institute of Archaeology of Tel Aviv University. Winona Lake, IN: Eisenbrauns, 2021.

Lipschits, Oded. "The Changing Faces of Kingship in Judah under Assyrian Rule." In *Changing Faces of Kingship in Syria-Palestine 1500–500 BCE*, edited by Agustinus Gianto and Peter Dubovský, 115–38. AOAT 459. Münster: Ugarit-Verlag, 2018.

Lipschits, Oded, Yuval Gadot, Benjamin Arubas, and Manfred Oeming. *What Are the Stones Whispering: 3000 Years of Forgotten History at Ramat Raḥel*. Winona Lake, IN: Eisenbrauns, 2017.

Lipschits, Oded, Omer Sergi, and Ido Koch. "Judahite Stamped and Incised Jar Handles: A Tool for Studying the History of Late Monarchic Judah." *Tel Aviv* 38 (2011): 5–41.

Litt, Thomas, Christian Ohlwein, Frank H. Neumann, Andreas Hense, and Mordechai Stein. "Holocene Climate Variability in the Levant from the Dead Sea Pollen Record." *Quaternary Science Reviews* 49 (2012): 95–105.

Maeir, Aren M., David Ben-Shlomo, Deborah Cassuto, Jeffrey R. Chadwick, Brent Davis, Adi Eliyahu Behar, Suembikya Frumin, Shira Gur-Arieh, Louise A. Hitchcock, et al. "Technological Insights on Philistine Culture: Perspectives from Tell Es-Safi/Gath." *Journal of Eastern Mediterranean Archaeology & Heritage Studies* 7 (2019): 76.

Maeir, Aren M., Eric L. Welch, and Maria Eniukhina. "A Note on Olive Oil Production in Iron Age Philistia: Pressing the Consensus." *PEQ* 153 (2021): 129–44.

Maitlis, Ytzhak. "Jerusalem, Wadi Zimra." *Excavations and Surveys in Israel* 10 (1991): 125–27.

Master, Daniel. M. "Economy and Exchange in the Iron Age Kingdoms of the Southern Levant." *BASOR* 372 (2014): 81–97.

Mazar, Amihai. *Timnah (Tel Batash) I: Stratigraphy and Architecture, Vol. 2: Text*. Qedem 37. Jerusalem: Institute of Archaeology, Hebrew University of Jerusalem, 1997.

Mazar, Amihai, Dvory Namdar, Nava Panitz-Cohen, Ronny Neumann, and Steve Weiner. "Iron Age Beehives at Tel Rehov in the Jordan Valley." *Antiquity* 82 (2008): 629–39.

Migowski, Claudia, Mordechai Stein, Sushma Prasad, Jörg F. W. Negendank, and Amotz Agnon. "Holocene Climate Variability and Cultural Evolution in the Near East from the Dead Sea Sedimentary Record." *Quaternary Research* 66 (2006): 421–31.

Na'aman, Nadav. "'The House-of-No-Shade Shall Take Away Its Tax from You' (Micah I 11)." *VT* 45, no. 4 (1995): 516–27.

Nagar, Annette. "Jerusalem, Tell el-Ful." *Hadashot Arkheologiyot* 126 (2014). Internet Edition: https://www.hadashot-esi.org.il/Report_Detail_Eng.aspx?id=10615&mag_id=121 (accessed August 21, 2023).

Namdar, Dvory, Oded Lipschits, Liora Freud, and Yuval Gadot, "Organic Content of YHWD-Stamped Storage Jars." In *Ramat Raḥel VI: The Babylonian-Persian Pit: Pottery Assemblage and Stamp Impressions*, edited by Oded Lipschits, Liora Freud, Yuval Gadot, and Manfred Oeming, 121–30. Monograph Series of the Institute of Archaeology of Tel Aviv University. Winona Lake, IN: Eisenbrauns, 2021.

Naveh, Zev, and Joel Dan. "The Human Degradation of Mediterranean Landscapes in Israel." In *Mediterranean Type Ecosystems*, edited by Francesco Di Castri and Harold A. Mooney, 373–90. Berlin; Heidelberg: Springer, 1973.

Ofer, Avi. "'All the Hill Country of Judah': From a Settlement Fringe to a Prosperous Monarchy." In *From Nomadism to Monarchy: Archaeological and Historical Aspects of Early Israel*, edited by Israel Finkelstein and Nadav Na'aman, 92–121. Jerusalem: Yad Izhak Ben-Zvi, 1994.

Onozuka, Takuzo. "Keeping Up with the Demand for Oil? Reconsidering the Unique Oil Presses from Late Bronze Age IIB to Iron Age IIA in the Southern Levant." *Orient* 47 (2012): 67–90.

Ovadia, Ruth. "Jerusalem, Giv'at Massu'a." *Excavations and Surveys in Israel* 12 (1993): 71–76.

Paz, Yitzhak, Oren Ackermann, Yoav Avni, Meni Ben-Hur, Michal Birkenfeld, Dafna Langgut, Sivan Mizrahi, Ehud Weiss, and Naomi Porat. "The Earliest Compost Pit? An Early Bronze Age Fertilized Agricultural Plot Discovered near Tel Yarmouth, Ramat Bet Shemesh, Israel." *Journal of Archaeological Science: Reports* 15 (2017): 226–34.

Porat, Naomi, Uri Davidovich, Yoav Avni, Gideon Avni, and Yuval Gadot. "Using OSL Measurements to Decipher Soil History in Archaeological Terraces, Judean Highlands, Israel: Using OSL to Decipher Soil History in Archaeological Terraces." *Land Degradation & Development* 29 (2018): 643–50.

Pritchard, James B. *Winery, Defenses, and Soundings at Gibeon*. Philadelphia: Penn Press, 1964.
Rainbird, Paul. "A Message for Our Future? The Rapa Nui (Easter Island) Ecodisaster and Pacific Island Environments." *World Archaeology* 33 (2002): 436–51.
Riehl, Simone. "Archaeobotanical Evidence for the Interrelationship of Agricultural Decision-Making and Climate Change in the Ancient Near East." *Quaternary International* 197 (2009): 93–114.
Rosen, Arlene Miller. *Civilizing Climate: Social Responses to Climate Change in the Ancient Near East*. Lanham: Rowman Altamira, 2007.
Roth, Helena, Yuval Gadot, and Dafna Langgut. "Wood Economy in Early Roman Period Jerusalem." *BASOR* 382 (2019): 71–87.
Sapir-Hen, Lidar. "Pax Assyriaca and the Animal Economy in the Southern Levant: Regional and Local-Scale Imperial Contacts." In *Rethinking Israel: Studies in the History and Archaeology of Ancient Israel, in Honor of Israel Finkelstein*, edited by Oded Lipschits, Yuval Gadot, and Matthew J. Adams, 341–53. Winona Lake, IN: Eisenbrauns, 2017.
Sapir, Neria, Nathan Ben-Ari, Liora Freud, and Oded Lipschits. "History, Economy and Administration in Late Iron Age Judah in Light of the Excavations at Mordor Arnona, Jerusalem." *Tel Aviv* 49.1 (2022): 32–53.
Sapir-Hen, Lidar, Yuval Gadot, and Israel Finkelstein. "Animal Economy in a Temple City and Its Countryside: Iron Age Jerusalem as a Case Study." *BASOR* 375 (2016): 103–18.
Sapir-Hen, Lidar, Yuval Gadot, and Israel Finkelstein. "Environmental and Historical Impacts on Long Term Animal Economy: The Southern Levant in the Late Bronze and Iron Ages." *Journal of Economic and Social History of the Orient* 57 (2014): 703–44.
Solimany, Gideon. "Jerusalem, Har Homa." *Hadashot Arkheologiyot* 124 (2012). Internet Edition: http://www.hadashot-esi.org.il/report_detail_eng.aspx?id=2020&mag_id=119 (accessed August 21, 2023).
Srebro, Haim, and Tamar Soffer. *The New Atlas of Israel: The National Atlas*. Survey of Israel. Jerusalem: The Hebrew University of Jerusalem, 2011.
Stager, Lawrence E. "Ashkelon and the Archaeology of Destruction: Kislev 604 BCE." *Eretz-Israel: Archaeological, Historical and Geographical Studies* 25 (1996): 61–74.
Stern, Ephraim. *Archaeology of the Land of the Bible: Vol. II: The Assyrian, Babylonian and Persian Periods. 732–332 BCE*. New York: Doubleday, 2001.
Storchan, Benyamin. "Jerusalem, 'Emeq Lavan." *Hadashot Arkheologiyot* 127 (2015).
Storchan, Benyamin. "Jerusalem, Ramat Shelomo." *Hadashot Arkheologiyot* 129 (2017).
Szanton, Nahshon. "The Rock-Cut Rooms and Cave 1: Evidence for Cultic Activity along the City of David's Eastern Slope in the Iron Age II." *New Studies on Jerusalem and Its Region* 19 (2013): 58–67 (Hebrew).
Thareani, Yifat. "The Empire and the 'Upper Sea': Assyrian Control Strategies along the Southern Levantine Coast." *BASOR* 375 (2016): 77–102.
Thareani, Yifat. "In the Service of the Empire: Local Elites and '*Pax Assyriaca*' in the Negev." *Eretz-Israel* 29 (2009): 184–91.
Ussishkin, David. "The Water Systems of Jerusalem During Hezekiah's Reign." In *Meilenstein: Festgabe für Herbert Donner zum 16. Februar 1995*, edited by Stefan Timm and Manfred Weippert, 298–307. Ägypten und Altes Testament 30. Wiesbaden: Harrassowitz, 1995.
Weiberg, Erika, Ryan E. Hughes, Martin Finné, Anton Bonnier, and Jed O. Kaplan. "Mediterranean Land Use Systems from Prehistory to Antiquity: A Case Study from Peloponnese (Greece)." *Journal of Land Use Science* 14 (2019): 1–20.

Weiss, Ehud. "'Beginnings of Fruit Growing in the Old World'—Two Generations Later." *Israel Journal of Plant Sciences* 62 (2015): 75–85.

Weiss, Ehud, and Mordechai E. Kislev. "Plant Remains as Indicators for Economic Activity: A Case Study from Iron Age Ashkelon." *Journal of Archaeological Science* 31 (2004): 1–13.

Weksler-Bdolah, Shlomit. "Alona." *Excavations and Surveys in Israel* 19 (1997): 68–70.

Williamson, Hugh G. M. *Isaiah 1–5: A Critical and Exegetical Commentary*. London: T&T Clark, 2006.

Winderbaum, Ariel. "Assur in Jerusalem: New Glyptic Evidence of the Assyrian Influence on Jerusalem." *New Studies in the Archaeology of Jerusalem and Its Region* 6 (2012): 83–104 (Hebrew).

Yechezkel, Azriel, and Amos Frumkin. "Spring Tunnels in Ancient Israel and the Jerusalem Hills: Physical, Geographical and Human Aspects." *Horizons in Geography* 96 (2019): 154–80 (Hebrew).

Yechezkel, Azriel, Amos Frumkin, and Shaul Tzionit. "Ancient Spring Tunnels of Jerusalem, Israel: Physical, Spatial, and Human Aspects." *Environmental Archaeology* 21 (2022): 323–41.

Younger, K. Lawson. "The Assyrian Impact on the Southern Levant in Light of Recent Study." *IEJ* 65 (2014): 179–204.

Zinger, Avraham. *Olive Cultivation*. Tel-Aviv: Ministry of Agriculture, 1985.

Zohary, Daniel, Maria Hopf, and Ehud Weiss. *Domestication of Plants in the Old World*. 4th edn. Oxford: Oxford University Press, 2012.

Zohary, Daniel, and Pinhas Spiegel-Roy. "Beginnings of Fruit Growing in the Old World." *Science* 187 (1975): 319–27.

Zohary, Michael. *Plant Life of Palestine: Israel and Jordan*. New York: Ronald, 1962.

Chapter 5

THE WILDERNESS AND THE SOWN IN THE LAND OF ISRAEL: HISTORICAL MAPPING, THE HUMAN FOOTPRINT, AND REMOTE SENSING

Noam Levin

Introduction

In this chapter I wish to combine the biblical text with historical (nineteenth century onwards) and modern mapping to make comparisons between the past (as described in the Hebrew Bible) and the present, and to offer some insights into the meaning of the desert as a wilderness area. As the wilderness and the sown land are not distinct categories, but rather two ends of a continuum, the same can be stated for desert and Mediterranean climate regions, as well as for areas inhabited by nomadic societies and areas inhabited by societies of farmers. The borders between all these are not fixed in space or in time, and are a function both of climate and of human activity. I open this chapter with citations from the Hebrew Bible, and then move on to demonstrate what can be inferred about desert and wilderness areas from modern approaches of mapping and from the point of view of modern conservation.

Chapter 3 of the book of Genesis ends with the expulsion of Adam and Eve from the Garden of Eden, and with God proclaiming to Adam:

"Because you did as your wife said and ate of the tree about which I commanded you, 'You shall not eat of it,' Cursed be the ground because of you; By toil shall you eat of it All the days of your life: Thorns and thistles shall it sprout for you. But your food shall be the grasses of the field; By the sweat of your brow shall you get bread to eat, Until you return to the ground—For from it you were taken."

(Gen. 3:17-19)

The expulsion from the Garden of Eden symbolizes the transition of human societies from those of hunters and gatherers, to farmers, as part of the agricultural revolution. The Fertile Crescent is often considered as one of the first regions in the world where the agricultural revolution took place after the last glacial maxima, and one of the centers where the domestication of animals and plants began.¹ The agricultural revolution, which started independently in a few focal areas, gradually expanded globally, leading to confrontations between communities of hunters and gatherers, and communities of farmers. One such confrontation is provided to us in the book of Genesis, between the two brothers of Esau and Jacob (Gen. 25:27): "When the boys grew up, Esau became a skillful hunter, a man of the outdoors; but Jacob was a mild man who stayed in camp," with the predicament that the society of farmers will take over that of the hunters and gatherers (Gen. 27:37, 40: "Isaac answered, saying to Esau, 'But I have made him master over you: I have given him all his brothers for servants, and sustained him with grain and wine … Yet by your sword you shall live, And you shall serve your brother'").

Over time, the global population has risen, with one of the major landscape transformations being that of reducing native vegetation cover and replacing large portions of it with agricultural vegetation.² The stages of land use transition often include the transition from natural ecosystems, via frontier clearing, to agricultural subsistence and small-scale farms, which culminate with urbanization on the one hand and intensive agriculture on the other.³ These stages took place in different times and at different paces across the globe. However, one of the common features is that when people started realizing the loss and threat to natural ecosystems and to wilderness areas, they started dedicating areas for conservation of nature, commonly known as protected areas, ever since the late nineteenth century.⁴ The understanding that wilderness areas are in a process of decline in both their area and state has led to ambitious efforts of rewilding as an approach to nature restoration.⁵ Given that global climate changes also affect remote unvisited areas, it may be claimed that "true" wilderness does not exist anymore in our era, which is known as the Anthropocene.⁶ While humankind

---

1. Jared Diamond and Peter Bellwood, "Farmers and Their Languages: The First Expansions," *Science* 300 (April 25, 2003): 597–603.

2. Kees Klein Goldewijk, Arthur Beusen, and Peter Janssen, "Long-Term Dynamic Modeling of Global Population and Built-up Area in a Spatially Explicit Way: HYDE 3.1," *The Holocene* 20, no. 4 (June 2010): 565–73.

3. Jonathan A. Foley et al., "Global Consequences of Land Use," *Science* 309, no. 5734 (July 22, 2005): 570–74.

4. James E. M. Watson et al., "The Performance and Potential of Protected Areas," *Nature* 515, no. 7525 (November 2014): 67–73.

5. Jamie Lorimer et al., "Rewilding: Science, Practice, and Politics," *Annual Review of Environment and Resources* 40, no. 1 (November 4, 2015): 39–62; Andrea Perino et al., "Rewilding Complex Ecosystems," *Science* 364 (April 26, 2019): article 6438.

6. Paul J. Krutzen, "The 'Anthropocene,'" in *Earth System Science in the Anthropocene: Emerging Issues and Problems*, ed. Ekhart Ehlers and Thomas Krafft (New York; Berlin; Heidelberg: Springer, 2006), 13–18.

has significantly altered terrestrial areas since the agricultural revolution, it is only in the twentieth century that most of the terrestrial ecosystems have been modified into intensely used anthromes.[7]

Wilderness in the Bible

The term wilderness, or wild lands, evokes the notion of remote and untouched ecosystems, where the presence of humans and the impacts of human activity are negligible or non-existent. Thus the wilderness is contrasted with the *oikoumenē*, the inhabited or habitable world. Etymologically, the word wilderness in English is explained as being derived from Old English, "wild-deor", where wild animals or wild deer can be found.[8] Another explanation is that wilderness is derived from the Old English word "weald," meaning forest. The American "Wilderness Act of 1964" provides us with the following definition: "A wilderness, in contrast with those areas where man and his own works dominate the landscape, is hereby recognized as an area where the earth and its community of life are untrammeled by man, where man himself is a visitor who does not remain."[9] Areas of wilderness are further defined as areas answering the following conditions: (i) having minimal human imprint, (ii) opportunities for unconfined recreation, (iii) an area of at least five thousand acres (~ 20 km^2), and (iv) of educational, scientific, or historical value. There is no single definition for the term wilderness, and it also depends on the point of view of the individual.[10] Another type of wilderness—a more recent one—is that which we humans are creating since the industrial revolution, and especially since the rise of vehicular transport. As noted by Horvath, with time, the land area devoted to cars (for traffic and for parking), which he terms "Machine space," is growing, thus creating an inorganic wilderness within our cities.[11] In this study I focus on the more classic definition of "natural" wilderness—remote areas where there are few, if any, settled areas with sedentary population.

In the Land of Israel there are no thick forests with well-developed and high trees as common to many of the wilderness areas of Europe or North America. In modern Hebrew, the term wilderness is often referred to as *Eretz Bereshit*

---

7. Erle C. Ellis, "Anthropogenic Transformation of the Terrestrial Biosphere," *Philosophical Transactions: Mathematical, Physical and Engineering Sciences* 369, no. 1938 (March 13, 2011): 1010–35.

8. Roderick Nash, *Wilderness and the American Mind* (New Haven: Yale University Press, 1967).

9. Michael J. McCloskey, "Wilderness Act of 1964: Its Background and Meaning," *Oregon Law Review* 45, no. 4 (1965): 288–321.

10. Stephen J. Carver and Steffan Fritz, eds., *Mapping Wilderness: Concepts, Techniques and Applications* (New York; Berlin; Heidelberg: Springer, 2016).

11. Ronald J. Horvath, "Machine Space," *Geographical Review* 64, no. 2 (April 1974): 167–88.

(ארץ בראשית), literally, the Land of Genesis, i.e., the land as it was in the beginning. Within the Bible, equivalent terms for wilderness often refer to desert areas, usually uninhabited, which were associated with the hardships and formative years of the Israelites on their Exodus from Egypt (but see Dalit Rom-Shiloni's study in this book, where she also explores additional terms that designate the wild in the Hebrew Bible, including those referring to "forest" areas). The desolate areas of the desert are also the places where encounters with God took place, not only for Moses, but also for others, such as Hagar and Ishmael. The desert terms for wilderness are also mentioned in various prophecies, contrasting fertile and populated areas with dry and uninhabited areas. Moreover, often in the HB, the desert wilderness is associated with negative values.[12]

Several terms are used in the HB for desert wilderness areas.[13]

1. *Midbar* (מדבר), meaning a desert, as in Isa. 41:18: "I will open up streams on the bare hills And fountains amid the valleys; I will turn the desert [*midbar*] into ponds, The arid land into springs of water." See also the definition of wilderness in contrast to sown land, in Jer. 2:2: "Go proclaim to Jerusalem: Thus said the LORD: I accounted to your favor The devotion of your youth, Your love as a bride—How you followed Me in the wilderness [*midbar*], In a land not sown." Note that in this verse in Jeremiah, the wilderness is portrayed positively, the place where Israel, as a young bride, lovingly pursued God.[14] Note, however, that the word *midbar* is derived from the verb *dbr*, and is often mentioned as grasslands, an area which is fit for raising and herding flocks,[15] as in Exod. 3:1 "Now Moses, tending the flock of his father-in-law Jethro, the priest of Midian, drove the flock into the **wilderness**, and came to Horeb, the mountain of God." Another example to this use of the term *Midbarot* (מדברות), is given in Mishnah Bava Kamma 7:7:[16] "It is forbidden to rear small herd animals in the Land of Israel, but it is permitted to rear them in Syria or in the **wilderness** in the Land of Israel." Several localities in Israel may have their names derived from this verb, signifying their possible association with

---

12. Robert Barry Leal, "Negativity Towards Wilderness in the Biblical Record," *Ecotheology* 10, no. 3 (December 2005): 364–81.

13. Narelle J. Coetzee, "Wild God in the Wilderness: Why Does Yahweh Choose to Appear in the Wilderness in the Book of Exodus?" (PhD diss., University of Birmingham, 2016).

14. Emily Jane Colgan, "O Land, Land, Land! Images of Land in Jeremiah and in New Zealand Poetry: Ecological Readings from Aotearoa" (PhD diss., University of Auckland, 2014).

15. Noga Hareuveni, *Desert and Shepherd in the Heritage of Israel* (Israel: Neot Kdumim, 1991); Etan Levine, "The Land of Milk and Honey," *Journal for the Study of the Old Testament* 25, no. 87 (2000): 43–57.

16. Translation taken from: https://www.sefaria.org/Mishnah_Bava_Kamma.7.7?lang=bi&with=all&lang2=en (accessed August 17, 2023).

grazing, such as *Debir* (דבר), as in Josh. 15:15: "From there he marched against the inhabitants of **Debir**."
2. *Shemama* (שממה), meaning a desolate area, as in Exod. 23:29: "I will not drive them out before you in a single year, lest the land become **desolate** and the wild beasts multiply to your hurt."
3. *Tsiya* (ציה), meaning a dry land, *Arava* (ערבה), meaning a steppe or a desert, as in Jer. 2:6: "They never asked themselves, 'Where is the LORD, Who brought us up from the land of Egypt, Who led us through the wilderness, A land of **deserts** and pits, A **land of drought** and darkness, A land no man had traversed, Where no human being had dwelt?'"
4. *Chorbah* (חרבה), meaning a wasteland, as in Ezek. 25:13: "assuredly, thus said the Lord GOD: I will stretch out My hand against Edom and cut off from it man and beast, and I will lay it in **ruins**; from Tema to Dedan they shall fall by the sword."
5. *Yeshimon* (ישמן), meaning a land without water, as in Deut. 32:10: "He found him in a desert region, in an empty howling **waste**."

Historical Mapping of Wilderness and the Sown Land of Israel

The border between agricultural areas settled by farmers and pastoralism with grazing areas settled by nomads is not constant in space nor in time, as can be learned from archeological evidence in the Negev Desert going back to the second millennia BCE.[17] Whereas in the past scholars often attributed the fluctuation of the border between the wilderness and the sown to climatic variability, geopolitical factors may have had more influence on this transition area and on land use, at least in the case of the Negev Desert.[18]

Classical historians, such as the fourteenth-century Ibn Khaldun and the twentieth-century Arnold Toynbee, noted the opposition between nomadic and sedentary societies as one of the central pillars of history, which may lead to the rise and fall of civilizations.[19] This contrast and rivalry between nomads, who occupy marginal lands in semi-arid and arid regions, and farmers is well established in the

---

17. Steve A. Rosen, "The Desert and the Pastoralist: An Archaeological Perspective on Human-Landscape Interaction in the Negev over the Millennia," *Annals of Arid Zone* 50 (2011): 1–15.

18. S. Thomas Parker, "Peasants, Pastoralists, and *Pax Romana*: A Different View," *BASOR* 265 (February 1987): 35–51; Israel Finkelstein et al., "The Archaeology and History of the Negev and Neighbouring Areas in the Third Millennium BCE: A New Paradigm," *Tel Aviv* 45, no. 1 (June 2018): 63–88; Yoav Avni, Gideon Avni, and Naomi Porat, "A Review of the Rise and Fall of Ancient Desert Runoff Agriculture in the Negev Highlands: A Model for the Southern Levant Deserts," *Journal of Arid Environments* 163 (April 2019): 127–37.

19. Robert Irwin, "Toynbee and Ibn Khaldun," *Middle Eastern Studies* 33, no. 3 (July 1997): 461–79.

HB. The well-known story of Cain (the farmer) and Abel (the shepherd) testifies to the conflict:

> Now the man knew his wife Eve, and she conceived and bore Cain, saying, "I have gained a male child with the help of the LORD." She then bore his brother Abel. Abel became a keeper of sheep, and Cain became a tiller of the soil. In the course of time, Cain brought an offering to the LORD from the fruit of the soil; and Abel, for his part, brought the choicest of the firstlings of his flock. The LORD paid heed to Abel and his offering, but to Cain and his offering He paid no heed. Cain was much distressed and his face fell.
>
> (Gen. 4:1-5)

The conflict between these two lifestyles is clearly expressed in the armed conflict between the Israelites (who at this stage were already a settled people) and nomadic societies in the book of Judges:

> After the Israelites had done their sowing, Midian, Amalek, and the Kedemites would come up and raid them; they would attack them, destroy the produce of the land all the way to Gaza, and leave no means of sustenance in Israel, not a sheep or an ox or an ass. For they would come up with their livestock and their tents, swarming as thick as locusts; they and their camels were innumerable. Thus they would invade the land and ravage it.[20]
>
> (Judg. 6:3-5)

The book of Joshua provides a geographic description of the division of the Land of Israel between the twelve tribes. While its grounding on historical reality is doubtful and debated,[21] this description does provide us with a view of the contrast between the land settled by the tribes of Israel (mostly in the Mediterranean and semi-arid areas) and the unsettled arid areas of the desert (Figure 5.1).

The first modern and reliable mapping of the Land of Israel was the Survey of Western Palestine, conducted by the Palestine Exploration Fund (PEF) in the 1870s, and published in 1881 (Figure 5.2c).[22] The twenty-six map sheets accompanying the survey at a scale of one inch to the mile (1:63,360) are well

---

20. The raid described in these sentences may resemble in some ways the raids of nomadic people in general on settled areas; see below examples for raids of Bedouins on settled areas in Palestine during the nineteenth century.

21. Israel Finkelstein, Amihay Mazar, and Brian B. Schmidt, eds., *The Quest for the Historical Israel: Debating Archaeology and the History of Early Israel: Invited Lectures Delivered at the Sixth Biennial Colloquium of the International Institute for Secular Humanistic Judaism, Detroit, October 2005*, Archaeology and Biblical Studies 17 (Atlanta: Society of Biblical Literature, 2007).

22. Claude Reignier Conder and Horatio Herbert Kitchener, *The Survey of Western Palestine: Memoirs of the Topography, Orography, Hydrography, and Archaeology*, 3 vols. (London: Committee of the Palestine Exploration Fund, 1881).

5. *The Wilderness and the Sown in the Land of Israel* 99

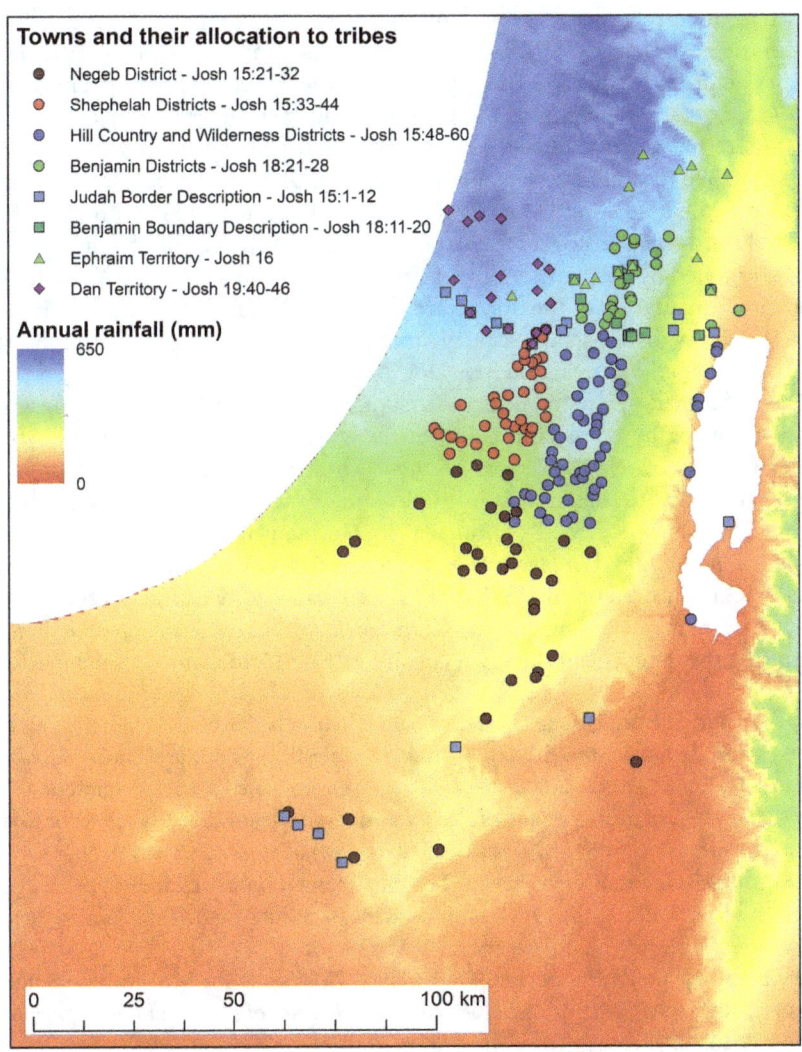

Figure 5.1 The location of towns and some of the twelve tribes according to the book of Joshua,[23] combined with average annual rainfall (for the years 1970–2000).[24]

23. From Christopher McKinny, "A Historical Geography of the Administrative Division of Judah: The Town Lists of Judah and Benjamin in Joshua 15:21-62 and 18:21-28" (PhD diss., Ramat Gan, Bar Ilan University, 2016).

24. From Stephen E. Fick and Robert J. Hijmans, "WorldClim 2: New 1-km Spatial Resolution Climate Surfaces for Global Land Areas," *International Journal of Climatology* 37, no. 12 (October 2017): 4302–15.

known for their relative accuracy,[25] and cover the biblical Promised Land, between Dan in the north and Be'er Sheva in the south, showing their land cover and land use just before the first *Aliya* (immigration) of the Zionist movement (1881), and the modern transformation of the Land of Israel.[26] In the PEF maps, the settled land where permanent villages and towns exist is mostly limited to areas with more than 300 mm/year (except along the coastal plain; Figure 5.2c).[27] Villages on the edge of the desert were often larger as a result of raids by Bedouins, which led the local inhabitants to concentrate in fewer villages.[28] These raids by the Bedouins were also noted by the "Survey of Western Palestine" in the 1870s.[29] A much more recent documentation of the northwards movement of Bedouins with their herds from the Negev towards the coastal plain of Israel during drought years in the early 1970s is provided by Levin and Ben-Dor.[30]

Kiepert provides us with one of the first maps of Israel/Palestine showing winter areas of grazing by nomads in desert areas, where annual vegetation follows the winter rains for a relatively short period.[31] These areas, depicted using a yellow hue on his map, are designated in the legend as "wilderness regions, i.e. winter grazing lands only occupied by nomads" (in German: *Wüstengebiete, d.h. nur von Nomaden bewohntes Winterweideland*; Figure 5.2a). The German cartographer Hans Fischer showed on his 1890 and 1911 maps what he termed as the "current limit of permanent settlement" (in German: *Jetzige Grenze seßhaften Wohnens*), delimiting the desert from the sown (Figure 5.2b).[32] Lieutenant-Colonel Frederick

25. Gad Schaffer and Noam Levin, "Reconstructing Nineteenth-Century Landscapes from Historical Maps—the Survey of Western Palestine as a Case Study," *Landscape Research* 41, no. 3 (April 2, 2016): 360–79; Noam Levin, "The Palestine Exploration Fund Map (1871–1877) of the Holy Land as a Tool for Analysing Landscape Changes: The Coastal Dunes of Israel as a Case Study," *The Cartographic Journal* 43, no. 1 (March 1, 2006): 45–67.

26. Gad Schaffer and Noam Levin, "Mapping Human Induced Landscape Changes in Israel Between the End of the 19th Century and the Beginning of the 21th Century," *Journal of Landscape Ecology* 7, no. 1 (January 1, 2014): 110–45.

27. Noam Levin, Ruth Kark, and Emir Galilee, "Maps and the Settlement of Southern Palestine, 1799–1948: An Historical/Gis Analysis," *Journal of Historical Geography* 36, no. 1 (January 2010): 1–18.

28. David Kallner, "Dura—a Typical Village on the Bedouin Frontier," *Bulletin of the Jewish Palestine Exploration Society* 14 (October 1, 1947): 30–37.

29. Conder and Kitchener, *The Survey of Western Palestine*.

30. Noam Levin and Eyal Ben-Dor, "Monitoring Sand Dune Stabilization Along the Coastal Dunes of Ashdod-Nizanim, Israel, 1945–1999," *Journal of Arid Environments* 58, no. 3 (August 2004): 335–55.

31. Heinrich Kiepert, *Neue Handkarte von Palaestina*, Map (Berlin: L. Kraatz, 1875).

32. Hans Fischer and H. Guthe, *Palästina*, 1:700,000 (Leipzig: Verlag der Geogr. Anstalt von Wagner & Debes, 1890), Pal 1261-C8, Jewish National and University Library, Laor Map Collection; Hans Fischer and H. Guthe, *Das Heutige Palästina* (Leipzig: Wagner & Debes, 1911), Bibelatlas in 20 Haupt und 28 Nebenkarten von Hermann Guthe, Ruth Kark private collection.

John Salmon, who served as Head of the British Mandate Survey of Palestine between 1933 and 1938, also attempted to distinguish between the desert and the sown. On the 1938, 1:100,000 topographic sheet of *Beth Lehem*, Salmon used a yellowish buff ground-tint to portray areas of crops and pasture, whereas the buff has been shaded off to white in the desert areas.[33] One of the last attempts during the British Mandate period to classify the quality of land for agricultural purposes was presented on a 1:1,000,000 map from 1946, titled "A Tentative Land Classification Map," on which the Judean Desert is classified as "wilderness" (very arid conditions, limited seasonal grazing), the Negev Desert is classified as "desert with scanty patches of cultivation only when rainfall is sufficient," and the northern Negev and the valley of *Be'er Sheva* were classified as "semi desert lowlands (seasonal pasture with patches of irrigation on favorable sites)" (Figure 5.2d).[34]

In the following year, the British Survey of Palestine issued a unique 1:250,000 scale map of the Negev entitled "Distribution of the Nomad Population of the Beersheba Sub-district."[35] Using aerial photos, the British have mapped all Bedouin tents in the Negev Desert, a feat which, as far as I am aware, has never been accomplished before, and is nowadays being done using high spatial resolution satellite images and deep learning techniques to map structures—e.g., in slums[36] and in refugee camps.[37] On this map (Figure 5.2c), all tents were depicted as red points, amounting to 7,859 tents altogether.[38] Mapping the tents provides another avenue for distinguishing between the sown (areas with fixed settlements) vs. the wilderness (areas of nomadic population). Note that most of the Bedouin tents were located in areas depicted as semi-desert lowlands with good loess soils (Figure 5.2d), and away from lands classified as "Good land" or settled uplands (Figure 5.2d), which were settled with villages and agricultural areas as shown on the PEF map (Figure 5.2c).[39]

---

33. Frederick John Salmon, "Some Notes on Conventional Signs for Topographical Maps," *The Geographical Journal* 89, no. 1 (January 1937): 50.

34. Survey of Palestine, "Map 5," 1:1,000,000, Maps Relating to the Report of the Anglo-American Committee of Enquiry Regarding the Problems of European Jewry and Palestine. Suppl. to Cmd. 6808 (London: His Majesty's Stationary Office, 1946), https://commons.wikimedia.org/wiki/File:WhitePaper.jpg#filelinks (accessed August 17, 2023).

35. Levin, Kark, and Galilee, "Maps."

36. Monika Kuffer, Karin Pfeffer, and Richard Sliuzas, "Slums from Space—15 Years of Slum Mapping Using Remote Sensing," *Remote Sensing* 8, no. 6 (May 27, 2016): 455.

37. Omid Ghorbanzadeh et al., "Dwelling Extraction in Refugee Camps Using CNN—First Experiences and Lessons Learnt," *International Archives of the Photogrammetry, Remote Sensing and Spatial Information Sciences* 42 (September 26, 2018): 161–66.

38. Seth J. Frantzman, Noam Levin, and Ruth Kark, "Counting Nomads: British Census Attempts and Tent Counts of the Negev Bedouin 1917 to 1948: British Census and Tent Counts of the Negev Bedouin," *Population, Space and Place* 20, no. 6 (August 2014): 552–68.

39. Frantzman, Levin, and Kark, "Counting Nomads."

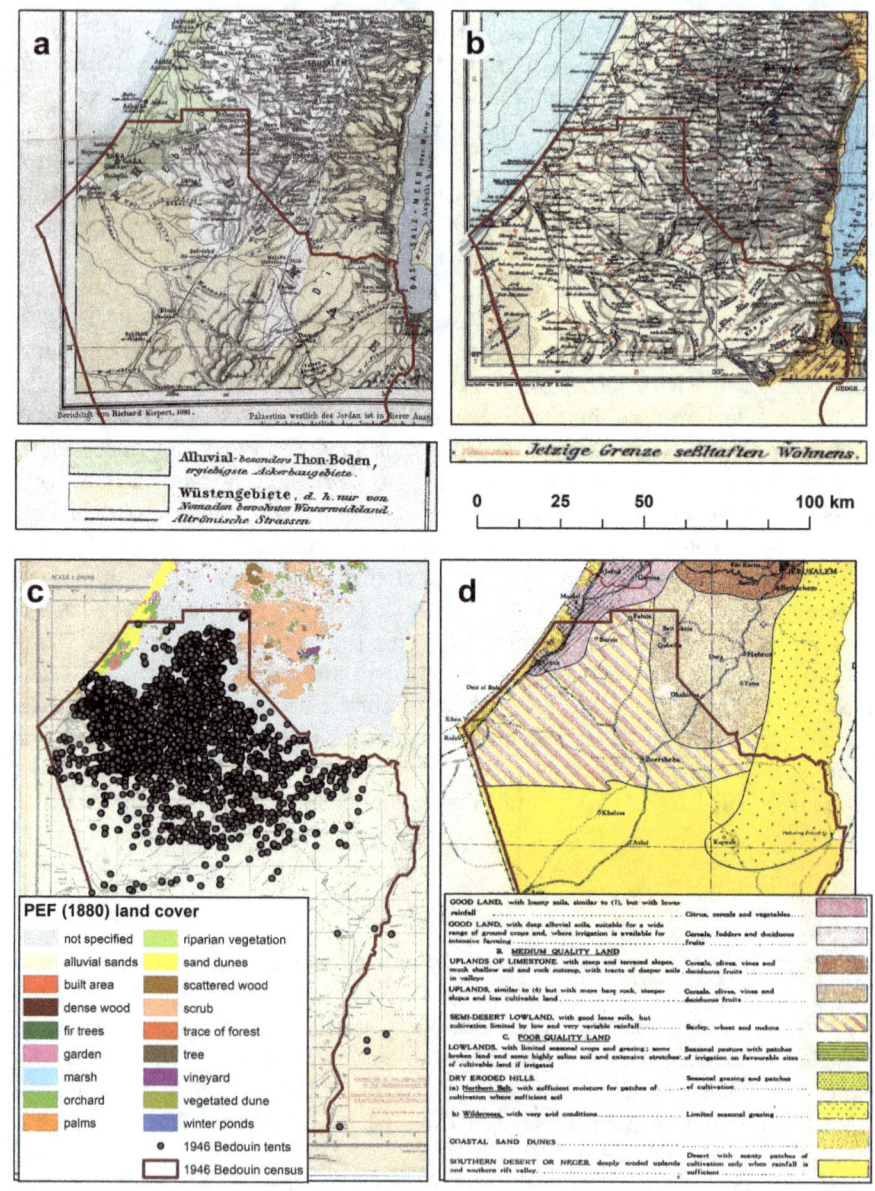

Figure 5.2 (a) Kiepert's (1875) map showing winter areas of grazing by nomads in desert areas in yellow;[40] (b) Fischer's 1911 map showing the "current limit of permanent settlement" in a red line;[41] (c) PEF (1880) land cover classes,[42] overlaying the 1946 British census of Bedouin tents (shown in grey circles); (d) The British Mandate 1946 "Tentative Land Classification Map."

40. Kiepert, "Neue Handkarte von Palaestina."
41. Fischer and Guthe, "Das Heutige Palästina."
42. Schaffer and Levin, "Mapping Human Induced Landscape Changes"; Schaffer and Levin, "Reconstructing Nineteenth-Century Landscapes."

Global Mapping of Wilderness Using GIS and Remote Sensing

Geographic Information Systems (GIS) are a software which enables the acquisition, storage, manipulation, analysis, and visualization of spatial information.[43] However, the first global mapping of wilderness areas was performed manually, using Jet Navigation Charts (at a scale of 1:2,000,000), where McCloskey and Spalding delineated all areas larger than 400,000 hectares located more than 6 km from developed features such as settlements and roads.[44] They found that about one-third of the world can be defined as wilderness, mostly in Arctic, Antarctic, and desert areas.

The first attempts to map wilderness areas using GIS were developed by the Australian geographer Robert Lesslie, and published in a series of papers,[45] first for the Australian National Wilderness Inventory, and later as the first global dataset of its kind for the World Conservation Monitoring Centre (Figure 5.3a).[46] Lesslie developed the wilderness continuum concept, which acknowledges that wilderness areas vary in their degrees of remoteness (from settlements and from access) and naturalness (aesthetic primitiveness and biophysical primitiveness).

A similar mapping approach for estimating landscape continuity was developed by the Open Landscape Institutes of the Society for the Protection of Nature in Israel (Figure 5.3d).[47] This approach is based on measuring the weighted distance from built-up areas, roads and other types of infrastructure. These anthropogenic features are then assigned weights based on expert estimation of their impact on their surroundings (e.g., different types of pollution or disturbance), assuming a linear decay function, where the slope of the decay function varies between different classes of built-up areas and roads.

---

43. Paul A. Longley et al., *Geographic Information Systems and Science* (Hoboken, NJ: John Wiley & Sons, 2005).

44. Michael J. McCloskey and Heather Spalding, "A Reconnaissance-Level Inventory of the Amount of Wilderness Remaining in the World," *Ambio* 18, no. 4 (January 1, 1989): 221–27.

45. Robert G. Lesslie and S. G. Taylor, "The Wilderness Continuum Concept and Its Implications for Australian Wilderness Preservation Policy," *Biological Conservation* 32, no. 4 (1985): 309–33; Robert G. Lesslie, Brendan G. Mackey, and Kathryn M. Preece, "A Computer-Based Method of Wilderness Evaluation," *Environmental Conservation* 15, no. 3 (October 1, 1988): 225–32; Robert G. Lesslie, "The Wilderness Continuum Concept and Its Application in Australia: Lessons for Modern Conservation," in *Mapping Wilderness*, ed. Stephen J. Carver and Steffen Fritz (New York; Berlin; Heidelberg: Springer, 2016), 17–33.

46. Robert G. Lesslie, *Global Wilderness* (Cambridge: UN-WCMC, 1998), dataset derived using the Digital Chart of the World 1993 version and methods based on the Australian National Wilderness Inventory (Robert G. Lesslie and M. Maslen, 1995), https://datadownload.unep-wcmc.org/datasets (accessed August 17, 2023).

47. Noam Levin et al., "Landscape Continuity Analysis: A New Approach to Conservation Planning in Israel," *Landscape and Urban Planning* 79, no. 1 (January 2007): 53–64.

Eric Sanderson from the Wildlife Conservation Society (WCS) and colleagues from the Center for International Earth Science Information Network (CIESIN) at Columbia University followed on the approach of Lesslie and developed a global mapping of the human footprint (Figure 5.3b),[48] which has been recently updated.[49] The human footprint aims to show the impacts of human activity on the Earth's ecosystems, by combining globally available data on population density, land transformation, accessibility, and night lights. These variables were weighted and combined to form a score ranging between 0 and 100. To map the "Last of the wild" areas globally, Sanderson et al. identified the ten largest contiguous areas within each biome where the human influence index fell below the cutoff of the "wildest" 10 percent.[50] A similar approach was also applied to identify the location and protection status of the world's remaining marine wilderness areas.[51] Overall, 23 percent of the Earth's land area and 13 percent of the Earth's oceans have been identified as the remaining wilderness areas, with five countries containing more than 70 percent of the world's wilderness (in descending order: Russia, Canada, Australia, the USA, and Brazil).[52]

Similar to the human footprint, Kennedy et al. globally quantified the human modification of the land (Figure 5.3d),[53] using a greater range of input variables representing anthropogenic stressors, more recent datasets, and the application of a ratio scale instead of ordinal or interval scales. The four maps presented in Figure 5.3 demonstrate that the outcomes of mapping wilderness (areas with low human footprint or low modification) vary between approaches, based on their input datasets (the stressors used), how they are transformed, and combined to form a final score.

48. Eric W. Sanderson et al., "The Human Footprint and the Last of the Wild," *BioScience* 52, no. 10 (2002): 891–904.

49. Oscar Venter et al., "Sixteen Years of Change in the Global Terrestrial Human Footprint and Implications for Biodiversity Conservation," *Nature Communications* 7, no. 1 (November 25, 2016): 1–11.

50. Sanderson et al., "The Human Footprint and the Last of the Wild."

51. James E. M. Watson et al., "Protect the Last of the Wild," *Nature* 563, no. 7729 (November 2018): 27–30; Kendall R. Jones et al., "The Location and Protection Status of Earth's Diminishing Marine Wilderness," *Current Biology* 28, no. 15 (2018): 2506–12.

52. Watson et al., "Protect the Last of the Wild."

53. Christina M. Kennedy et al., "Managing the Middle: A Shift in Conservation Priorities Based on the Global Human Modification Gradient," *Global Change Biology* 25, no. 3 (March 2019): 811–26.

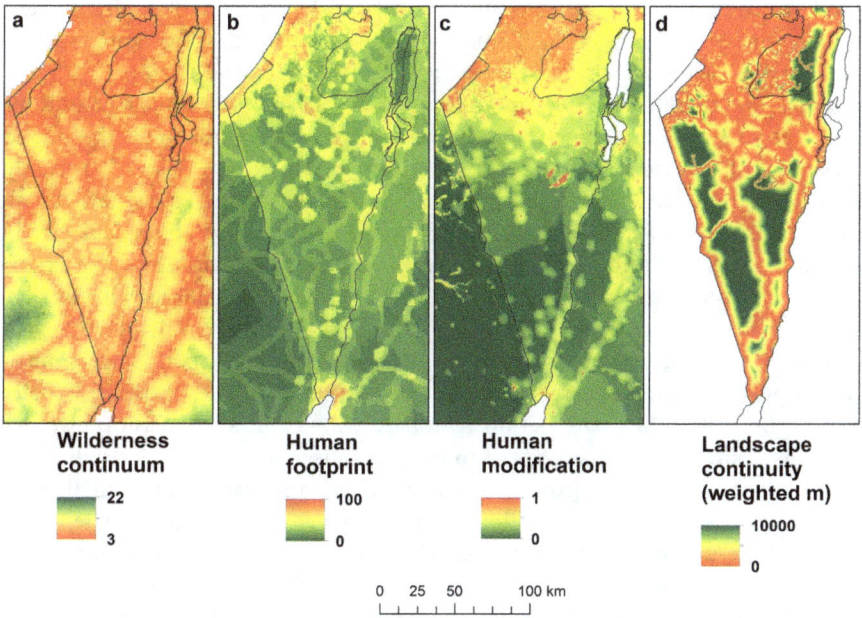

Figure 5.3 A comparison of approaches for mapping wilderness: (a) the wilderness continuum of Lesslie;[54] (b) the human footprint of WCS, CIESIN;[55] (c) the global human modification layer of Kennedy et al.;[56] (d) the landscape continuity.[57]

Spatial and Temporal Variability of Wilderness

The mapping of the extent of settled areas or the mapping of the wilderness as a binary variable disregards the natural variability of our world. True to the popular inspirational quotes attributed to Heraclitus, "There is nothing permanent except change," and Buddha, "Nothing is permanent; Everything is subject to change; Being is always becoming," our world is constantly changing, in space and in time. Consequently, the boundaries of wilderness and desert areas are fixed neither spatially nor temporally. Acknowledging the dynamics of the boundary of the desert requires measurements of meteorological parameters on the one

---

54. Lesslie, *Global Wilderness*.

55. Wildlife Conservation Society and Center for International Earth Science Information Network, "Global Human Footprint (Geographic), v2 (1995–2004)," Socioeconomic Data and Applications Center, 2005, https://sedac.ciesin.columbia.edu/data/set/wildareas-v2-human-footprint-geographic (accessed August 17, 2023).

56. Kennedy et al., "Managing the Middle."

57. Levin et al., "Landscape Continuity Analysis."

hand (from meteorological stations and satellites) as well as mapping of land cover properties (using satellite images). Climate zone classifications (such as the Köppen-Geiger classification[58]) are usually based on long-term (thirty years) averages, and therefore do not capture the annual variability in climate conditions. Using annual meteorological data, however, is useful for mapping the annual variability of climate zones, as done by Bruins for the Negev Desert,[59] using the P/PET (the ratio between precipitation and potential evapotranspiration) climate classification approach. The location of the 200 mm isohyet (representing the border between the arid and semi-arid regions) in Israel moves northward in dry years and southwards in rainy years. In extreme years, the 200 mm isohyet has transitioned by up to 50 km (Figure 5.4).[60] The 200 mm isohyet mostly occurs within hot semi-arid climates (type "BSh" according to the Köppen-Geiger climate classification), the area in Israel where the Bedouin population was mostly located during the British Mandate period (compare with Figure 5.2). Pastoralism and nomadism are sometimes suggested to be a land use and lifestyle type which are better suited for facing environmental changes (as is the case with marginal desert areas where nomadic people are often found), given that nomadic societies are more mobile, and can follow resources when and where they are available.[61] Note that the 200 mm isohyet transitions much more in the northern Negev or in the northern part of the Jordan Valley along the north–south axis than in the Judean Desert along the east–west axis. The relative fixed location of the 200 mm isohyet in the Judean Desert is because it is a rain-shadow desert, with the Judean Desert forming because of the orographic drying of moist air as it descends from the mountains eastwards towards the Dead Sea.

Because of high inter-annual variability of rainfall in semi-arid and arid areas, it is more difficult to identify statistically significant trends of climate change in

58. Hylke E. Beck et al., "Present and Future Köppen-Geiger Climate Classification Maps at 1-Km Resolution," *Scientific Data* 5, no. 1 (December 18, 2018): 1–12.

59. Hendrik J. Bruins, "Ancient Desert Agriculture in the Negev and Climate-Zone Boundary Changes During Average, Wet and Drought Years," *Journal of Arid Environments* 86 (November 2012): 28–42.

60. Baruch Ziv et al., "Trends in Rainfall Regime over Israel, 1975–2010, and Their Relationship to Large-Scale Variability," *Regional Environmental Change* 14, no. 5 (October 2014): 1751–64.

61. Marius Warg Næss, "Climate Change, Risk Management and the End of *Nomadic Pastoralism*," *International Journal of Sustainable Development & World Ecology* 20, no. 2 (April 2013): 123–33.

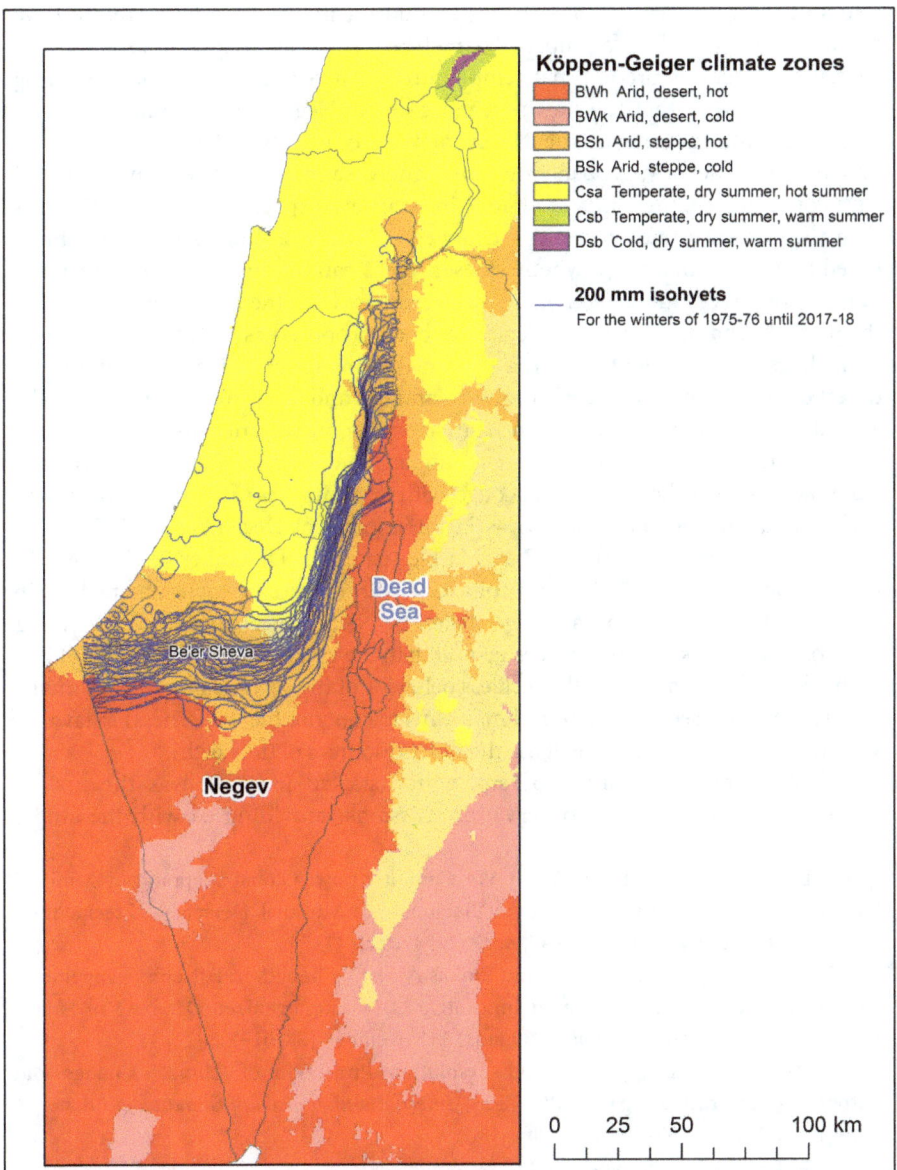

Figure 5.4 Köppen-Geiger climate zones,[62] overlaid by annual rainfall isohyets of 200 mm (representing the border between the arid and semi-arid (Mediterranean) regions; isohyets were calculated from rainfall data of the Israel Meteorological Service), for all the years between 1975–6 and 2017–18. Note the large inter-annual variability in the north–south location of the 200 mm isohyet.

62. Beck et al., "Present and Future."

arid and semi-arid areas.[63] Statistically significant increases in temperature have already been recorded for most of Israel between the period of 1950–2017.[64] Climate projections predict that temperatures will rise in all of Israel including the Negev Desert, that the northern parts of the Negev will become drier, and that the southern parts of the Negev may become exposed to an increase in precipitation intensity, probably due to an increase in convective activity there.[65] As a consequence, the climatic regions in Israel are expected to shift northwards with the current trends of climate change.[66] While desert areas may be defined based on their climatology, whether desert areas can be considered as wilderness or not depends on human activity within desert areas. In the face of desertification, the path of urbanization of the Negev has been proposed as a preferable one over agricultural development, as it may lessen the impact of human activity on the desert environment.[67] To clearly monitor land use and land cover changes globally as well as over the Negev, space-borne imagery is now routinely used.

A new understanding of our place as humans in the world, and of the Earth as a closed ecosystem, ushered in the space age, with iconic images of the Earth from space, such as the astronauts' photos known as Earthrise (taken on December 24, 1968; NASA photograph AS08-14-2383) and Blue Marble (taken on December 7, 1972; NASA photograph AS17-148-22727), and coincided with the rise of environmentalism in the early 1970s.[68] These visual images taken by NASA astronauts emphasized that our world can be likened to a spaceship sailing in the vast emptiness of space and that humankind should abandon the reckless behavior of the so-called cowboy economy (where the world seems infinite and man aims to conquer the wilderness) in favor of spaceman economy (acknowledging the finite resources of the Earth).[69]

NASA's Landsat satellite program, which started in 1972, was the first of many environmental Earth observation missions, providing us with the ability

63. Efrat Morin, "To Know What We Cannot Know: Global Mapping of Minimal Detectable Absolute Trends in Annual Precipitation: Minimal Detectable Precipitation Trends," *Water Resources Research* 47, no. 7 (July 2011): 47–55.

64. Yizhak Yosef, Enric Aguilar, and Pinhas Alpert, "Changes in Extreme Temperature and Precipitation Indices: Using an Innovative Daily Homogenized Database in Israel," *International Journal of Climatology* 39, no. 13 (November 15, 2019): 5022–45.

65. Assaf Hochman et al., "High-Resolution Projection of Climate Change and Extremity over Israel Using COSMO-CLM," *International Journal of Climatology* 38, no. 14 (November 2018): 5095–106.

66. Beck et al., "Present and Future."

67. Boris A. Portnov and Uriel N. Safriel, "Combating Desertification in the Negev: Dryland Agriculture vs. Dryland Urbanization," *Journal of Arid Environments* 56, no. 4 (March 2004): 659–80.

68. Donald J. Wuebbles, "Celebrating the 'Blue Marble,'" *Eos, Transactions American Geophysical Union* 93, no. 49 (December 4, 2012): 509–10.

69. Kenneth E. Boulding, "The Economics of the Coming Spaceship Earth," in *The Costs of Economic Growth*, ed. Peter A. Victor, The International Library of Critical Writings in Economics Series 275 (1966. Reprint, Northampton, MA: Edward Elgar Pub, 2013), 54–62.

to continuously monitor the Earth from space at various spatial and temporal resolutions.[70] Landsat images as well as those of many other sensors are freely available for everyone to use for the benefit of humankind, thanks to the recognition and vision of governments and space agencies. The platform of Google Earth Engine allows the required computer storage and analysis power needed to run global analyses using entire archives of satellite images, to monitor changes and better understand the impacts of climate change and of human activities.[71]

The Negev Desert has undergone many changes since the late nineteenth century, when it was sparsely populated, mostly with a nomadic Bedouin population, and hardly any permanent settlements, other than along the coastal plain of Gaza.[72] The Ottoman Empire established the town of *Be'er Sheva* in 1900 to assert their sovereignty over the Negev's Bedouin population. Since the late nineteenth century and through the period of the British Mandate over Palestine, the Bedouin population was slowly transitioning from a nomadic to a semi-nomadic society, growing various cereals over an area which amounted to up to 2,500 km^2 in rainy years.[73] Following the establishment of the State of Israel, new towns and agricultural settlements were founded in the Negev (mostly in the north of the Negev and along the Arava Valley), which, along with afforestation efforts, the expansion of irrigated agriculture to the Negev, and the designation of protected areas as well as many military training areas, have transformed the landscape of the Negev, where there are ongoing land disputes between the State of Israel and the Bedouins.[74]

70. Donald T. Lauer, Stanley A. Morain, and Vincent V. Salomonson, "The Landsat Program: Its Origins, Evolution, and Impacts," *Photogrammetric Engineering and Remote Sensing* 63, no. 7 (1997): 831–88; Michael A. Wulder et al., "Current Status of Landsat Program, Science, and Applications," *Remote Sensing of Environment* 225 (May 2019): 127–47.

71. Noel Gorelick et al., "Google Earth Engine: Planetary-Scale Geospatial Analysis for Everyone," *Remote Sensing of Environment* 202 (December 2017): 18–27.

72. Levin, Kark, and Galilee, "Maps."

73. Portnov and Safriel, "Combating Desertification in the Negev."

74. Arnon Soffer and Julian V. Minghi, "Israel's Security Landscapes: The Impact of Military Considerations on Land Uses," *The Professional Geographer* 38, no. 1 (February 1986): 28–41; Shlomo Swirski, "Current Plans for Developing the Negev: A Critical Perspective," trans. Ruth Morris, Information on Equality and Social Justice in Israel (Tel Aviv: Adva Center, January 1, 2007); Eran Feitelson, "The Four Eras of Israeli Water Policies," in *Water Policy in Israel*, ed. Nir Becker (New York; Berlin; Heidelberg: Springer, 2013), 15–32; Emily McKee, "Performing Rootedness in the Negev/Naqab: Possibilities and Perils of Competitive Planting: Performing Rootedness," *Antipode* 46, no. 5 (November 2014): 1172–89; Yoav Galai, "Narratives of Redemption: The International Meaning of Afforestation in the Israeli Negev," *International Political Sociology* 11, no. 3 (September 1, 2017): 273–91; Havatzelet Yahel and Ruth Kark, "Land and Settlement of Israel's Negev Bedouin: Official (Ad Hoc) Steering Committees, 1948-1980," *British Journal of Middle Eastern Studies* 45, no. 5 (October 20, 2018): 716–41.

One of the common approaches to estimating vegetation cover from space is using the Normalized Difference Vegetation Index (NDVI),[75] a spectral index based on the red and infra-red bands, where high NDVI values indicate more biomass of photosynthetic vegetation. Examining time series of NDVI between 2000 and 2014, Levin found that most of the detected landscape changes (as indicated via changes in NDVI) were related to human activities (mostly related to agriculture and urbanization).[76] Levin identified that only in certain areas could trends in NDVI be directly attributed to climatic variability, mostly along the transition areas between the semi-arid and arid zones, as in the sand dunes in the north-western Negev[77] and amongst planted forest areas in the north of the Negev.[78] Whereas traditional approaches for mapping vegetation assign static classes of land cover or land use (as in Figure 5.5a, b), remote sensing enables us to quantify and map the variability in vegetation cover (e.g., using NDVI; Figure 5.5c).

The ever-increasing human activity in the Negev Desert of Israel is also evident from night-time lights satellite images of the Earth. Artificial lights are a unique signature of human activity, and a commonly used approach to map changes in human presence and in economic activity (Figure 5.6a).[79] Another approach for

---

75. Compton J. Tucker, "Red and Photographic Infrared Linear Combinations for Monitoring Vegetation," *Remote Sensing of Environment* 8, no. 2 (May 1979): 127–50.

76. Noam Levin, "Human Factors Explain the Majority of Modis-Derived Trends in Vegetation Cover in Israel: A Densely Populated Country in the Eastern Mediterranean," *Regional Environmental Change* 16, no. 4 (April 2016): 1197–211.

77. Merav Seifan, "Long-Term Effects of Anthropogenic Activities on Semi-Arid Sand Dunes," *Journal of Arid Environments* 73, no. 3 (March 2009): 332–7; Zehava Siegal, Haim Tsoar, and Arnon Karnieli, "Effects of Prolonged Drought on the Vegetation Cover of Sand Dunes in the Nw Negev Desert: Field Survey, Remote Sensing and Conceptual Modeling," *Aeolian Research* 9 (June 2013): 161–73.

78. Michael Dorman et al., "Forest Performance During Two Consecutive Drought Periods: Diverging Long-Term Trends and Short-Term Responses Along a Climatic Gradient," *Forest Ecology and Management* 310 (December 2013): 1–9; David Helman, et al., "Detecting Changes in Biomass Productivity in a Different Land Management Regimes in Drylands Using Satellite-Derived Vegetation Index," *Soil Use and Management* 30, no. 1 (March 1, 2014): 32–39.

79. Noam Levin et al., "Remote Sensing of Night Lights: A Review and an Outlook for the Future," *Remote Sensing of Environment* 237 (February 2020): article 111443.

80. Michael Zohary, *Vegetation of Israel and Adjacent Areas*, Beihefte zum Tübinger Atlas des Vorderen Orients. Reihe A, Naturwissenschaft 7 (Wiesbaden: In Kommission bei L. Reichert, 1982).

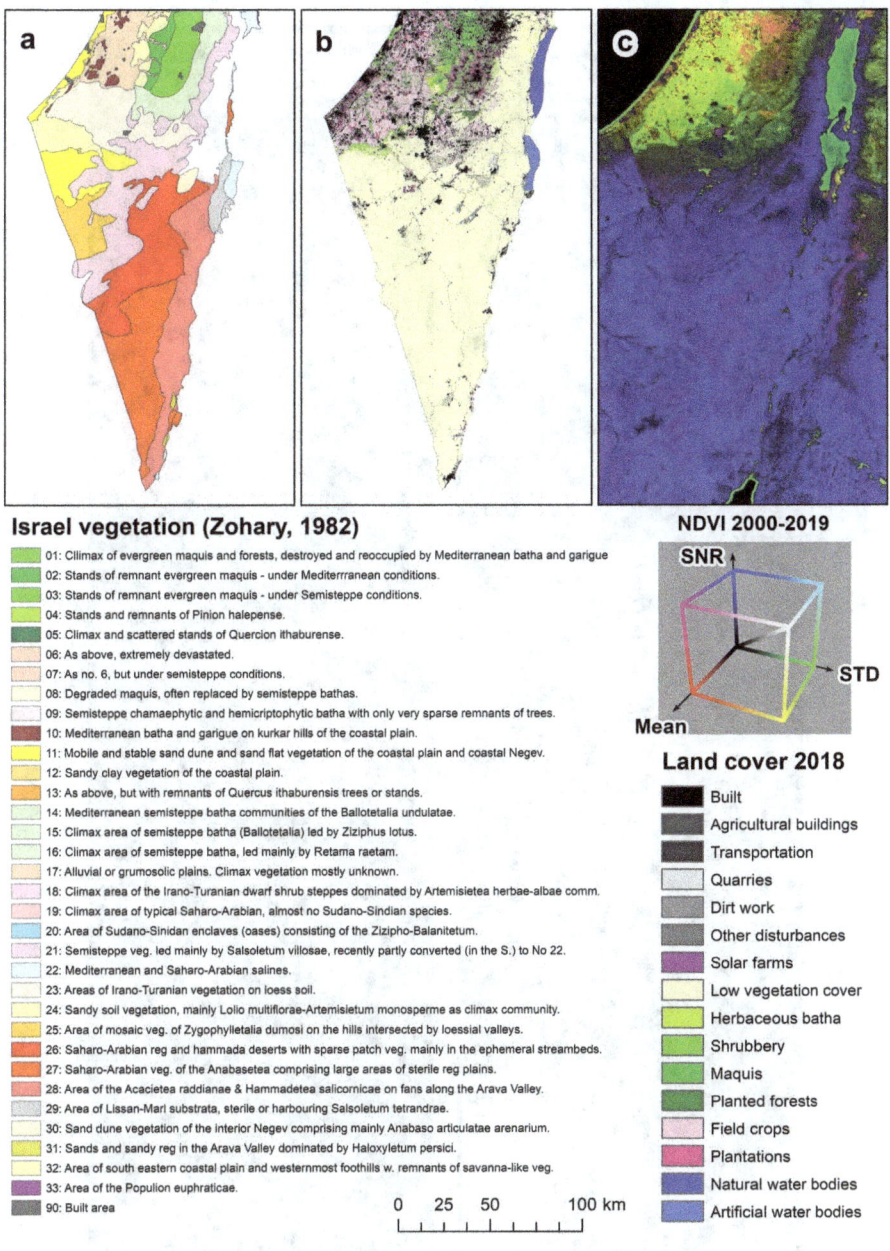

Figure 5.5 Land cover and vegetation maps of Israel: (a) Israel vegetation according to Zohary;[80] (b) land cover of Israel, based on the MAARAG (2018), as of 2018; note that much of the area previously inhabited by nomadic Bedouins during the British Mandate period has been converted to field crops; (c) temporal variability for 2000–19 in the 16-day values of the Normalized Difference Vegetation Index (NDVI), based on MODIS data; the mean values were colored in red, the standard deviation (STD) values in green, and the signal to noise ratio (SNR; the ratio between the mean and the standard deviation) in blue. Areas shown in green hues in Figure 5.5c indicate annual vegetation (bright green being mostly field crops, and "weaker" green referring to natural herbaceous vegetation), whereas areas shown in orange hues in Figure 5.5c mostly refer to Mediterranean maquis, planted forests and tree plantations. Areas shown in blue hues in Figure 5.5c are mostly very arid areas with little vegetation.

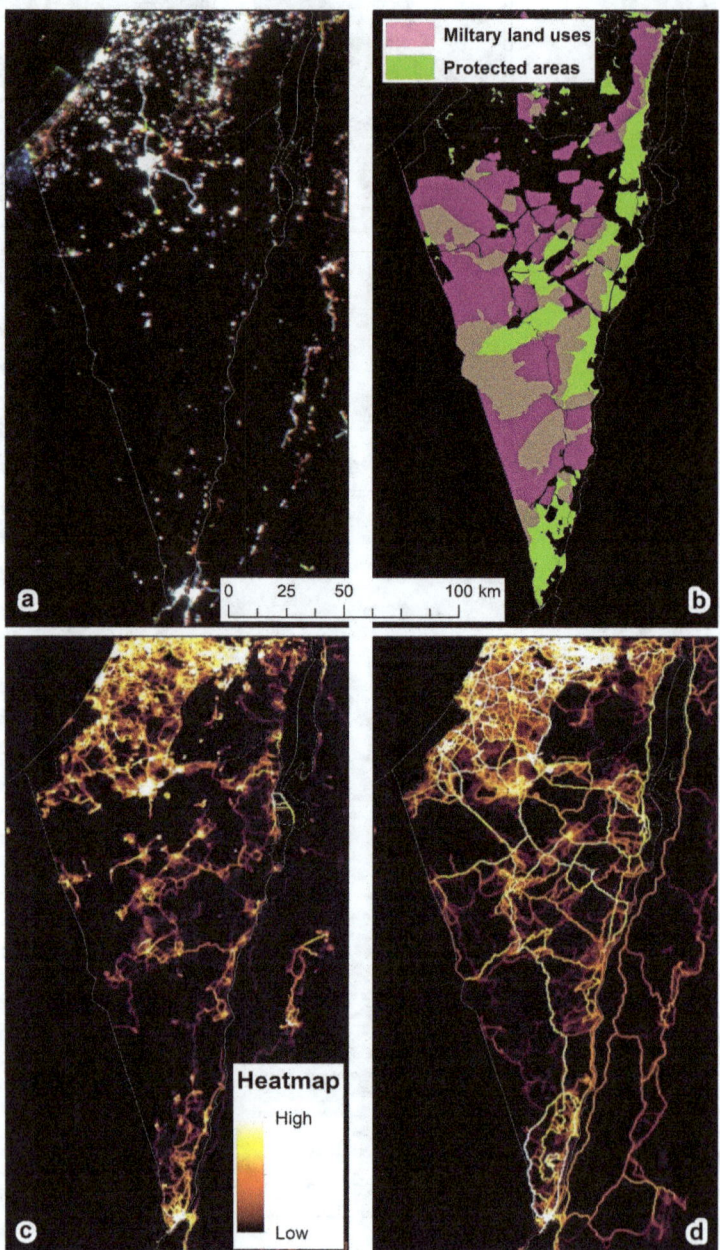

Figure 5.6 (a) VIIRS nighttime lights, false color composite of October 2019 (red), October 2015 (green), and October 2012 (blue); white areas represent areas which were lit in all three years; (b) protected areas (in green) and military land uses (in pink), and the overlaps between them; (c) strava heatmap showing areas frequently used by hikers and runners; (d) strava heatmap showing areas frequently used by bikers (bicycles). Images © Strava and OpenStreetMaps (and their contributors).

mapping human activity is based on volunteered geographic information available from social media,[81] as in the case of heat maps available from various sports tracking applications, such as Strava.[82] While night lights imagery mostly shows continuous human presence (cities, villages, industrial areas, etc.), sports tracking applications present us with temporary human activity, where people are present when doing sporting activities such as hiking, running, and biking (Figure 5.6c, d). The combination of night lights and social media data demonstrates the ever-increasing presence of people in the desert areas, which were once considered wilderness. Whereas substantial portions of the Negev and Judean deserts of Israel are managed as protected areas, large areas are also used by the army as military training areas, often with a dual use of both nature reserves and military (Figure 5.6b). The extensive areas where people are present in the Negev Desert raises the question whether there are any areas which can still be called wilderness amongst the many uses and needs of the growing population of the modern State of Israel?

Conclusions

"True wilderness" may no longer exist in the deserts of the Negev and Judea; however, the role of the desert as a place for spiritual self-discovery and connection with nature persists, following the tradition of the HB, and also as part of the modern Israeli tradition of hiking and exploration, for which the Sinai Peninsula (especially when it was under Israeli control, between 1967 and 1979) served as a type of a lost paradise.[83] Desert tourism is expanding in the Negev,[84] and several alternative communities have developed there as well (such as the Kibbutz of Ne'ot Smadar in 1989, Desert Ashram in 2002, and Arava Spiritual Centre in 2014).

With climate change, climatic zones within the Negev Desert will undoubtedly change as they have changed in the past.[85] However, given technological advances,

81. Michael F. Goodchild and Linna Li, "Assuring the Quality of Volunteered Geographic Information," *Spatial Statistics* 1 (May 2012): 110–20.

82. https://www.strava.com/heatmap (accessed August 17, 2023); Juha Oksanen et al., "Methods for Deriving and Calibrating Privacy-Preserving Heat Maps from Mobile Sports Tracking Application Data," *Journal of Transport Geography* 48 (October 2015): 135–44.

83. Smadar Lavie and Dani Rabinowitz, "Sinai for the Coffee Table: Birds, Bedouins and Desert Wanderlust," *MERIP Middle East Report*, no. 150 (January 1988): 40–44.

84. Joshua Schmidt and Natan Uriely, "Tourism Development and the Empowerment of Local Communities: The Case of Mitzpe Ramon, a Peripheral Town in the Israeli Negev Desert," *Journal of Sustainable Tourism* 27, no. 6 (June 3, 2019): 805–25.

85. Anton Vaks et al., "Middle-Late Quaternary Paleoclimate of Northern Margins of the Saharan-Arabian Desert: Reconstruction from Speleothems of Negev Desert, Israel," *Quaternary Science Reviews* 29, no. 19–20 (September 2010): 2647–62.

human habitation in the Negev is constantly increasing and human activity is ever more present. Given the changes in human presence and in climate, one of the challenges is understanding current changes in vegetation in the desert areas—to what degree can they be attributed to changes in human land use, and to what degree can they be explained by climatic factors?

When trying to understand the landscape of the Land of Israel within the HB, we are facing even greater challenges—not just of understanding what were the climate and land use of different areas in different periods, but also of understanding the terminology itself—what did the writers of the HB mean when they used the different terms for wilderness? Our improved understanding of the spatial and temporal variability of the climate and vegetation in the deserts of Israel in the twentieth and twenty-first centuries can assist us in identifying areas that were likely more or less stable for societies of farmers, herders, and nomads, also in the times of the Bible.

Bibliography

Avni, Yoav, Gideon Avni, and Naomi Porat. "A Review of the Rise and Fall of Ancient Desert Runoff Agriculture in the Negev Highlands: A Model for the Southern Levant Deserts." *Journal of Arid Environments* 163 (April 2019): 127–37.

Beck, Hylke E., Niklaus E. Zimmermann, Tim R. McVicar, Noemi Vergopolan, Alexis Berg, and Eric F. Wood. "Present and Future Köppen-Geiger Climate Classification Maps at 1-Km Resolution." *Scientific Data* 5, no. 1 (December 18, 2018): 1–12.

Boulding, Kenneth E. "The Economics of the Coming Spaceship Earth." In *The Costs of Economic Growth*, edited by Peter A. Victor, 54–62. The International Library of Critical Writings in Economics Series 275. 1966. Reprint, Northampton, MA: Edward Elgar Pub, 2013.

Bruins, Hendrik J. "Ancient Desert Agriculture in the Negev and Climate-Zone Boundary Changes During Average, Wet and Drought Years." *Journal of Arid Environments* 86 (November 2012): 28–42.

Carver, Stephen J., and Steffan Fritz, eds. *Mapping Wilderness: Concepts, Techniques and Applications*. New York; Berlin; Heidelberg: Springer, 2016.

Coetzee, Narelle J. "Wild God in the Wilderness: Why Does Yahweh Choose to Appear in the Wilderness in the Book of Exodus?" PhD diss., University of Birmingham, 2016.

Colgan, Emily Jane. "O Land, Land, Land! Images of Land in Jeremiah and in New Zealand Poetry: Ecological Readings from Aotearoa." PhD diss., University of Auckland, 2014.

Conder, Claude Reignier, and Horatio Herbert Kitchener. *The Survey of Western Palestine: Memoirs of the Topography, Orography, Hydrography, and Archaeology*. 3 vols. London: Committee of the Palestine Exploration Fund, 1881.

Diamond, Jared, and Peter Bellwood. "Farmers and Their Languages: The First Expansions." *Science* 300 (April 25, 2003): 597–603.

Dorman, Michael, Tal Svoray, Avi Perevolotsky, and Dimitrios Sarris. "Forest Performance During Two Consecutive Drought Periods: Diverging Long-Term Trends and Short-Term Responses Along a Climatic Gradient." *Forest Ecology and Management* 310 (December 2013): 1–9.

Ellis, Erle C. "Anthropogenic Transformation of the Terrestrial Biosphere." *Philosophical Transactions: Mathematical, Physical and Engineering Sciences* 369, no. 1938 (March 13, 2011): 1010–35.

Feitelson, Eran. "The Four Eras of Israeli Water Policies." In *Water Policy in Israel*, edited by Nir Becker, 15–32. New York; Berlin; Heidelberg: Springer, 2013.

Fick, Stephen E., and Robert J. Hijmans. "WorldClim 2: New 1-km Spatial Resolution Climate Surfaces for Global Land Areas." *International Journal of Climatology* 37, no. 12 (October 2017): 4302–15.

Finkelstein, Israel, Matthew J. Adams, Zachary C. Dunseth, and Ruth Shahack-Gross. "The Archaeology and History of the Negev and Neighbouring Areas in the Third Millennium BCE: A New Paradigm." *Tel Aviv* 45, no. 1 (June 2018): 63–88.

Finkelstein, Israel, Amihay Mazar, and Brian B. Schmidt, eds. *The Quest for the Historical Israel: Debating Archaeology and the History of Early Israel: Invited Lectures Delivered at the Sixth Biennial Colloquium of the International Institute for Secular Humanistic Judaism, Detroit, October 2005*. Archaeology and Biblical Studies 17. Atlanta: Society of Biblical Literature, 2007.

Fischer, Hans, and H. Guthe. "Das Heutige Palästina." Leipzig: Wagner & Debes, 1911. Bibleatlas in 20 Haupt und 28 Nebenkarten von Hermann Guthe. Ruth Kark private collection.

Fischer, Hans, and H. Guthe. "Palästina." 1:700,000. Leipzig: Verlag der Geogr. Anstalt von Wagner & Debes, 1890. Pal 1261-C8. Jewish National and University Library, Laor Map Collection.

Foley, Jonathan A., Ruth DeFries, Gregory P. Asner, Carol Barford, Gordon Bonan, Stephen R. Carpenter, F. Stuart Chapin, et al. "Global Consequences of Land Use." *Science* 309, no. 5734 (July 22, 2005): 570–74.

Frantzman, Seth J., Noam Levin, and Ruth Kark. "Counting Nomads: British Census Attempts and Tent Counts of the Negev Bedouin 1917 to 1948: British Census and Tent Counts of the Negev Bedouin." *Population, Space and Place* 20, no. 6 (August 2014): 552–68.

Galai, Yoav. "Narratives of Redemption: The International Meaning of Afforestation in the Israeli Negev." *International Political Sociology* 11, no. 3 (September 1, 2017): 273–91.

Ghorbanzadeh, Omid, Dirk Tiede, Zahra Dabiri, Martin Sudmanns, and Stefan Lang. "Dwelling Extraction in Refugee Camps Using CNN—First Experiences and Lessons Learnt." *International Archives of the Photogrammetry, Remote Sensing and Spatial Information Sciences* 42 (September 26, 2018): 161–66.

Goodchild, Michael F., and Linna Li. "Assuring the Quality of Volunteered Geographic Information." *Spatial Statistics* 1 (May 2012): 110–20.

Gorelick, Noel, Matt Hancher, Mike Dixon, Simon Ilyushchenko, David Thau, and Rebecca Moore. "Google Earth Engine: Planetary-Scale Geospatial Analysis for Everyone." *Remote Sensing of Environment* 202 (December 2017): 18–27.

Hareuveni, Noga. *Desert and Shepherd in the Heritage of Israel*. Israel: Neot Kdumim, 1991.

Helman, David, et al. "Detecting Changes in Biomass Productivity in a Different Land Management Regimes in Drylands Using Satellite-Derived Vegetation Index." *Soil Use and Management* 30, no. 1 (March 1, 2014): 32–39.

Hochman, Assaf, Paola Mercogliano, Pinhas Alpert, Hadas Saaroni, and Edoardo Bucchignani. "High-Resolution Projection of Climate Change and Extremity over Israel Using COSMO-CLM." *International Journal of Climatology* 38, no. 14 (November 2018): 5095–106.

Horvath, Ronald J. "Machine Space." *Geographical Review* 64, no. 2 (April 1974): 167–88.
Irwin, Robert. "Toynbee and Ibn Khaldun." *Middle Eastern Studies* 33, no. 3 (July 1997): 461–79.
Jones, Kendall R., et al. "The Location and Protection Status of Earth's Diminishing Marine Wilderness." *Current Biology* 28, no. 15 (2018): 2506–12.
Kallner, David. "Dura—a Typical Village on the Bedouin Frontier." *Bulletin of the Jewish Palestine Exploration Society* 14 (October 1, 1947): 30–37.
Kennedy, Christina M., James R. Oakleaf, David M. Theobald, Sharon Baruch-Mordo, and Joseph Kiesecker. "Managing the Middle: A Shift in Conservation Priorities Based on the Global Human Modification Gradient." *Global Change Biology* 25, no. 3 (March 2019): 811–26.
Kiepert, Heinrich. "Neue Handkarte von Palaestina." Map. Berlin: L. Kraatz, 1875.
Klein Goldewijk, Kees, Arthur Beusen, and Peter Janssen. "Long-Term Dynamic Modeling of Global Population and Built-up Area in a Spatially Explicit Way: HYDE 3.1." *The Holocene* 20, no. 4 (June 2010): 565–73.
Krutzen, Paul J. "The 'Anthropocene'." In *Earth System Science in the Anthropocene: Emerging Issues and Problems*, edited by Ekhart Ehlers and Thomas Krafft, 13–18. New York; Berlin; Heidelberg: Springer, 2006.
Kuffer, Monika, Karin Pfeffer, and Richard Sliuzas. "Slums from Space—15 Years of Slum Mapping Using Remote Sensing." *Remote Sensing* 8, no. 6 (May 27, 2016): 455.
Lauer, Donald T., Stanley A. Morain, and Vincent V. Salomonson. "The Landsat Program: Its Origins, Evolution, and Impacts." *Photogrammetric Engineering and Remote Sensing* 63, no. 7 (1997): 831–88.
Lavie, Smadar, and Dani Rabinowitz. "Sinai for the Coffee Table: Birds, Bedouins and Desert Wanderlust." *MERIP Middle East Report*, no. 150 (January 1988): 40–4.
Leal, Robert Barry. "Negativity Towards Wilderness in the Biblical Record." *Ecotheology* 10, no. 3 (December 2005): 364–81.
Lesslie, Robert G. *Global Wilderness*. Cambridge: UN-WCMC, 1998. Dataset derived using the Digital Chart of the World 1993 version and methods based on the Australian National Wilderness Inventory (R. Lesslie and M. Maslen, 1995). Available online: https://datadownload.unep-wcmc.org/datasets (accessed August 17, 2023).
Lesslie, Robert G. "The Wilderness Continuum Concept and Its Application in Australia: Lessons for Modern Conservation." In *Mapping Wilderness*, edited by Stephen J. Carver and Steffen Fritz, 17–33. New York; Berlin; Heidelberg: Springer, 2016.
Lesslie, Robert G., Brendan G. Mackey, and Kathryn M. Preece. "A Computer-Based Method of Wilderness Evaluation." *Environmental Conservation* 15, no. 3 (October 1, 1988): 225–32.
Lesslie, Robert G., and S. G. Taylor. "The Wilderness Continuum Concept and Its Implications for Australian Wilderness Preservation Policy." *Biological Conservation* 32, no. 4 (1985): 309–33.
Levin, Noam. "Human Factors Explain the Majority of Modis-Derived Trends in Vegetation Cover in Israel: A Densely Populated Country in the Eastern Mediterranean." *Regional Environmental Change* 16, no. 4 (April 2016): 1197–211.
Levin, Noam. "The Palestine Exploration Fund Map (1871–1877) of the Holy Land as a Tool for Analysing Landscape Changes: The Coastal Dunes of Israel as a Case Study." *The Cartographic Journal* 43, no. 1 (March 1, 2006): 45–67.

Levin, Noam, and Eyal Ben-Dor. "Monitoring Sand Dune Stabilization Along the Coastal Dunes of Ashdod-Nizanim, Israel, 1945–1999." *Journal of Arid Environments* 58, no. 3 (August 2004): 335–55.

Levin, Noam, Ruth Kark, and Emir Galilee. "Maps and the Settlement of Southern Palestine, 1799–1948: An Historical/Gis Analysis." *Journal of Historical Geography* 36, no. 1 (January 2010): 1–18.

Levin, Noam, Christopher C. M. Kyba, Qingling Zhang, Alejandro Sánchez de Miguel, Miguel O. Román, Xi Li, Boris A. Portnov, et al. "Remote Sensing of Night Lights: A Review and an Outlook for the Future." *Remote Sensing of Environment* 237 (February 2020): article 111443.

Levin, Noam, Hava Lahav, Uri Ramon, Ayelet Heller, Guy Nizry, Asaf Tsoar, and Yoav Sagi. "Landscape Continuity Analysis: A New Approach to Conservation Planning in Israel." *Landscape and Urban Planning* 79, no. 1 (January 2007): 53–64.

Levine, E. "The Land of Milk and Honey." *Journal for the Study of the Old Testament* 25, no. 87 (2000): 43–57.

Longley, Paul A., Michael F. Goodchild, David J. Maguire, and David W. Rhind. *Geographic Information Systems and Science*. Hoboken, NJ: John Wiley & Sons, 2005.

Lorimer, Jamie, Chris Sandom, Paul Jepson, Chris Doughty, Maan Barua, and Keith J. Kirby. "Rewilding: Science, Practice, and Politics." *Annual Review of Environment and Resources* 40, no. 1 (November 4, 2015): 39–62.

McCloskey, Michael J. "Wilderness Act of 1964: Its Background and Meaning." *Oregon Law Review* 45, no. 4 (1965): 288–321.

McCloskey, Michael J. and Heather Spalding. "A Reconnaissance-Level Inventory of the Amount of Wilderness Remaining in the World." *Ambio* 18, no. 4 (January 1, 1989): 221–27.

McKee, Emily. "Performing Rootedness in the Negev/Naqab: Possibilities and Perils of Competitive Planting: Performing Rootedness." *Antipode* 46, no. 5 (November 2014): 1172–89.

McKinny, Christopher "A Historical Geography of the Administrative Division of Judah: The Town Lists of Judah and Benjamin in Joshua 15:21–62 and 18:21–28." PhD diss., Bar Ilan University, 2016.

Morin, Efrat. "To Know What We Cannot Know: Global Mapping of Minimal Detectable Absolute Trends in Annual Precipitation: Minimal Detectable Precipitation Trends." *Water Resources Research* 47, no. 7 (July 2011): 47–55.

Næss, Marius Warg. "Climate Change, Risk Management and the End of *Nomadic* Pastoralism." *International Journal of Sustainable Development & World Ecology* 20, no. 2 (April 2013): 123–33.

Nash, Roderick. *Wilderness and the American Mind*. New Haven: Yale University Press, 1967.

Oksanen, Juha, Cecilia Bergman, Jani Sainio, and Jan Westerholm. "Methods for Deriving and Calibrating Privacy-Preserving Heat Maps from Mobile Sports Tracking Application Data." *Journal of Transport Geography* 48 (October 2015): 135–44.

Parker, S. Thomas. "Peasants, Pastoralists, and *Pax Romana*: A Different View." *BASOR* 265 (February 1987): 35–51.

Perino, Andrea, Henrique M. Pereira, Laetitia M. Navarro, Néstor Fernández, James M. Bullock, Silvia Ceauşu, Ainara Cortés-Avizanda, et al. "Rewilding Complex Ecosystems." *Science* 364, no. 6438 (April 26, 2019): eaav5570.

Portnov, Boris A., and Uriel N. Safriel. "Combating Desertification in the Negev: Dryland Agriculture vs. Dryland Urbanization." *Journal of Arid Environments* 56, no. 4 (March 2004): 659–80.

Rosen, Steve A. "The Desert and the Pastoralist: An Archaeological Perspective on Human-Landscape Interaction in the Negev over the Millennia." *Annals of Arid Zone* 50 (2011): 1–15.

Salmon, Frederick John "Some Notes on Conventional Signs for Topographical Maps." *The Geographical Journal* 89, no. 1 (January 1937): 50.

Sanderson, Eric W., Malanding Jaiteh, Marc A. Levy, Kent H. Redford, Antoinette V. Wannebo, and Gillian Woolmer. "The Human Footprint and the Last of the Wild." *BioScience* 52, no. 10 (2002): 891–904.

Schaffer, Gad, and Noam Levin. "Mapping Human Induced Landscape Changes in Israel Between the End of the 19th Century and the Beginning of the 21st Century." *Journal of Landscape Ecology* 7, no. 1 (January 1, 2014): 110–45.

Schaffer, Gad, and Noam Levin. "Reconstructing Nineteenth-Century Landscapes from Historical Maps—the Survey of Western Palestine as a Case Study." *Landscape Research* 41, no. 3 (April 2, 2016): 360–79.

Schmidt, Joshua, and Natan Uriely. "Tourism Development and the Empowerment of Local Communities: The Case of Mitzpe Ramon, a Peripheral Town in the Israeli Negev Desert." *Journal of Sustainable Tourism* 27, no. 6 (June 3, 2019): 805–25.

Seifan, Merav. "Long-Term Effects of Anthropogenic Activities on Semi-Arid Sand Dunes." *Journal of Arid Environments* 73, no. 3 (March 2009): 332–7.

Siegal, Zehava, Haim Tsoar, and Arnon Karnieli. "Effects of Prolonged Drought on the Vegetation Cover of Sand Dunes in the NW Negev Desert: Field Survey, Remote Sensing and Conceptual Modeling." *Aeolian Research* 9 (June 2013): 161–73.

Soffer, Arnon, and Julian V. Minghi. "Israel's Security Landscapes: The Impact of Military Considerations on Land Uses." *The Professional Geographer* 38, no. 1 (February 1986): 28–41.

Survey of Palestine. "Map 5." 1:1,000,000. Maps Relating to the Report of the Anglo-American Committee of Enquiry Regarding the Problems of European Jewry and Palestine. Suppl. to Cmd. 6808. London: His Majesty's Stationary Office, 1946. Available online: https://commons.wikimedia.org/wiki/File:WhitePaper.jpg#filelinks (accessed August 17, 2023).

Swirski, Shlomo. "Current Plans for Developing the Negev: A Critical Perspective." Translated by Ruth Morris. Information on Equality and Social Justice in Israel. Tel Aviv: Adva Center, January 1, 2007.

Tucker, Compton J. "Red and Photographic Infrared Linear Combinations for Monitoring Vegetation." *Remote Sensing of Environment* 8, no. 2 (May 1979): 127–50.

Vaks, Anton, Miryam Bar-Matthews, Alan Matthews, Avner Ayalon, and Amos Frumkin. "Middle-Late Quaternary Paleoclimate of Northern Margins of the Saharan-Arabian Desert: Reconstruction from Speleothems of Negev Desert, Israel." *Quaternary Science Reviews* 29, no. 19–20 (September 2010): 2647–62.

Venter, Oscar, Eric W. Sanderson, Ainhoa Magrach, James R. Allan, Jutta Beher, Kendall R. Jones, Hugh P. Possingham, et al. "Sixteen Years of Change in the Global Terrestrial Human Footprint and Implications for Biodiversity Conservation." *Nature Communications* 7, no. 1 (November 25, 2016): 1–11.

Watson, James E. M., Nigel Dudley, Daniel B. Segan, and Marc Hockings. "The Performance and Potential of Protected Areas." *Nature* 515, no. 7525 (November 2014): 67–73.

Watson, James E. M., Oscar Venter, Jasmine Lee, Kendall R. Jones, John G. Robinson, Hugh P. Possingham, and James R. Allan. "Protect the Last of the Wild." *Nature* 563, no. 7729 (November 2018): 27–30.

Wildlife Conservation Society and Center for International Earth Science Information Network. "Global Human Footprint (Geographic), v2 (1995–2004)." Socioeconomic Data and Applications Center, 2005. Available online: https://sedac.ciesin.columbia.edu/data/set/wildareas-v2-human-footprint-geographic (accessed April 9, 2020).

Wuebbles, Donald J. "Celebrating the 'Blue Marble.'" *Eos, Transactions American Geophysical Union* 93, no. 49 (December 4, 2012): 509–10.

Wulder, Michael A., Thomas R. Loveland, David P. Roy, Christopher J. Crawford, Jeffrey G. Masek, Curtis E. Woodcock, Richard G. Allen, et al. "Current Status of Landsat Program, Science, and Applications." *Remote Sensing of Environment* 225 (May 2019): 127–47.

Yahel, Havatzelet, and Ruth Kark. "Land and Settlement of Israel's Negev Bedouin: Official (Ad Hoc) Steering Committees, 1948–1980." *British Journal of Middle Eastern Studies* 45, no. 5 (October 20, 2018): 716–41.

Yosef, Yizhak, Enric Aguilar, and Pinhas Alpert. "Changes in Extreme Temperature and Precipitation Indices: Using an Innovative Daily Homogenized Database in Israel." *International Journal of Climatology* 39, no. 13 (November 15, 2019): 5022–45.

Ziv, Baruch, Hadas Saaroni, Roee Pargament, Tzvi Harpaz, and Pinhas Alpert. "Trends in Rainfall Regime over Israel, 1975–2010, and Their Relationship to Large-Scale Variability." *Regional Environmental Change* 14, no. 5 (October 2014): 1751–64.

Zohary, Michael. *Vegetation of Israel and Adjacent Areas*. Beihefte zum Tübinger Atlas des Vorderen Orients. Reihe A, Naturwissenschaft 7. Wiesbaden: In Kommission Bei L. Reichert, 1982.

Chapter 6

SPATIAL LANGUAGE OF THE WILD: *YAʿAR, MIDBAR, AND ŚĀDEH*

Dalit Rom-Shiloni

Introduction

Accepting the convention that the "wild" (or "wilderness") designates a realm beyond human reach and, thus, (supposedly) beyond human intervention,[1] I espouse in this chapter the recognition, expressed by other scholars (geographers and sociologists, among others), that there are not really firm borders between the domestic and "the wild." The relative proximity of these two realms, as well as the interactions between them, are here investigated through the focus on three lexemes among the terms that demarcate the "wild" in the HB (Hebrew Bible): יער ("forest/thickets"), מדבר ("desert/wilderness"), and שדה ("[1] field, [2] territory, [3] steppe, open country, wild"; only the third meaning pertains to our topic).[2] Each of these terms has been discussed independently;[3] יער and מדבר have had a formative role throughout the ages and in different western cultures in constructing the notions of "the wild" (and wilderness).[4]

---

1. For definitions of wild/wilderness, see Roderick Nash, *Wilderness and the American Mind* (New Haven and London: Yale University Press, 1967), 1–7. One major methodological question concerns the tension between these human perspectives on "the wild," and the ancient history of any wild area discussed, which might in fact have been domesticated in earlier periods. Thus, one needs to take into consideration the relativity and the ever-changing status of regions as wild/domestic.

2. Other possible terms for "the wild" are: הר "mountain" (e.g., Josh. 17:15, 18), and the various synonyms of מדבר—e.g., ישימון (e.g., 1 Sam. 23:19; Isa. 43:20); ערבה (e.g., 1 Sam. 23:24; Isa. 35:1). The present discussion cannot treat them all.

3. The bibliographical references are too vast to mention. For יער ("thicket, undergrowth, wood" as also "forest"), see *HALOT* 422–2; as well as Martin J. Mulder, "יער *yaʿar*," *TDOT* 6: 208–17, and references there. For מדבר ("desert, wilderness"), see *HALOT* 546–47; Shmaryahu Talmon, "מדבר *midbar*; ערבה *ʿaraba*," *TDOT* 8: 87–118, and references there. More recently and with a clearly ecological perspective read theologically, see Robert B. Leal, *Wilderness in the Bible: Toward a Theology of Wilderness* (New York: Peter Lang, 2004). For שדה, see *HALOT* 1307–9; Gerhard Wallis, "שדה *sadeh;* שדי *šaday*," *TDOT* 14: 37–45, and references there.

4. Nash, *Wilderness*, 8–23.

The goals of the present chapter are twofold. First, I want to discuss these three terms in relation to one another. Although they differ substantially from one another in the physical landscapes they denote, they do have at least one major characteristic in common—they are each perceived as being beyond the borders of human residence. Second, studying these three specific terms should help us detect more general biblical perceptions of "the wild," and answer the questions: how did biblical authors describe "the wild"? What did they actually know about it? How did they portray human interactions with "the wild"?

Methodologically, such questions may be understood by utilizing the conceptual framework of social spatiality studies, as developed mainly by Henri Lefebvre and Edward W. Soja.[5] Though significant differences obtain between them, first Lefebvre and then Soja reformulated earlier understandings of human geography.[6] Lefebvre searched for a theoretical construct that would integrate three long-observed categories of space: "first, the *physical*—nature, the Cosmos; secondly, the *mental*, including logical and formal abstractions; and thirdly, the *social*." He argued that social space is "indistinguishable from mental space" and from physical space, and therefore adduced a notion of space as a triad "of the perceived, the conceived, and the lived," or in spatial terms: "spatial practice, representations of space, representational spaces."[7] For Soja, "trialectical thinking" is by definition inclusive of all three spaces; he coined the phrase "the trialectics of spatiality."[8] In Soja's framework: Firstspace is "perceived space," the concrete, "empirical space … directly sensible and open, within limits, to accurate measurement and description."[9] Secondspace is "conceived/conceptualized space." Soja accepted Lefebvre's emphasis on "conceived" space as the dominant notion of space in any

---

5. Henri Lefebvre, *The Production of Space*, trans. D. Nicholson-Smith (Oxford: Blackwell, 1991)—the French book was published first in 1974; a revised version followed in 1984—and Edward W. Soja, *Thirdspace: Journeys to Los Angeles and Other Real-and-Imagined Places* (Cambridge, MA: Blackwell, 1996); Edward W. Soja, *Postmodern Geographies: The Reassertion of Space in Critical Social Theory* (London: Verso, 1989). See the Introduction to the present volume.

6. For an introduction to this field and its relevance for HB studies, consult Jon Berquist, "Introduction: Critical Spatiality and the Uses of Theory," in *Constructions of Space I: Theory, Geography, Narrative*, ed. Claudia V. Camp and Jon L. Berquist, LHBOTS 481 (New York and London: T&T Clark, 2008), 1–12.

7. Lefebvre, *Production of Space*, 39–40. On pp. 11–27, he discussed the theoretical background that led him to reformulate these three aspects of the "social character of space."

8. Soja, *Thirdspace*, 70.

9. Soja, *Thirdspace*, 66. Lefebvre's (*Production of Space*, 38) "spatial practice," or "perceived space" is similar to Soja's "Firstspace" category. Gerda de Villiers ("From the Walls of Uruk: Reflections on Space in the Gilgamesh Epic," in *Constructions of Space V: Place, Space and Identity in the Ancient Mediterranean World*, ed. Gert T. M. Prinsloo and Christl M. Maier, LHBOTS 576 [New York: Bloomsbury, 2013], 143–58, esp. 143–44) pointed out the difference between "place" and "space"; Soja's Firstspace refers to "place."

society, since according to Soja, formulating conceived space designates "control over knowledge, signs and codes; over the means of deciphering spatial practice and hence over the production of spatial knowledge."[10] Therefore, such conceived mental spaces represent power and ideology. Soja added to that category also the idea of "utopian thought and vision."[11] Soja's Thirdspace parallels only partially Lefebvre's "representational-lived spaces."[12] Both Lefebvre and Soja pointed out the dynamic connections between all three types of space "with no one inherently privileged *a priori.*"[13] However, more than Lefebvre's representational space, Soja's Thirdspace not only is intrinsically connected to his previous two categories, but also accentuates notions of opposition—of "counterspaces," of struggles which may attend "relations of dominance, subordination, and resistance" to dominant orders, and give rise to perceptions of otherness within human groups.[14] Soja termed this process "thirding-as-Othering."[15]

The framework of these three social spaces may be relevant to each of the three HB terms under consideration here, יער, מדבר, and שדה.[16] They each project a notion of a "perceived space"—that is, a concrete, "empirical space ... directly sensible and open, within limits, to accurate measurement and description."[17] However, quite immediately these same terms devolve to more general notions of "conceived spaces"—that is, literary portrayals of places (or regions) that involve more abstract (at times even metaphorical) understandings of these places. Literary constructions of space intrinsically embed ideas and ideologies concerning these wild spaces.[18] Hence, to advance more the second goal of this chapter, I intend to broaden the study of these biblical "wilds" as "conceived spaces," by observing several specific implications they have for broader anthropological and

10. Soja, *Thirdspace*, 66–67; and Lefebvre, *Production of Space*, 38–39.

11. Soja, *Thirdspace*, 67.

12. Lefebvre (*The Production of Space*, 33, 39) characterized "representational spaces" as "associated images and symbols," even coded ones, that designate the "clandestine or underground side of social life."

13. Soja, *Thirdspace*, 68.

14. Soja, *Thirdspace*, 67–68.

15. Soja, *Thirdspace*, 81–82.

16. Several HB scholars have introduced Lefebvre's and Soja's studies to our field; see Jon Berquist, "Critical Spatiality and the Construction of the Ancient World," in *"Imagining" Biblical Worlds: Studies in Spatial, Social, and Historical Constructs in Honor of James W. Flanagan*, ed. David M. Gunn and Paula M. McNutt, JSOTSup 359 (Sheffield: Sheffield Academic, 2002), 14–29; Claudia V. Camp, "Introduction," in *Constructions of Space II: The Biblical City and Other Imagined Spaces*, ed. Jon L. Berquist and Claudia V. Camp, LHBOTS 490 (New York: T&T Clark, 2008), 1–17. For other references, see the Introduction to the present volume.

17. As Soja (*Thirdspace*, 66) explained: "Spatial practice ... is thus presented as both medium and outcome of human activity, behavior, and experience."

18. Soja, *Thirdspace*, 67–68.

theological conceptions in the HB. Furthermore, the discussion of the HB "wilds" allows me to further develop one major feature of social Thirdspace, related to Soja's notion of "thirding-as-Othering." That is to say, to understand both the physical and conceptual aspects of "the wild" in the HB, it will also be helpful to consider HB usage of these terms in relation to "dominance, subordination, and resistance" in human/nonhuman interactions.[19] Throughout, I pay particular attention to the significance of fluid boundaries within "the trialectics of spatiality," and between "the domestic" and "the wild," as also to the possibilities and consequences of crossing borders between them.

Biblical Portrayals of "the wild": Seven Descriptive Parameters

Beyond the shared feature of being spaces outside the borders of human residence, יער ("forest, thicket"), מדבר ("desert, wilderness"), and שדה ("wild steppe") each characterize different "wild" regions and landscapes of the Bible's terrain. My study of the approximately sixty occurrences of יער, some 270 of מדבר, and over 300 occurrences of שדה, indicates that biblical authors were familiar with additional points these three terms have in common.

This can be seen in the many examples where יער, מדבר, and שדה are used interchangeably. While there is a clear gradual difference between שדה as "cultivated field," and יער as the most extreme wild region (e.g., Mic. 3:12; Jer. 26:18), שדה as "wild steppe" is also used alongside יער, in the pair יער/שדה (in 1 Sam. 14:25; 2 Sam. 18:6; Ezek. 39:10); as well as in apposition (יער השדה נגב, "the brushland of the Negeb," Ezek. 21:2).[20] "the wild" fauna of the יער is designated as חית השדה (Hos. 2:14). The pair מדבר/יער occurs only once (Ezek. 34:25), whereas the pair שדה/מדבר occurs in several narratives—e.g., in describing Joseph's venture into Dothan (Gen. 37:15, 17):[21]

> So he sent him from the valley of Hebron. When he reached Shechem, (15) a man came upon him wandering in the fields (וימצאהו איש והנה תעה בשדה) ... (v. 17) ... So Joseph followed his brothers and found them at Dothan ... (22) ... And Reuben went on, "Shed no blood! Cast him into that pit out in the wilderness (אל הבור הזה במדבר), but do not touch him yourselves."

19. Lefebvre (*The Production of Space*) and Soja (*Thirdspace*, 67–70) were alerted to the (human) political forces that shape social spaces, particularly Thirdspace, which allows struggles for liberation and emancipation by diverse groups, mainly subordinate, peripheral and marginalized minorities. Hence, for both theories, the conception of otherness remains within human groups. See pp. 138–41 below.

20. Thus NJPS. Moshe Greenberg (*Ezekiel 21–37*, AB 22A [New York: Doubleday, 1997], 415) reads the construction as an apposition, "the scrub country, the Negeb."

21. The story does not specify the distance between that שדה in the area of Shechem and Dothan (which may be some 20 km apart), and does not tell of where that pit was found, except for designating it as in the מדבר. Geographically, that area of shepherding stretches north-east of Shechem, on the northern borders of the Samaria Desert.

Such a close interchange of שדה and מדבר occurs also in relation to Joshua's war in the desert east of Ai, Josh. 8:15, 24: "(v. 15) ... Joshua and all Israel fled in the direction of the wilderness (וינסו דרך המדבר) ... (v. 24) When Israel had killed all the inhabitants of Ai who had pursued them into the open wilderness (בשדה במדבר)." Note also Ezek. 29:5: "And I will fling you into the desert (ונטשתיך המדברה) ... You shall be left lying in the open (על פני השדה תפול)"; and the paired constructions: חית השדה/המדבר ("the wild beast/the wilderness," Isa. 43:20), נאות מדבר/כל עצי השדה ("the pastures of the wilderness/all the trees of the countryside," Joel 1:19) or בהמות שדה/נאות המדבר ("the very beasts of the field/the pastures of the wilderness," Joel 1:20; 2:22, בהמות שדי/נאות מדבר "beasts of the field/pastures in/of the wilderness").[22]

While each of those phrases has its own meaning and context, they demonstrate that biblical authors took each of the three terms, יער, מדבר, and שדה, as in some sense parallel terms denoting "the wild." But what makes each of these terms a designation of "the wild"?

Seven Parameters of "the wild"

I started my search for an answer with the more obvious terms (in a sense), יער and מדבר, identifying geographical parameters of "the wild" in the HB uses of each of these. Gradually I realized that although very different in their spatial features— יער is primarily characterized by landscape and botany (i.e., by phytogeographical) terms, whereas מדבר is primarily described by landscape and climate terms—there are shared categories that mark each of them as wild. I then added שדה, in its three meanings, to the mix. My investigation led to the recognition of seven descriptive parameters (i.e., of Firstspace, "perceived space"), all based on HB occurrences, from which we may derive the biblical conceptions of "the wild" connoted through these three terms (i.e., as Secondspace, "conceived space").

The first four parameters refer to geographical and biological information integrated with sporadic details found in the HB concerning locations (a); landscape characteristics (b) (including climatological characteristics); flora (c); and fauna (d). The other three parameters extend our perceptions of biblical portrayals of "the wild" by looking at human geography, anthropological aspects of interaction between the domestic and "the wild": human presence (e); human intervention (f); and "the wild" as a source of threat and danger to humans (g). These seven parameters, indeed, illustrate the proximity between the perceived and the conceived spaces.

As can be seen from Table 6.1, יער, מדבר, and שדה as "wild steppe" share some general features as remote locations (a), away from human residence. They clearly differ in their landscape characteristics (b), but they share the presence of wild flora (c) and wild fauna (d), though they differ in the types of animals found. These three spaces also share three parameters of human geography. HB references to each suggest that human presence (e) is rare, and thus that human intervention (f) is

---

22. The lexical boundaries between יער and שדה (and likewise הר) are occasionally breached by the ancient Versions (e.g., LXX to 2 Sam. 18:6). See Mulder, "יער ya'ar," 216.

Table 6.1 Seven parameters of "the wild": יַעַר, מִדְבָּר, and שָׂדֶה

	(a) Locations	(b) Landscape characteristics	(c) Flora	(d) Fauna	(e) Human presence	(f) Human intervention	(g) The wild's threat and danger
יַעַר Forest/thickets	1. Lebanon and Bashan Mountains 2. The Carmel and Central Mountain range in Israel	1. Mountains surroundings of 1500–3088 m. and up to 1500 mm precipitation 2. Mediterranean phytogeographical region, 400–1100 m and 700–800 mm precipitation	Uncultivated forest, hardwood אלון, ברוש, עץ שמן, סבך היער אלה אלון לבנה	Undomesticated כל חיתו (יער) בהמות יער דב ארי חזי [חזיר]	Rare	Rare	Maximal
מִדְבָּר Border of the desert	Eastern deserts	Varied 400–300 mm precipitation	Cultivated	Domesticated	Cities, farmers, and shepherds, "desert dwellers"	Partial in cities, cultivated fields roads, wells	Threat from the desert
מִדְבָּר Desert/wilderness	Eastern deserts, Negev, Sinai, deserts on Trans-Jordan	Varied, highly arid areas 200 mm precipitation or less	Uncultivated, scarce ציה צמאה, מדברה, הרבות, ארץ ערובה נחה [אפל] שלהבת להבה	Undomesticated, scarce תנים, שרף שרוף, פתן, צפעוני birds of prey	Rare, passers-by	None	Maximal

	(a) Locations	(b) Landscape characteristics	(c) Flora	(d) Fauna	(e) Human presence	(f) Human intervention	(g) The wild's threat and danger
שדה Cultivated field	Agricultural zone around cities, human settlements	Varied cultivated zones, 400 mm precipitation and up	Cultivated	Domesticated	Constant	Maximal	Minimal
שדה Territory/possession	Private: national/regional	Varied	Cultivated and/or mixed	Domesticated and/or mixed	Constant and/or mixed	Maximal and/or mixed	Minimal and/or mixed
שדה Wild steppe/open country	Unclear, farther remote Often within Eastern and Southern deserts	Varied in proximity to יער and כרמל	Uncultivated שדה שבי, שדה זרה, עץ השדה, חציר, קמשונים שדה, שדה יער	Undomesticated חית השדה, בהמת השדה, זר בעל, תנים, חמור, אילה בשדה (? אתאן בנות יען)	Rare, passers-by	Minimal (roads, wells)	Maximal

either completely absent (in reference to the desert), or at most rare—for example, when the need arises for roads to cross through forest or steppe (e.g., Josh. 20:31), or when events of war compel (e.g., 1 Sam. 14:25). Accordingly, the element of threat and danger (g) is a major characteristic for each of the realms of "the wild." This may be seen in several poetic or prophetic contexts—e.g., consolation prophecies that reverse natural conditions: וישבו במדבר לבטח וישנו ביערים "and they shall live secure in the wasteland, they shall even sleep in the woodland" (Ezek. 34:25). A brief description of יער and מדבר on the basis of these parameters will illustrate their usefulness.

Four geographical regions west and east of the Jordan are mentioned in the HB as covered by יער "forest/thickets" (or by the related term סבך, "thickets"):[23] (1) the Lebanon and Bashan mountains to the north (e.g., 2 Kgs 19:23); (2) the central mountain range of Ephraim (e.g., Josh. 17:15-18), Benjamin, and Judah (e.g., 1 Sam. 14; 22:5); single references to יער in (3) the Negeb (e.g., Ezek. 21:2, 3); and (4) the Trans-Jordan mountains (e.g., Isa. 21:13). These regions may be reconstructed as forested by virtue of regional names with יער (e.g., יער אפרים, in 2 Sam. 18:6, 8; or הר אפרים, Josh. 17:15-18); toponyms with the term (e.g., קרית יערים, Josh. 9:17; שדי יער, Ps. 132:6); or references to specific trees that are typical of the Mediterranean phytogeographical region (e.g., 2 Sam. 18:9; Hos. 4:13).[24] In relation to the mountains of Benjamin and Judah, the יער denotes the highlands, in distinction from the low-lying שפלה (e.g., Isa. 32:19: וברד ברדת היער ובשפלה תשפל עיר, "It will hail when the forest goes down, and in the lowlands the city will be laid low").[25] These higher altitude areas (400–1100 m high) generally receive 700–800 mm precipitation per year. Such phytogeographical conditions make the forest an attractive habitat for wild animals, which may be described in general terms (e.g., חיתו יער, "beast of the forest," Isa. 56:9) or specified by name (e.g., אריה, "lion," Amos 3:4; חזיר "wild boar," Ps. 80:14).

The deserts mentioned in the HB stretch over regions west of the Jordan, as far south as the Sinai Peninsula (and Egypt), and east in the Trans-Jordan. These areas generally receive less than 200 mm precipitation per year. In addition, the regions west of the Jordan—i.e., the eastern deserts of Samaria (Manasseh, Ephraim, Benjamin) and Judah—may be characterized as "deserts in the shadow of rain"—i.e., areas that are east of the watershed line. These arid areas allow only scant cover of desert flora (e.g., קוצי המדבר and הברקנים, "desert thorns and briers," Judg. 8:7) and wild desert fauna (e.g., בכרה, "she-camel," and פרה, "wild ass," Jer. 2:23, 24), which differ dramatically from the trees and larger animals of the יער. In terms of

---

23. For a detailed discussion, consult DNI Bible entry, יער "forest/Chapparal."

24. Most of these references to specific trees, אלון (oak, *Quercus*) and אלה (terebinth, *Pistacia palaestina*, 2 Sam. 18:9), are to individual trees at specific sites, mostly cultic (e.g., Gen. 35:4, 8; Josh. 24:26; Judg. 9:37; 1 Sam. 10:3). Nevertheless, their distribution over the central mountain range validates the information concerning the spread of forests in these regions.

25. Translated thus by Joseph Blenkinsopp, *Isaiah 1–39*, AB 19 (New York: Doubleday, 2000), 432.

the human parameters, the desert is described as uninhabited, as not even a place to pass through (e.g., Jer. 2:6), and a place of mortal danger (e.g., Gen. 21:14).

There are two major exceptions indicated by the table, which suggest a "test group" to these characteristics of "the wild." The first is the כרמל ("the borders of the desert"), a narrow north–south belt (about 5 to 10 km wide) on the higher mountains of the eastern Benjamin and Judean Deserts. Enjoying 500–300 mm of yearly precipitation, this region still allows for agriculture and shepherding, and, thus, is sporadically domesticated (1 Sam. 25). The *Carmel*, thus, contains domesticated fauna (d) and cultivated flora (c) (e.g., 2 Chron. 26:10). Set on the borders of the desert, the *Carmel* features some human presence (e) within and around the cities and villages (e.g., Teqoa, Amos 1:1; or Anathoth, Jer. 1:1); human intervention (f) is partial and restricted (e.g., 1 Sam. 25:2); and the region is under constant threat of drought (g), and of human intruders that may come from the desert (e.g., 1 Sam. 22, 24, 25).

Second, the two more conventional meanings of שדה, "cultivated field" and "territory, possession" are *not* defined by their geographical locations, they could be anywhere. However, "cultivated fields" may differ from the "wild steppe" by their climate conditions, as the former are restricted to regions of 400 mm precipitation and more. Therefore, placing the many references of שדה in its three very different meanings on this table of seven parameters of "the wild" presents important challenges to the study of the biblical "wilds."

I will therefore devote the bulk of the discussion below to the particular characteristics of שדה. The discussion aims to show that not only are these parameters helpful for pinning down uses of שדה as "wild steppe," but they may also be used to reconstruct broader biblical conceptions of "the wild," as well as distinctions between "wild" and "domesticated" spaces.

Perceptions of "Wilds": The Challenges of שדה

In the more than 300 occurrences of this term in the HB, שדה (along with שדי) stands for three quite different spatial entities: (1) a cultivated field; (2) a territory or possession; (3) a wild steppe.[26]

---

26. שדה occurs 297 times in the HB. The word שדי with its 13 occurrences may stand for שדה as "field"—e.g., Deut. 32:13; Jer. 4:17; Hos. 10:4; 12:12; Lam. 4:9—or "steppe"—e.g., Isa. 56:9; Joel 2:22; Pss. 8:8; 50:11; 80:14; 104:11 (שדי in Ps. 96:12 appears in 1 Chron. 16:32 as השדה). It may also serve as a calque for the Akkadian *šadû*, KUR, "mountain" (*CAD* Š, 1, 49–58); e.g., Jer. 18:14; and possibly Ps. 96:12. Note that *šadû* may also connote "open country, steppeland" (*CAD* Š, 58–9; see Gilg. M. iv 10); in Gilg. Y. vi 261 it parallels *ṣēru*, "hinterland, open country, steppeland" (see *ṣēru* A 3 *CAD* Ṣ, 141–47; and note *CAD* Ṣ, *ṣeru* A3 3' b, where *ṣeru* is used for agriculture, 142–43). Furthermore, *šadû*, KUR, "mountain" also stands in construction with desert—e.g., *huribtu ša* KUR-*i ašar laššu šammu* "the desert of the open country where there is no vegetation" (Jean-Vincent Scheil, *Annales de Tukulti Ninip II, roi d'Assyrie 889–884*, Bibliothèque de l'École des hautes études 178 [Paris: Musée du Louvre, 1909], Tn. II 63). For the Akkadian etymology, and its connotations of mountain,

שדה as Cultivated Field

In the sense of "cultivated field," שדה denotes the agricultural zone surrounding residential areas (see Table 6.2).²⁷ Thus, in terms of locations designated by this term (a), שדה describes lands contiguous to every human settlement that allows for agriculture—that is (b), in areas that can count on more than 400 mm precipitation per year (e.g., the Qiriat ʿArba/Hebron area given to the Kohathite Levitical clans

Table 6.2 Seven parameters of "the wild": שדה as cultivated field

	(a) Locations	(b) Landscape characteristics	(c) Flora	(d) Fauna	(e) Human presence	(f) Human intervention	(g) The wild's threat and danger
שדה Cultivated field	Agricultural zone around cities, human settlements	Varied cultivated zones, 400 mm precipitation and up	Cultivated	Domesticated	Constant	Maximal	Minimal

highland, and steppe, see Alexander Heidel, "A Special Usage of the Akkadian Term *Šadû*," *JNES* 8 (1949): 233–5. I thank Noga Ayali-Darshan and Nathan Wassermann for their helpful comments on this point. William H. Propp ("On Hebrew *śāde[h]*, 'Highland,'" *VT* 37 [1987]: 230–36) proposed introducing a separate lexical category for those texts where שדה/שדי refer to (or stand in parallelism to) mountains or highlands (Num. 23:14; Judg. 5:19; 2 Sam. 1:21; Jer. 13:27; 17:3; 18:14; Ps. 1:11; Job 40:20). However, the many other occurrences of שדה with reference to various locations and topographies (see discussion below) mitigate against taking שדה as topographically demarcated. Wallis ("שדה *sadeh*; שדי *šaday*," 37–45) chose to accentuate the basic meaning "field" for שדה, and thus distinguished between "developed fields" over against "undeveloped fields"—that is, fields that contain features of the wild. I believe the following discussion does more justice to the various meanings of שדה in the HB.

27. Note the connection between קרית ארבע/חברון מגרשיה, שדה העיר, חצריה ("Qiriat ʿArba/Hebron the pastures around it, the fields of the town, and its villages") in Josh. 21:11-12; and between בתים, חצרות, שדת ("the houses, the courtyards, and the fields") in Exod. 8:9, which demarcate human-constructed surroundings, and recognize the distinctions between them. See Juval Portugali, "'*Arim, Banot, Migrashim* and *Haṣerim*: The Spatial Organization of Eretz Israel in the 12th–10th Centuries BCE according to the Bible," *Eretz Israel* (1983): 282–90 (Hebrew). The pairs עיר/שדה ("city/country," e.g., Deut. 28:3, 16; Jer. 14:17-18; 32:17-18; Ezek. 7:15) and בית/שדה ("house/field [outside]," e.g., Gen. 39:5; Deut. 5:21; Mic. 2:2) show these categories of human residence and agricultural lands as geographically proximate, and yet as distinctive spaces. In Jer. 35:6-9, בית and שדה designate locations of permanent human residency, ownership, and cultivation, which the Rechabites were commanded to eschew in order to adopt a (semi-)nomadic lifestyle. In some instances, the triad בתים, שדות, כרמים ("houses, fields, vineyards") occurs—e.g., Jer. 32:15; 35:9; Ps. 107:36; Neh. 5:3, 11.

and to Caleb, Josh. 21:10-12). Cultivated plant life (c) is grown in the שדה;[28] it may be indicated by the general term כל עשב השדה ("all the grasses of the field"), that consists mostly of grains and legumes (e.g., והפשתה והשערה, "flax and barley," Exod. 9:22, 25; והחטה והכסמת, "wheat and emmer," Exod. 9:31-32); and fruit trees (e.g., ועץ השדה יתן פריו, "and the trees of the field their fruit," Lev. 26:4).[29] This realm features domesticated fauna (d), described as "the livestock in your fields"—i.e., horses, donkeys, camels, cattle, and sheep (Exod. 9:3), and note Deut. 11:15: ונתתי עשב בשדך לבהמתך ("I will also provide grass in your fields for your cattle").[30] Both flora and fauna in this realm serve as sources of food for the closest human settlements (e.g., Gen. 41:48). With regard to the presence of human beings (e), the agricultural function of שדה requires daily movement between the houses of the city and the cultivated fields. This, in turn, marks the שדה as a realm subject to constant (maximal) human intervention (f); and, thus, as a realm that poses minimal danger to human beings ([g], see, e.g., Exod. 23:16; Josh. 9:32, 43). Hence, in this sense of cultivated fields around human settlements, the שדה connotes productive and positive conditions of relative safety.

28. For the broad range of agricultural products of the שדה, see Joel 1:10-12; these included different kinds of grains (e.g., Gen. 37:7) and lentils (e.g., 2 Sam. 23:11). Such variety seems to be behind the phrase זרע [ה]שדה ("seed of the fields," as verb or noun, in Gen. 47:24; Exod. 23:16; Lev. 19:19; 25:3, 4; 27:16; Deut. 14:22; 28:38; Ps. 107:37). The general term כל עשב השדה ("all the grasses of the field," e.g., Exod. 9:22, 25, 31-32) points to cultivated plant life. Likewise, the variety of activities connected with the שדה all have to do with growing crops (e.g., Lev. 19:9, 19; 23:22; 25:3-5, 12, 31, 34; Deut. 24:19). Compare to עשב השדה in Gen 3:18 that denotes uncultivated flora, and thus refers to the third meaning of שדה, below.

29. שדה may indicate a place where fruit trees grow—e.g., Exod. 10:5; Judg. 9:27; Ezek. 17:8; Joel 1:12. It is also paired with כרם ("vineyard," e.g., Lev. 25:3-4; 1 Sam. 8:14). The phrase עץ השדה ("tree of the field") may stand for the cultivated fruit-trees of domestic agriculture—e.g. Exod. 10:5: כל העץ הצמח לכם מן השדה ("all your trees that grow in the field"; and note also כל פרי העץ "all the fruit of the trees," v. 15), similar to the phrase ועץ השדה יתן פריו ("and the trees of the field yield their fruit"; note also the parallel terms עץ השדה, in Lev. 26:4 and עץ הארץ, in Lev. 26:20). Ezekiel 34:27 and 36:30 follow Lev. 26, so that עץ השדה (and פרי העץ) refer to agriculture products. Note, however, that Ezekiel also repeatedly used עץ השדה (and often the plural עצי השדה) to refer to the high trees of Lebanon, thus to uncultivated trees (Ezek. 17:24; 31:4-6, 15; 39:10; and similarly for flora in the Negev, 21:2).

30. For examples of the שדה as the place to herd sheep and cattle, see Exod. 9:19, 21; Num. 22:4 (including oxen); and 1 Sam. 11:5. Laws in Exod. 22:4-5 concerning damages to the שדה and כרם specify damages caused by grazing animals and by fire that catches the grains, and reflect the tensions between farmers and shepherds.

שדה as Territory or (National) Possession

In its second meaning, שדה as "territory or possession" (see Table 6.3) may indicate a region of unspecified measurements and undefined borders, presented as a private property in the possession of its owner and his family, clan, or tribe (e.g., שדה עפרון אשר במכפלה אשר לפני ממרא, "Ephron's land in Machpelah, near Mamre," Gen. 23:17; or חלקת שדה נבות היזרעאלי, "the field of Naboth the Jezreelite," 2 Kgs 9:25).[31] While these private possessions may be understood as "cultivated fields"—that is, in terms of the seven parameters, they share the features of שדה described above previous section—they could refer to a varied landscape (b), with mixed flora and fauna features ([c] and [d]). Note, for instance, that Ephron's land (Gen. 23:17) includes the field, its trees, and the cave that was at its edge (v. 9; and see vv. 11, 13, 19-20), thus much beyond a "cultivated field."

On a broader scale, however, the שדה may indicate a national or communal territory (e.g., שדה אדום, "the country of Edom," Judg. 5:4; שדה פלשתים, "the territory of the Philistines," in 1 Sam. 6:1; שדה אפרים and שדה שמרון, "the Ephraimite country and the district of Samaria," Obad. 19), without specification of breadth or borders; thus it may mark a region known to be the residence of a particular national group.[32] In these national contexts, שדה as territory is a geopolitical term, which probably includes both "cultivated fields" and wild areas. In terms of the seven parameters of "the wild," this usage generally does not yield information about specific landscape characteristics (b) or features that indicate human intervention (f)—thus, I allowed myself to label these as "varied" (see Table 6.3). Descriptions of flora and fauna ([c] and [d]) are also generally avoided. The only clear evidence of human presence and intervention ([e] and [f]) may be seen in the political inclusion of an entire region under the control of a national-political entity (whether tribes, or kingdoms).

Table 6.3 Seven parameters of "the wild": שדה as territory, possession

	(a) Locations	(b) Landscape characteristics	(c) Flora	(d) Fauna	(e) Human presence	(f) Human intervention	(g) The wild's threat and danger
שדה Territory/ possession	Private, national/ regional	Varied	Cultivated and/or mixed	Domesticated and/or mixed	Constant and/or mixed	Maximal and/or mixed	Minimal and/or mixed

31. This same property, designated as כרם (נבות) ("[Naboth's] vineyard," in 1 Kgs 21:1-4, 16, 18), becomes King Yehoram's graveyard.

32. In those contexts, שדה often stands in parallel to the terms ארץ (e.g. ארצה שעיר שדה אדום "the land of Seir, the country of Edom," Gen. 32:4; Ps. 78:12), אדמה ("ground," e.g., Joel 1:10), and on the private-tribal sphere to נחלה ("territory," e.g., Judg. 20:6; Ruth 4:5), and אחזה ("holding," e.g., Lev. 27:16, 22; Josh. 21:12).

שדה *as Wild Steppe*

In its third meaning, שדה as "wild steppe" (see Table 6.4) may be found anywhere in biblical terrain, in any landscape, beyond the cultivated fields outside residential cities or villages, until the areas farthest away from human habitation ([a] and [b]).[33] Moving from north to south through biblical territory, we find a number of occurrences of שדה in this sense: (i) the שדה in *Ya'ar Ephraim* (2 Sam. 18:6);[34] (ii) the area surrounding *'Ai* (Josh. 8:24-29): ויהי ככלות ישראל להרג את כל ישבי העי בשדה במדבר אשר רדפום בו ("When Israel had killed all the inhabitants of Ai who had pursued them into the open wilderness," v. 24)—the phrase בשדה במדבר conveys the location of that steppe by the Ai in the Judean desert—and (iii) the description in several places of David hiding from Saul in the שדה (e.g., 1 Sam. 19:3; 20:5, 11, 24, 35; 25:15)—in terms of the narrative, this use of שדה points geographically to the desert areas east of *Gibeah*, and in the Judean Desert as far southeast as *Carmel* and *Maon* (1 Sam. 25:15; and see the discussion of מדבר below).[35] These narrative locations interestingly (and possibly, coincidentally) point to regions on the borders of the arid areas in Israel, and to the eastern and southern deserts.[36]

Table 6.4 Seven parameters of "the wild": שדה as wild steppe

	(a) Locations	(b) Landscape characteristics	(c) Flora	(d) Fauna	(e) Human presence	(f) Human intervention	(g) The wild's threat and danger
שדה Wild steppe/ open country	Unclear, farther remote, often within eastern and southern deserts	Varied in proximity to מדבר and יער	Uncultivated שיח השדה, עשב השדה, עץ השדה, דודאים, המן, גפן שדה, פקעת שדה	Undomesticated הדשה תיח, בהמת השדה, דב שכול, לביא, תנים, אילת בשדה, פראים, בנות יענה(?)	Rare, passers-by	Minimal (roads, wells)	Maximal

33. Cf. Wallis, "שדה *sadeh*," 43.

34. Whether יער אפרים ("Ephraim Forest") was east or west of the Jordan has been debated; see P. Kyle McCarter, *II Samuel*, AB 9B (Garden City, NY: Doubleday, 1984), 405.

35. Going further south, to the western Negev, in Gen. 24, Isaac leaves the residential area and wanders around in the שדה, v. 63: ויצא יצחק לשוח בשדה ("And Isaac went out walking in the field"); v. 65: מי האיש הלזה ההלך בשדה לקראתנו ("Who is that man walking in the field toward us?"). Since Isaac was visible to Rebecca and to Abraham's servant on their way south, this wandering might have been at a farther area distanced from the family tent.

36. Another example of the variety of landscapes and locations of שדה in this sense may be learned from Exod. 16. The manna was found in close proximity to the residential camp (סביב למחנה, vv. 13b-15), an area subsequently labeled שדה (v. 25). As a feature of the wandering stories in the Sinai desert (16:10, 14, 32), שדה here should be understood as a fairly dried and wild steppe (clearly not a cultivated field; cf. Exod. 1:14). Without going into

In terms of its flora (c), the שדה is characterized by wild plant species, generally termed שיח השדה ("shrub of the steppe," Gen. 2:5) and עשב השדה ("grasses of the steppe," Gen. 2:5), or עץ השדה ("tree(s) of the steppe," e.g., Ezek. 17:24). A few species of specific wild plants are also mentioned: דודאים בשדה ("mandrakes in the steppe/open country," Gen. 30:14, 16); the manna (Exod. 16:25); and גפן שדה ("wild vine," which produces פקעת שדה, "wild gourd," 2 Kgs 4:39).[37] Most important to notice is that in this meaning, שדה is characterized as wild according to all seven parameters.

In terms of fauna (d), wild animals may be found in the שדה, generally termed חית השדה ("wild beasts," e.g., Gen. 2:19, 20),[38] or בהמת השדה ("beasts of the steppe," e.g., 1 Sam. 17:44—but in v. 46: חית הארץ, "beasts of the earth,"—and Joel 1:19-20), and distinguished from עוף השמים ("the birds of the sky," e.g., Gen. 2:19, 20). In most of the occurrences of חית השדה there is no specification of species (e.g., Jer. 12:9; Ezek. 34:5, 8; Hos. 2:14).[39]

Among the rarely mentioned animals associated with the שדה in this sense, we read of (only) three predators:[40] a female bear, 2 Sam. 17:8: כי גברים המה ומרי נפש המה

the long interpretive traditions concerning the manna, this meaning of שדה characterizes the manna as a type of wild flora (see Gen. 30:14; 2 Kgs 4:39), taken to be a divine gift (לחם מן השמים, "bread from the sky," Exod. 16:4) and supplied to sustain the people over the Sabbath (Exod. 16:21-30, 31-36). Hence, this specific third meaning of שדה is of importance.

37. Wild flora are considered to be not lasting and not valuable in 2 Kgs 19:26, for example, where the Assyrian king's defeated enemies are portrayed as dried out shrubs of the field, היו עשב שדה וירק דשא ("They were but grass of the steppe/open country and green herbage").

38. חית השדה also occurs in 2 Kgs 14:9; Jer. 27:5-6; Job 5:23; 40:20; Ps. 104:11 חיתו שדי "wild beasts"; and often with עוף השמים, "birds of the sky," e.g., 2 Sam. 21:10; Ezek. 31:6, 13); note also כל עוף הרים and זיז שדי ("every bird of the mountains" and "the creatures of the field," Ps. 50:11). Similar combinations are seen with חית הארץ, e.g., Gen. 1:30; 9:2; Ezek. 29:5; 32:4; and with four components, including רמש האדמה ("all creeping things that move on the ground") and דגי הים ("fish of the sea") in Ezek. 38:20; Hos. 2:20.

39. In this context we may also consider the repeated prophetic curse proclaimed against the kings of Israel. Using the pair שדה/עיר ("field/city"), this curse distinguishes between dogs, which represent beasts of prey that live within human residences and birds of prey that are active in the wild: המת לירבעם [/לבעשא / לאחאב] בעיר יאכלו הכלבים והמת לו בשדה יאכלו עוף השמים ("Anyone belonging to Jeroboam [/ to Baasha / to Ahab] who dies in the town shall be devoured by dogs; and anyone who dies in the open country shall be eaten by the birds of the air," 1 Kgs 14:11; 16:4; 21:24). This same distinction between the human settlements and "the wild" may be behind the reference to the exposing of human corpses which were not respectfully buried—e.g., in reference to Jezebel: והית [ק: והיתה] נבלת איזבל כדמן על פני השדה בחלק יזרעאל ("and the carcass of Jezebel shall be like dung on the steppe [NJPS: ground], in the field of Jezreel," 2 Kgs 9:37; see also 1 Kgs 21:23; 2 Kgs 9:10, 36; and Jer. 9:21); compare to the parallel phrase והיו לדמן על פני האדמה ("they shall become dung upon the face of the earth," Jer. 8:2; 16:4; 25:33; and similarly in Ps. 83:11).

40. The following list should therefore be taken as random and clearly partial data, based only on the literary occurrences of שדה alongside mentions of specific animal species.

כדב שכול בשדה ("for [your father and his men] are courageous fighters, and they are as desperate as a bear in the wild robbed of her whelps"); תנים ("jackals," Isa. 43:20); and a לביא ("lion") in parallelism to חית השדה ("wild beast," Hos. 13:8). In addition, there are references to two herbivores, אילת בשדה ("the hind in the steppe/open country") in Jeremiah's description of the great drought (Jer. 14:1-6, v. 5); פראים ("wild asses," Ps. 104:11); and one may possibly add birds of prey, בנות יענה (though often translated as "ostriches," Isa. 43:20).[41]

All this information together creates an interesting picture. In comparison to the ample information available concerning the locations, flora, and fauna of the שדה as "cultivated field," the information about the actual features of שדה as "wild steppe/open country" is fairly minimal. Within many references, only minor details may be gathered concerning landscape characteristics and plant or animal life. Could this be coincidental? Table 6.1 above shows that this phenomenon occurs also in reference to the flora and fauna of the יער and the מדבר.

Considering the three parameters of interaction between the domestic and "the wild" in the שדה as "wild steppe/open country," human presence (e) may be characterized as temporary, as passing through, not as long term. Among those who pass through are shepherds (e.g., Gen. 37:15; Exod. 9:3, 19, 21-22, 25),[42] hunters (e.g., Gen. 25:27, 29, Esau is איש שדה, "a wild-man"), and individuals on journeys (e.g., Num. 23:14; 1 Kgs 11:29; Ezek. 16:6, 8).[43] In addition, we are told that traitors, transgressors, and criminals may be found in this שדה (e.g., David pursued by Saul, 1 Sam. 20:5, 24; 25:15).[44] Therefore, human intervention (f) is very limited, occurring only on extraordinary occasions—for example, when roads must be opened (e.g., Num. 22:23; 2 Sam. 20:11-12),[45] or wells must be dug

41. While often translated as "ostrich(es)," בנות יענה are characterized as birds of prey (or in the contexts of predators) in Isa. 13:21; 34:13; 43:20; Mic. 1:8; Job 30:29; see the DNI Bible entry: Syrian Ostrich (?) / Little Owl (?), בת יענה, יענים, *Struthio camelus syriacus* (?) / *Athene noctua* (?). https://dni.tau.ac.il/dictionary-entry/syrian-ostrich-little-owl-בת-יענים-יענה-struthio-camelus-syriacus-athene-noctua/

42. As mentioned above, it is difficult to decide whether shepherding zones were still considered within the cultivated areas or beyond them. See 1 Sam. 11:5.

43. Ezekiel 16:1-8 uses the image of the desertion of the newly-born Jerusalem by throwing the infant upon the field: ותשלכי על פני השדה (vv. 2-3). As argued by Meir Malul ("Adoption of Foundlings in the Bible and Mesopotamian Documents: A Study of Some Legal Metaphors in Ezekiel 16.1-7," *JSOT* 46 [1990]: 97–126), on the basis of Mesopotamian adoption laws, throwing the baby onto the שדה marks the desertion of the foundling, and legally any passer-by is entitled to pick the baby up and adopt her (vv. 6, 8). Legally, the שדה is thus a no-man's land.

44. It is of interest that merchants are not mentioned explicitly as crossing the שדה, nor the יער or the מדבר (cf. Gen. 37:25, where ארחת ישמעאלים, "a caravan of Ishmaelites," travels the main roads of the *Gilead* on its way to Egypt, though these roads clearly pass through areas of steppe/open country and desert).

45. This area of the road (מסלה or דרך) and the שדה around it is the setting for the internal war between Israel and Benjamin on the roads leading to Beth El and Gibeah. The troops walk on the מסלות, "the roads," and the casualties are spread over the שדה (Judg. 20:31).

(e.g., Gen. 29:2). Thus, the שדה as "wild steppe/open country" poses dangers to humans (g) from both human and animal sources—חית השדה endanger those who venture here (e.g., 2 Sam. 21:10; Ezek. 33:27; 34:8); the שדה is an isolated area, where war, murder, and rape may occur; it is also a realm where illegitimate cults may be performed (Lev. 17:5; Jer. 13:27). These dangers occur because this area is perceived as empty of humans and normal human activity, and under no societal control (e.g., Deut. 22:23-29).

שדה *as a Realm of Fluid Boundaries*

Notwithstanding the preceding description, there is a more elusive meaning of שדה that is harder to pin down. Several examples may serve to illustrate this complexity.

(1) שדה as realm of conflict and violence. Conflicts can occur when two persons are "alone in the steppe," ויהי בהיותם בשדה. These meetings end in severe violence, either murder (2 Sam. 14:6: וינצו שניהם בשדה ואין מציל ביניהם "The two of them came to blows out in the fields/steppe where there was no one to stop them"; and see Gen. 4:8; Deut. 21:1) or rape (Deut. 22:25-27).[46] Where is such an area located in reference to domestic settlements? A criminal event that lacks witnesses must happen in a remote place, but it is nevertheless a remote place to which humans have access.[47]

---

46. Deuteronomy 22 discusses a cluster of marriage laws (Deut. 22:23-29), including laws that discuss the sexual harassment of a young, engaged girl in two separate locations, within a city (vv. 23-24), and in the שדה (vv. 25-27). The great difference between the two locations is the question of whether the girl would be heard if she screamed. If she is hurt in the שדה, her life is spared, because even if she screamed, she would not have been heard (v. 27). For the present discussion, the important point is that שדה stands in opposition to the city, it is the area *outside* the human-settled arena. This sense of שדה as a remote area is further clarified in the Temple Scroll's discussion of this law (66:4-5): ואם בשדה מצאה האיש את האשה במקום רחוק וסתר מהעיר ("and if in the field/steppe did the man find the woman in a remote and hidden place away from the city"); see Elisha Qimron, *The Temple Scroll: A Critical Edition with Extensive Reconstructions* (Beer Sheba: Ben-Gurion University of the Negev Press; Jerusalem: Israel Exploration Society, 1996), 91; Jeffrey H. Tigay, *Deuteronomy 17–34*, Mikra leIsrael (Tel Aviv: Am Oved; Jerusalem: The Hebrew University Magnes Press, 2016), 557 (Hebrew).

47. The unexpected meeting between Jeroboam and Ahiah the Shilonite on the road (1 Kgs 11:29-39) also specifies that ושניהם לבדם בשדה ("and when the two were alone in the open country," v. 29). While this meeting turns out to be a positive one for the partners, it clearly takes place under great stress and benefits from secrecy (vv. 30-31). The only other geographical detail we get is that it was בדרך ("on the way," v. 29; indeed the Lucianic revision of LXX repeats בדרך also at the end of the verse, whereas LXX shows a different text lacking the entire phrase; see Zipora Talshir, *The Alternative Story of the Division of the Kingdom (3 Kingdoms 12:24a–z)*, Jerusalem Biblical Studies 6 (Jerusalem: Simor, 1993), 103–106). This short anecdote does not even allow us to know the route Jeroboam took leaving Jerusalem.

(2) שדה as place of ritual separation. Within the ritual legal sphere, the description of the purification ceremony of the leper on the first day of his purification (Lev. 14) tells of the priest's actions outside of the residential area (i.e., the camp, v. 3), including the release of a living bird in the שדה: ושלח את הצפר החיה על פני השדה ("to set the live bird free in the open country," v. 7). The meaning of שדה here is clarified in the next section, in the details of a similar procedure for the purification of a house with "leprosy" (vv. 48-53). Here, the apposition of שדה to "*outside* the city" articulates the separation between them: ושלח את הצפר החיה אל מחוץ לעיר אל פני השדה ("he shall set the live bird free outside the city in the open country," v. 53). At face value, these verses designate two circles of human residence, the city and the שדה outside of it; but once the bird is set free, it has no borders, and thus the שדה immediately contains both the cultivated zone and much beyond it—that is, "the wild."[48]

(3) שדה as revelation zone. Manoach's wife sits alone in the שדה, where she is fairly far away from her husband (Judg. 13:9-10), when God's angel reveals himself to her for the second time.[49] Was she sitting still within the cultivated fields, or did she distance herself even farther away, where no other humans (not even her husband) could see her?

(4) Wars repeatedly take place in the שדה, outside cities.[50] Yet again the question remains—were those wars conducted in close vicinity, just outside the city walls? Or did they primarily take place in more remote and open areas, beyond the cultivated zones of the cities, and only in the event of success, approach the city walls (e.g., Josh. 8:24; Judg. 9:39-45)?

The point I would like to stress here is that, especially in such ambiguous contexts, the use of שדה does not necessarily allow us to evaluate in concrete ways whether the biblical event described took place in the cultivated agricultural zone around human settlements or in a more distant and uncultivated,

---

48. Jacob Milgrom (*Leviticus 1–16*, AB 3A [New York: Doubleday, 1991], 840) pointed out the wide range of meanings for שדה in this context (with its Akkadian parallel, see n. 26 above); in his commentary for vv. 33-53 he referred to Mesopotamian and Hittite parallels, rituals of house purifications in which birds are sent either to the underworld (in Hurrian ritual) or to the heavens (in Mesopotamian and other Hittite rituals, pp. 864–65, 881–82).

49. Commentators have pointed out the intentional distancing of Manoach, see Barry G. Webb, *Judges*, NICOT (Grand Rapids, MI: Eerdmans, 2012), 354; Yairah Amit (*Judges*, Mikra LeIsrael [Tel Aviv and Jerusalem: Am Oved and Magnes, 1999], 220 [Hebrew]) suggested that the major focus of the current story moves from the birth of Samson to the revelation, which is, therefore, accentuated and elaborated through repetitions. I would also call attention to the geographical distancing of the event.

50. The following list of references are all war stories in which the שדה is mentioned as the battlefield: Josh. 8:24; Judg. 9:39-45; 20:31; 1 Sam. 4:2; 14:4-5, 15, 25; 2 Sam. 10:6-8; 11:11, 23; 18:6; 20:11-12; 2 Kgs 7:1-2, 12. This עיר/שדה pairing serves also in judgment prophecies, Jer. 6:25; 14:17-18; Ezek. 7:15; 33:27; and in the prophecy against Tyre, Ezek. 26:6, 8.

"wild" area. The former possibility may be seen, for instance, in 2 Sam. 23:11, where Shammah son of Age the Ararite fights the Philistines and saves a field sown with lentils: חלקת השדה מלאה עדשים. The latter sense seems to be the case, for instance, in 2 Sam. 18:6, which brings together שדה and יער in ויצא העם השדה לקראת ישראל ותהי המלחמה ביער אפרים ("The troops marched out into the open to confront the Israelites, and the battle was fought in the forest of Ephraim").[51] What I find to be of crucial importance is the recognition that biblical writers have no specific terminology to distinguish between the domestic zone and the wild, open country. Rather, שדה is used for all three of the abovementioned meanings (field, territory, and wild steppe/open country).

Intermediate Conclusions

The lexical flexibility of שדה leads me back to the reasons for my decision to integrate these three very different terms (יער, מדבר, and שדה) in the search for biblical definitions of "the wild." Describing each of the three meanings of שדה according to those parameters of "the wild" illustrates the significant differences between them. The distinctions between the biblical uses of שדה as human-made and cultivated field, on the one hand, and wild steppe/open country, on the other, demonstrate (at least) one benefit of my articulation of these seven "parameters of the wild," as they enable us to more comprehensively delineate the occurrences of שדה as wild steppe/open country.

But there are at least two additional lessons to learn from the biblical usage of this one word, שדה, for these three different spaces. First, even more than יער and מדבר, שדה is the term that at face value illustrates the conceptual proximity of the domestic and "the wild" in the biblical purview, and the lack of any real borders between them. Second, the complexities of שדה illustrate the usefulness of Lefebvre's and Soja's social spatial theory and raise the possibility of extending it beyond the realm of human (social) spaces. The three different meanings of שדה, along with its ambiguous occurrences, demonstrate the inadequacy of presuming solely binary relationships between the domestic and "the wild," and accentuate the need to consider more complex interactions between spatial relationships. I here take up Soja's notion of "thirding-as-Othering" in various human social contexts,[52] and suggest that biblical portrayals of "wilds," and שדה as an illustration of them, independently affirm tendencies of "othering" "the wild," presenting it as dangerous, and beyond human reach. These observations provide us with a new standpoint from which to consider the broader conceptions of "the wild" operating in the HB.

---

51. LXX 2 Sam. 18:6 translates the שדה with εἰς τὸν δρυμὸν ("in the forest"); LXX seems to adapt the mention of MT שדה here to יער, in analogy with the place name mentioned at the end of this verse יער אפרים. See McCarter, *II Samuel*, 400.

52. See Soja, *Thirdspace*, 60; and see the entire discussion on pp. 60–70.

Conceptions of "the wild" in the HB and Some of their Implications

The Transition from "Perceived" to "Conceived" Spaces of "the wild"

The foregoing discussion has suggested that biblical spaces perceived as "wild" share a fairly clear definition: such areas may be physically very close to human habitations and yet beyond the boundaries of human residence by virtue of their locations, landscape characteristics, flora, and fauna. Humans are rarely present in such spaces, passing through or otherwise intervening in them only rarely; these spaces are perceived as generally dangerous to human beings. This last element, in particular, moves us to the realm of "the wild" as conceived space; that is, (in this case) the perception of danger comes to define שדה, יער, and מדבר (and at times to even link them together).

I want to suggest three additional features that are central to biblical conceptions of "the wild" as represented by the terms יער, מדבר, and שדה; these features illustrate the fluidity of the boundaries between domestic and wild zones on the level of conceived spaces. First, the biblical "wilds" are presented and conceptualized through what I would call *the tension of distances*: that is, the tension between proximity/familiarity and remoteness/unfamiliarity. On the one hand, all these areas may be physically proximate to humans and to human settlements.[53] As discussed above, this is most clearly represented by שדה, which time and again blurs the boundaries between cultivated zones and the wild steppe/open country. The יער poses a looming realm of danger to humans on the roads (e.g., 2 Kgs 2:24), outside or encroaching on their cities (e.g., Jer. 5:6; 21:14). Likewise, many stories located on the borders of the Judean (eastern) deserts (e.g., 1 Sam. 24, 25, 26; and see the prophecies of Jeremiah) indicate an extraordinary familiarity with life conditions in the desert as physically proximate to regular human activity. These descriptions clearly distinguish between the (nearby) borders of the deserts, which still allow human residence and agricultural activity, and the (more remote) dry and dangerous desert areas (e.g., Jer. 2:6, 31). Yet, despite this physical proximity, this seeming familiarity with the desert (as represented by the biblical depictions

---

53. This close proximity of "the wild" to the domestic in the HB stands in distinction to the distance between domestic and "wild" in the Mesopotamian epic of Gilgamesh; Gilgamesh goes as far north as the cedar forests of Lebanon, then westward and eastward to the ends of the world, beyond the "Mashu Mountains" or "the Twin Mountains" in his search for Utnapishtim (whose name means "distance"); see de Villiers, "From the Walls of Uruk," 147–55; and Wayne Horowitz, *Mesopotamian Cosmic Geography*, Mesopotamian Civilizations 8 (Winona Lake, IN: Eisenbrauns, 1998), 97. In our modern context, the HB conceptions of the wild are thus very different also from the American (as well as the European, Canadian, Australian, etc.) "wilds" in both perceived and conceived arenas. As presented by Nash (*Wilderness*, 44–66, 67–83), the American notion of "the wild" is much larger in territory, in scope, in remoteness from human settlements, and for different reasons has been conceived in romantic or nationalistic ways.

of flora, fauna, and danger to humans) appears still to be very limited, almost stereotypical. Hence, the desert as conceived space remains quite an unfamiliar, remote, and dangerous area, almost beyond reach, and beyond the borders of social life and order.

This feeling of remoteness and unfamiliarity (the sense of "otherness" pertaining to "the wild") is based not only on the minimal human role, but also on the literary tendency of biblical writers to describe the flora and fauna of these areas only in general terms (e.g., עץ השדה/עצי היער, or חית השדה/חיתו יער).[54] In a similar vein, the יער is portrayed only from the outside (often observed from a distance), and the flora and fauna of the שדה as wild steppe stand in dramatic contrast to the familiar flora and fauna of the cultivated field. Hence, the seven descriptive parameters serve to sharpen our awareness of this contrasting dynamic inherent in these biblical spatial terms.

Second, human interaction with "the wild" (יער, מדבר, and שדה) is rare, i.e., humans do not enter "the wild" unless absolutely necessary. HB stories of interaction with "the wild" do not show adventurous journeys into it, nor "victories" over it.[55] Rather, all three arenas pose great danger to humans, whether from animal sources (predators) or human ones (brigands, rapists, or enemy forces, e.g., Deut. 22:25). Hence, on a regular basis, humans for the most part pass outside the יער (e.g., 2 Kgs 2:25); remain on the borders of the מדבר (e.g., 1 Sam. 25; cf. Jer. 2:6); and walk only on the roads through the שדה (e.g., Judg. 20:31). In the

---

54. One might even raise the possibility that these general phrases demonstrate only a *minimal acquaintance* with the flora and fauna (and possibly other geographical features) specific to each "wild" region. However, there are, of course, other fauna and flora species mentioned in the HB whose habitats are not marked as one of these three regions discussed here; e.g., the leopard (נמר), whose habitat is the remote mountains of the north (Song 4:8).

55. Compare to the Gilgamesh epic, where the hero subdues Humbaba, appointed by Enlil to guard the cedar forests, and thus gains control over the area and cuts its trees; see Samuel N. Kramer, "Gilgamesh and the Land of the Living," *Journal of Cuneiform Studies* 1 (1947): 3–46. Note the contrast with Assyrian royal ideology, which glorified climbing the farther Lebanon mountains, reaching their high forests, and even cutting them down. This hubristic ideology is reflected, e.g., in 2 Kgs 19:23 || Isa. 37:24, which describe the unreachable "wild" arena of the Lebanon mountains and its high thick trees, cedars and cypresses. The boasting of these passages imitates repeated formulae in royal Assyrian inscriptions which describe this achievement of arriving in the Lebanon forests to acquire these luxurious building-materials for royal buildings, e.g., RINAP 3/1: 178 Sennacherib 22, col. iii, lines 11; RINAP 3/2: 308–10, Sennacherib 222, and more; see Shawn Z. Aster, *Reflections of Empire in Isaiah 1–39: Responses to Assyrian Ideology* (Atlanta: SBL, 2017), 265–69. Quite similar royal ideology may be reflected in the royal buildings of Jerusalem (2 Sam. 5:11-12; 1 Kgs 5:15-26; 6:14-22; 7:2-12), primarily in the construction of the royal building בית יער הלבנון, built of cedars that imitate a "living forest" (1 Kgs 7:2-5). See Nogah Hareuveni (in association with Helen Frenkley), *Shrubs and Trees in Israel Heritage* (Kiryat Ono: Neot Kedumim, 1984), 101–10 (Hebrew).

HB, humans stay away from "the wild"; they would not voluntarily enter these spaces, however proximate, unless circumstances compel.⁵⁶

Third, *interaction with "the wild" is almost always concerned with violence.* Human intrusion into the יער, for instance, comprises efforts to annihilate it for the benefit of humans (e.g., Josh. 17:15-18; Deut. 19:5); to intensify the general destruction of the nearby city through fire (e.g., Jer. 21:14); or to conduct war (e.g., 2 Sam. 18:6).⁵⁷ In such circumstances, the יער is the arena for animal or human violence against other humans (e.g., 2 Sam. 18:8).

The tension of distances (remoteness and unfamiliarity), the infrequent human interaction in these spaces (by mere presence or by intervention), and the element of violence are three components that construct the notion of "the wild" in the HB as a stereotypical "other" and dangerous space. They add to the physical characteristics of "the wild" the conceived sense of fear and enmity between humans and "the wild."

Some Implications for Biblical Anthropology and Theology

Both the descriptive parameters relating to human interaction with "the wild" and the conceptions of distance, unfamiliarity, and danger noted above reveal a broader shared conception, a highly *anthropocentric conception of space*, which sets clear boundaries between human arenas including nearby, human-made, open spaces, and "wild" spaces.⁵⁸ Human arenas are "safe"; "the wild" is not. This is, of course, a stereotypic division restricted to the distinction of the domestic from "the wild"; although the human arena is clearly not free of evil and social threats of human sources.⁵⁹ The ambiguity of the uses of our target terms, especially שדה, testifies to

---

56. This HB (and ANE in general) treatment of "the wild" differs from the common modern ideas of suppressing the wild/wilderness, and from the romantic (and postmodern) positive approach toward the wild (see Nash, *Wilderness*, 44–83), and see the Introduction to the present volume.

57. See n. 56 above. For a similar dynamic in the Gilgamesh epic, see that as a symbol of victory against Humbaba, Gilgamesh cuts the great trees there; see de Villiers, "From the Walls of Uruk," 150–51.

58. This distinction between the domestic and "the wild" may at times reflect rigid, formulaic, traditional, references to this or that conception of "the wild" or wilderness, not reflective of actual experience—e.g., in descriptions of the Sinai desert; or the terms חית השדה, עץ השדה, etc.

59. This anthropocentric conception of space is shared by other ancient Near Eastern cultures; see Bernd Janowski, "Das biblische Weltbild: Eine methodologische Skizze," in *Das biblische Weltbild und seine altorientalischen Kontexte*, ed. Bernd Janowski and Beate Ego, FAT 32 (Tübingen: Mohr Siebeck, 2001), 3–26; Angelika Berlejung, "Weltbild/Kosmologie," in *Handbuch theologischer Grundbegriffe zum Alten und Neuen Testament*, ed. Angelika Berlejung and Christian Frevel (Darmstadt: Wissenschaftliche Buchgesellschaft, 2006), 65–72; de Villiers, "From the Walls of Uruk," 147–56.

the biblical writers' negotiations of unsafe space—that is, space (whether proximate or distant) that is out of human control. This conception deserves a longer discussion, as I believe that this anthropocentric conception is basic to HB (ancient) conceptions of nature in general.[60]

Theologically speaking, these three "wilds" (יער, מדבר, and שדה), out of the sphere of human control, can each be seen as under divine control, and in that way illustrate three theological principles.[61] First, *salvation from "the wild" or judgment inflicted by it is in YHWH's hands alone* (e.g., Lev. 26:6, 22).[62]

> Lev. 26:6: I will grant peace in the land, and you shall lie down untroubled by anyone; I will give the land respite from vicious beasts (והשבתי חיה רעה מן הארץ), and no sword shall cross your land.

> Lev. 26:22: I will loose wild beasts against you (והשלחתי בכם את חית השדה), and they shall bereave you of your children and wipe out your cattle. They shall decimate you, and your roads shall be deserted.

Second, HB authors commonly *leave transformations between the domestic and "the wild" to the sovereignty of YHWH*. For either judgment or benevolence, prophetic literature introduces YHWH to transform the ecological systems of his own land, as well as the lands of other peoples. The examples are numerous and well-known.[63]

Worth mentioning are references to the three terms of "the wild," יער, מדבר, and שדה, in judgment prophecies against Israel/Judah, where these terms for "the wild" serve to emphasize the completeness of the described destruction. The

---

60. Job 38:26 presents a real exception to this anthropocentric conception, within YHWH's speech to Job. YHWH proclaims that he gives rain on regions vacant of humans: להמטיר על ארץ לא איש מדבר לא אדם בו ("to rain down on uninhabited land, on the wilderness where no man is").

61. One conception I have not explored here for reasons of space is the notion of מדבר as place of connection with God (e.g., the wilderness experience). This conception of "the wild" is perceived to have positive theological value (e.g., Hos. 2:15-24; Ezek. 20:32-38); it is likewise based on the notion that the physical realm of מדבר is not a human territory but God's.

62. This theological principle/conception prevails also in the ANE. See the Sumerian City Laments, e.g., Piotr Michalowski, *The Lamentation over the Destruction of Sumer and Ur* (Winona Lake, IN: Eisenbrauns, 1989), lines 126-32, 143-46, 222, 346-49; Jerrold S. Cooper, *The Curse of Agade* (Baltimore, MD: Johns Hopkins University Press, 1983), lines 257, 279-80, etc.

63. For example, as repeatedly advocated by the prophets, the success of each עיר and its שדה, as well as their destruction, is interdependent (e.g., Isa. 5:8-10; 32:9-14; Mic. 1:6-7); and see n. 27 above.

domesticated zone is so profoundly annihilated that it turns into "the wild" יער, e.g., Hos. 2:14: והשמתי גפנה ותאנתה ... ושמתים ליער ואכלתם חית השדה ("I will lay waste her vines and her fig trees, … I will turn them into brushwood, and beasts of the field shall devour them"; note also Isa. 7:23-25; Ps. 80:13-18).[64] In Jer. 26:18 and Mic. 3:12, the degradation may include the city, and even the Temple; the city is reduced to the status of a cultivated field, and the Temple reverts to יער, etc. By contrast, consolation prophecies turn those annihilated, desolated zones back into the most productive cultivated fields, e.g., Isa. 51:3: "Truly the LORD has comforted Zion, comforted all her ruins; He has made her wilderness like Eden (וישם מדברה כעדן), Her desert like the Garden of the LORD (וערבתה כגן יהוה). Gladness and joy shall abide there, thanksgiving and the sound of music" (see also Isa. 32:15-16; Ezek. 34:25-30).[65] This theological conception is also profoundly anthropocentric, even ethnocentric, since YHWH's transformations of these ecological systems (of his own land as well as those of other peoples) are solely to punish or benefit his own people.

Even the מדבר participates in transformations between the domestic and "the wild." While humans cannot change climatological and ecological conditions, prophetic passages present YHWH as transforming the desert as a feature of either annihilation or restoration. In judgment prophecies, the land (even the world, תבל) is transformed into a devastated area like the desert (e.g., Isa. 14:17; Jer. 4:11).[66] Consolation prophecies, on the other hand, turn desolated regions into cultivated, plentiful areas (Isa. 32:15-16; 51:3; Joel 2:21-27); dry lands into lands of flowing waters (Isa. 35:1, 6; 43:19-20); and vacant regions, devoid of humans, into a land that roads traverse (Isa. 43:19); unsafe areas will be transformed into completely safe ones, so that people can settle safely in the desert and sleep in the forests (Ezek. 34:25, employing Lev. 26:5-6).[67]

Third, I want to call attention to the difference of directionality—in biblical terms, crossing borders between the domestic and "the wild" has been observed as moving beyond the familiar human realm of activity into unknown space.

64. Without using the terms יער/שדה, Isa. 7:23-25 portrays the same picture of destruction, where the cultivated vineyards turn into thickets (שמיר ושית) and require bow and arrows to defend them from predators; v. 25 proclaims that cultivated spaces on the mountains will become herding places (which may thus be standing for the more ambiguous sense of שדה).

65. The same reversal of destruction to restoration recurs in prophecies of consolation that do not use these terms—e.g., Hos. 2:16-25 (though חית השדה does appear in 2:20); Amos 9:11-15; and many more.

66. See also Isa. 16:1, 8; 27:10; 50:2; Communal Lament, 64:9; Jer. 4:26; 9:9-11; 12:10, 12; 23:10; 50:12; Ezek. 6:13-14; Hos. 2:5; 13:15; Joel 1:19-20; 2:3; and 4:19 against Egypt and Edom; Zeph. 2:13, against Assyria and Nineveh; Mal 1:2-3, against Esau/Edom.

67. On a more conceptual level, YHWH himself is to return from exile, leading his people to the land (Isa. 40:3; Jer. 31:2; compare to this same idea in Zech. 1:16-17; 8:1-3, yet with no reference to an ecological transformation). This line of transformation in the natural habitat is presented in Ps. 65:10-14, as a result of YHWH's giving rain.

However, in theological contexts, since "the wild" is part of the divine sphere and under YHWH's control, YHWH can reverse this process, bring "the wild" into the domestic realm, annihilating the human arena, just as he is able to extend the domestic at the expense of "the wild" for the benefit of his people. While the discussion of each of these terms demonstrates the opposition between perceptions of the domestic and "the wild," the physical proximity between those spaces and the lack of any borders between them allowed HB authors to manipulate this opposition for theological reasons.

Conclusions

I want to close this study of the fluid boundaries between the domestic and "the wild" by framing my observations within Soja's "trialectics of spatiality."[68] On the levels of Firstspace, perceived space, and Secondspace, conceived space, the distinction between the two senses of שדה ("cultivated field" and "wild steppe/open country"), seems challenging. Lexically, these two meanings are undistinguishable, as שדה is used for both. Therefore, the seven parameters of "the wild" suggest other helpful geographical parameters to differentiate between them, and those parameters carry us already from the perceived to the conceived spaces. Secondspace, the conceived space of "the wild," is represented by a plethora of references in the HB, which could lead to the conclusion that biblical authors did maintain a binary division of spaces, clearly distinguishing domestic from "wild," although boundaries between them may be vague and undefined.[69] However, when it comes to the possibilities and consequences of crossing borders between the domestic and "the wild," this study shows how relevant is Soja's conception of Thirdspace, with the concomitant notion of "thirding-as-Othering." This concept helps us to understand the dynamics of references to "the wild" as alien, fearful, insecure, beyond human reach. "Thirding-as-Othering" pushes biblical "wilds" into God's domain, transforming physical space into the theological medium of divine action, which God transforms at will, for better or for worse, as an aspect of judgment and redemption.

Acknowledgments

This research is supported by the Israel Science Foundation (grant no. ISF 1884/19). I am grateful to Mark Boda for working with me on this project, and to the colleagues involved in the Annual Meeting SBL section: "Nature Imagery and Conceptions of Nature in the Bible" (2019–21). I am further indebted to Dr. Ruth Clements for her thoughtful comments.

---

68. Soja, *Thirdspace*, 73–82; see fig. 2b, p. 74.

69. The repeated pair עיר/שדה often includes under עיר all human-made spaces (further distinguished as מגרשים, חצרות, שדות), see n. 27 above.

Bibliography

Amit, Yairah. *Judges*. Mikra LeIsrael. Tel Aviv and Jerusalem: Am Oved and Magnes, 1999 (Hebrew).
Aster, Shawn Z. *Reflections of Empire in Isaiah 1–39: Responses to Assyrian Ideology*. Atlanta: SBL, 2017.
Berlejung, Angelika. "Weltbild/Kosmologie." In *Handbuch theologischer Grundbegriffe zum Alten und Neuen Testament*, edited by Angelika Berlejung and Christian Frevel, 65–72. Darmstadt: Wissenschaftliche Buchgesellchaft, 2006.
Berquist, Jon L. "Critical Spatiality and the Construction of the Ancient World." In *"Imagining" Biblical Worlds: Studies in Spatial, Social, and Historical Constructs in Honor of James W. Flanagan*, edited by David M. Gunn and Paula M. McNutt, 14–29. JSOTSup 359. Sheffield: Sheffield Academic, 2002.
Berquist, Jon L. "Introduction: Critical Spatiality and the Uses of Theory." In *Constructions of Space I: Theory, Geography, Narrative*, edited by Claudia V. Camp and Jon L. Berquist, 1–12. LHBOTS 481. New York and London: T&T Clark, 2008.
Blenkinsopp, Joseph. *Isaiah 1–39*. AB 19. New York: Doubleday, 2000.
Camp, Claudia V. "Introduction." In *Constructions of Space II: The Biblical City and Other Imagined Spaces*, edited by Jon L. Berquist and Claudia V. Camp, 1–17. LHBOTS 490. New York: T&T Clark, 2008.
Cooper, Jerrold S. *The Curse of Agade*. Baltimore: Johns Hopkins University Press, 1983.
George, Mark K. "Introduction." In *Constructions of Space IV: Further Developments in Examining Ancient Israel's Social Space*, edited by Mark K. George, 1–22. LHBOTS 569. New York: T&T Clark, 2013.
Hareuveni, Nogah, in association with Helen Frenkley. *Shrubs and Trees in Israel's Heritage*. Kiryat Ono: Neot Kedumim, 1984 (Hebrew).
Heidel, Alexander. "A Special Usage of the Akkadian Term Šadû." *JNES* 8 (1949): 233–35.
Horowitz, Wayne. *Mesopotamian Cosmic Geography*. Mesopotamian Civilizations 8. Winona Lake, IN: Eisenbrauns, 1998.
Janowski, Bernd. "Das biblische Weltbild: Eine Methodologische Skizze." In *Das biblische Weltbild und seine altorientalischen Kontexte*, edited by Bernd Janowski and Beate Ego, 3–26. FAT 32. Tübingen: Mohr Siebeck, 2001.
Kramer, Samuel N. "Gilgamesh and the Land of the Living." *JCS* 1 (1947): 3–46.
Lefebvre, Henri. *The Production of Space*. Oxford: Blackwell, 1991.
Malul, Meir. "Adoption of Foundlings in the Bible and Mesopotamian Documents: A Study of Some Legal Metaphors in Ezekiel 16.1-7." *JSOT* 46 (1990): 97–126.
McCarter, P. Kyle. *II Samuel*. AB 9B. Garden City, NY: Doubleday, 1984.
Michalowski, Piotr. *The Lamentation over the Destruction of Sumer and Ur*. Winona Lake, IN: Eisenbrauns, 1989.
Milgrom, Jacob. *Leviticus 1–16*. AB 3A. New York: Doubleday, 1991.
Mulder, Martin J. "רעי Ya'ar." *TDOT* 6 (1990): 208–17.
Nash, Roderick. *Wilderness and the American Mind*. New Haven and London: Yale University Press, 1967.
Portugali, Juval. "*Arim, Banot, Migrashim* and *Haṣerim*: The Spatial Organization of Eretz Israel in the 12th–10th Centuries BCE according to the Bible." *Eretz Israel* 17 (1983): 282–90 (Hebrew).
Propp, William H. "On Hebrew *śāde(h)*, 'Highland.'" *VT* 37 (1987): 230–36.

Qimron, Elisha. *The Temple Scroll: A Critical Edition with Extensive Reconstructions*. Beer Sheba and Jerusalem: Ben-Gurion University of the Negev Press and Israel Exploration Society, 1996.
Soja, Edward W. *Thirdspace: Journeys to Los Angeles and Other Real-and-Imagined Places*. Cambridge, MA: Blackwell, 1996.
Talmon, Shemaryahu. "מדבר *midbar*; ערבה *'araba*." *TDOT* 8 (1997): 87–118.
Talshir, Zipora. *The Alternative Story of the Division of the Kingdom (3 Kingdoms 12:24a–z)*. Jerusalem Biblical Studies 6. Jerusalem: Simor, 1993.
Tigay, Jeffrey H. *Deuteronomy 17–34*. Mikra LeIsrael. Tel Aviv and Jerusalem: Am Oved and Magnes, 2016 (Hebrew).
Villiers, Gerda de. "From the Walls of Uruk: Reflections on Space in the Gilgamesh Epic." In *Constructions of Space V: Place, Space, and Identity in the Ancient Mediterranean World*, edited by Gert T. M. Prinsloo and Christl M. Maier, 143–58. LHBOTS 576. New York: Bloomsbury, 2013.
Wallis, Gerhard. "שדה *sadeh*; שדי *šaday*." *TDOT* 14 (2004): 37–45.
Webb, Barry G. *Judges*. NICOT. Grand Rapids, MI: Eerdmans, 2012.

Ancient Sources

Gilg. M. iv 10; Gilg. Y. vi 261.
RINAP 3/1:178 Sennacherib 22, col. iii, lines 11; RINAP 3/2:308–10, Sennacherib 222.
Tn. II 63 Jean-Vincent Scheil, *Annales de Tukulti Ninip II, roi d'Assyrie 889–884* (Bibliothèque de l'École des hautes études 178; Paris: Musée du Louvre, 1909).

Chapter 7

NATURE AND CRITICAL SPATIALITY: A RESPONSE

Jon L. Berquist

This volume marks the initial publication of the DNI Bible Supplements series, reflecting the work of the SBL Nature Imagery and Conceptions of Nature in the Bible section and also the larger Dictionary of Nature Imagery of the Bible (DNI Bible) website (https://dni.tau.ac.il). This project, in its multiple manifestations, has already made a significant contribution to biblical scholarship and is poised to do much more. The project is inherently critical by combining the insights of many disciplines (biblical studies, ANE studies, classics, archaeology, reception history— but also a range of life sciences including botany, zoology, climatology, and more) and bringing them into productive conversation with each other. This generates an immense opportunity to place scientific data into our biblical scholarship, both correcting and complexifying the many passages with explicitly named flora and fauna, but also the entirety of texts for which landscape and geographical context are implicitly present. There is high potential for connecting ancient texts with lived experience, through a strategy of de-centering the human focus that has obsessed generations of analysis. In this volume, we see animals, plants, landscapes, and geography as active participants, and perhaps even as subjects, alongside the humans with whom they interact. I cannot claim to imagine the full realm of possibilities to emerge with this shift in thinking. This first volume is already a major foray into these possibilities, with much more to come from these and other scholars.

The final chapter, by **Dalit Rom-Shiloni**, forms an excellent closing point for any reader, and especially for one such as me, with interests in spatial theory.[1] She

---

1. For an introduction to critical spatial theory in biblical studies, please see my earlier work: Jon L. Berquist, "Critical Spatiality and the Construction of the Ancient World," in *"Imagining" Biblical Worlds: Studies in Spatial, Social and Historical Constructs in Honor of James W. Flanagan*, ed. David M. Gunn and Paula M. McNutt, JSOTSup 359 (Sheffield: Sheffield Academic Press, 2002), 14–29; idem, "Introduction: Critical Spatiality and the Uses of Theory," in *Constructions of Space I: Theory, Geography, Narrative*, ed. Claudia V. Camp and Jon L. Berquist, LHBOTS 481 (New York and London: T&T Clark, 2008), 1–12; idem, "Theories of Space and Construction of the Ancient World," in *Foundations for Sociorhetorical Exploration: A Rhetoric of Religious Antiquity Reader*, ed. Vernon K. Robbins, Robert H. von Thaden Jr., and Bart B. Bruehler, Rhetoric of Religious Antiquity 4 (Atlanta: SBL Press, 2016), 151–76.

effectively uses the work of Henri Lefebvre and Edward Soja (among others) in critical spatiality to ground her work, allowing an explication of her thesis that wild and domestic are not firmly delineated spaces with clear boundaries between them. Instead, they are in some ways perceptions (which may change with the perceiver, or with time, or intention) and in some ways actions (how one responds to space and interacts with it). This in no way diminishes the realities of physical differences among various spaces, but it foregrounds the human cognition and use of space as well as that space's inhabitants. Whatever boundaries exist are fluid, impermanent, and permeable.

Rom-Shiloni's close reading of texts and her focus on specific words and their deployment form a standard and a foundation for further work in this area. Her typologies are well documented and quite nuanced. Clearly, the key words have multiple meanings, and these are treated in detail. I am particularly impressed by the development of fluid boundaries (in the section "שדה as a Realm of Fluid Boundaries," pp. 136–38) in connection with understandings of Thirdspace. Thus, a physical area denoted by a singular word becomes many options for specific kinds of action/interaction. For me, this represents a significant theoretical advance, recognizing the interrelatedness of space and activity in a greater specificity than has been understood before. This is a crucial point in an appropriate de-centering of the human; although human choice in usage of space is still a significant factor, the space shapes tendencies and patterns of human use. I wonder, therefore, if we should also speak of *animal construction* of space, and perhaps even *geological construction* of space, as well as human construction. Does the wild induce opportunities for conflict, ritual, and more, as well as serve as a container for human activities of the same?

The chapter leaves the reader wanting more. The typology offered for these words for the wild is compelling, perhaps even neater than a discussion of the wild should be. I wonder what other factors are at play. Is it possible to observe any change in the meanings of these words for the wild over time, or among the social classes of authors, or in different locations of writing? In the contemporary world, our terms for landscape vary at least somewhat due to such factors. If that is not observably the case in the Hebrew Bible, does that indicate something of a limited time and space of the writing of these texts as a performance of a living language? If so, what does this vocabulary tell us about the text's written history?

The chapter by **Alexander Coe Stewart** features a book of Amos that is more wildly populated than I had recognized. In this well-documented and well-illustrated contribution, the reader can begin to see the possibilities for this line of scholarly inquiry to reshape our perceptions of specific books and literary products. Nature is a power and a force in the book of Amos, as a whole and in the many constituent parts of fauna, flora, and landscape. All are in the deity's awareness and control. I wonder if this is part of Amos's meaning, that God is as present in the wild as in the temple and in the cities. In the midst of some hope that the future can be more tame, God's unsafeness seems emphasized, especially in the present moment. Given that Amos's speeches supposedly occur in cities (and cities as well as nations are mentioned throughout), there seems to be an opportunity for more attention to the interface not only of the wild vis-à-vis the cultivated, but

7. Nature and Critical Spatiality: A Response   149

also in relationship to the urban. Does Amos redefine the urban as wild (due to its injustice), or is the urban a waystation for the reader on the path from the wild to the divinely cultivated?

In **Dorit Pomerantz**'s article on wild animals outside the walls, she identifies four realms for human/carnivore interaction—hunting, zoological gardens, war, and herding. The serious treatment of these realms includes both the lived experience of authors or tradents and the realities of access to literature from other regions. This is an important methodological distinction, worthy of attention for future approaches. Can we find traces of these two sources' conversation with each other? Perhaps the distinctions of critical spatiality would be beneficial here; one can learn about animals through Firstspace or through Secondspace, and it may be that differing or complementary knowledges would ensue. Would different authors consider one or the other source to be more normative in their portrayal? In particular, I wonder if the metaphoric, figural, or poetic mentions of carnivores might be more influenced by the literary portrayals, or if later texts would evince more awareness of international literature?

An application of the wild/domestic spaces to the Song of Songs is the subject of the chapter by **Martien A. Halvorson-Taylor**, with an emphasis on the metaphorical as is appropriate to the chosen text. More so than other contributions in this volume, this treatment reminds the reader that the language of the Song does not necessarily use the same vocabulary and referents as in other parts of the Hebrew Bible. Thus, the variety of meanings within nature imagery are given strong consideration, examining the Song's use in particular. Within the context of Song 2:8-17, there is a strong reflection on the nature imagery used to describe the woman and her setting, which gives support for questioning the commonplace assumption that the woman is shown to be in a house while the man is depicted as ranging more widely. Indeed, both occupy a variety of figurative spaces. Because of the metaphorical nature of the book and of this scholarly approach, it becomes more challenging to think of Firstspace depictions in the Song, but this only makes the Secondspace conceptions all the more fluid. The arrangement of metaphors become all the more wild in their juxtaposition; none of them stay stable for long enough to be domesticated or even easily understood.

Dafna Langgut and **Yuval Gadot** bring a more archaeological, politicized, and imperial sensitivity to issues of landscape. They seek to understand, in particular, some of the changes in landscape brought about by human actors in the Shephelah during Assyrian domination. They present an intriguing thesis: during this time period, the Shephelah began to focus on olive production, and the Judean Highlands specialized in grape production. Both clearly reflect human influence that reshaped landscape through intentional action, whether or not on the part of the empire. The multidisciplinary archaeobotanical approach is rigorous and compelling. In their conclusions, they move into the economics of such intensification, showing significant support for the idea that the Assyrian Empire used both agricultural reprioritizations and commerce among connected regions of the empire as part of their imperial project. Ramifications for a variety of Assyrian-period biblical texts become apparent, as well as conversations with the sociology of imperialization.

As such, this contribution offers a solid beginning for a number of other scholarly works that move from archaeological and botanical to the textual and cultural. The benefits of this volume's and this project's interdisciplinarity are striking and will be wide-ranging in effect.

Noam Levin addresses geographical concerns, bringing together concerns of mapping with the findings of contemporary remote sensing, a new way to gather data with historical as well as geographic import. The specific focus of the chapter is on the areas of sown land, a type of landscape that indicates intense human-land interaction as well as human-plant contact. Remote sensing allows for much more nuanced understandings of current geographical and ecological diversity, as well as the changing uses of land over recent times—but the implications are clearly wider. By seeing climate variation and ecological responses over a span of a century or more, we gain a much deeper appreciation for the malleability of the landscape under human intervention, and for the resilience of the land itself to perdure during times of societal change. This is a prime example of the value of human geographical study for the understanding of the ancient world; although we may not be able to track precise conditions during a given year of ancient Israel, a knowledge of the land will assist us in knowing the possibilities and the patterns at work in these settings. The chapter also serves as a good reminder that even twenty-five centuries ago was still modern time, at least in comparison to the depths of geologic time.

As a whole, this volume represents more than a beginning full of promise; it is a landmark in and of itself. All of the chapters deserve continued reflection as their rich implications take root in new scholarly directions. The multidisciplinary nature of this volume and its underlying DNI Bible project sets a fecund course, and over time we can expect to see more extended interchange between disciplinary areas, as the dialogue becomes two-way and multi-nodal. For those of us who believe in the power of interdisciplinarity, especially when it can integrate humanistic and data-driven scientific approaches, this volume represents a significant step into a more knowledgeable future. To the extent that a focus on nature imagery assists biblical scholars in taking seriously the created and altered world that humans inhabit, at times tenuously, this volume is an even greater contribution.

Bibliography

Berquist, Jon L. "Critical Spatiality and the Construction of the Ancient World." In *"Imagining" Biblical Worlds: Studies in Spatial, Social and Historical Constructs in Honor of James W. Flanagan*, edited by David M. Gunn and Paula M. McNutt, 14–29. JSOTSup 359. Sheffield: Sheffield Academic Press, 2002.

Berquist, Jon L. "Introduction: Critical Spatiality and the Uses of Theory." In *Constructions of Space I: Theory, Geography, Narrative*, edited by Claudia V. Camp and Jon L. Berquist, 1–12. LHBOTS 481. New York and London: T&T Clark, 2008.

Berquist, Jon L. "Theories of Space and Construction of the Ancient World." In *Foundations for Sociorhetorical Exploration: A Rhetoric of Religious Antiquity Reader*, edited by Vernon K. Robbins, Robert H. von Thaden Jr., and Bart B. Bruehler, 151–76. Rhetoric of Religious Antiquity 4. Atlanta, GA: SBL Press, 2016.

Chapter 8

BEYOND THE NATURE-CULTURE DIVIDE: A RESPONSE

Anselm C. Hagedorn

The title of this fascinating collection of essays calls to mind structural-functionalist dichotomies of nature/culture suggesting that there are clearly defined boundaries. That this is not the case is made abundantly clear by all contributions to the volume. Rather than evoking strict boundaries, the individual articles stress the fluidity of the concepts and focus on the possibility of crossing from one space into the other (and back). This focus acknowledges the increasing awareness in modern anthropology and the attention of anthropologists to the problem within their discipline that there exists a plethora of definitions for culture but hardly any for "nature."[1] It may be simply a sign of anthropological disdain, but I have the feeling that this is not wholly accurate as it is frequently noted in the relevant literature that the boundaries between nature and culture are blurry at best. Marylin Strathern,[2] for example, in her influential study on exchange and gender in Melanesia has drawn attention to the fact that categories such as "wild" and "domestic" are social constructs of Western society, which transform nature into both a modern term and a term of modernity.[3]

Mark Boda's and Dalit Rom-Shiloni's volume is a powerful statement that the Hebrew Bible can offer some valuable contributions to the debate, when situated in a larger interpretative framework, and the editors succeed in integrating textual and archaeological data.

---

1. Cultural critics seem to agree that nature is "perhaps the most complex word in the [English] language"; Maureen McNeil, "Nature," in *New Keywords: A Revised Vocabulary of Culture and Society*, ed. Tony Bennett, Lawrence Grossberg, and Meaghan Morris (Oxford: Blackwell, 2005), 235–9, at 235, quoting Raymond Williams.

2. See Marylin Strathern, *The Gender of the Gift: Problems with Women and Problems with Society in Melanesia*, Studies in Melanesian Anthropology (Berkeley: University of California Press, 1988).

3. Matthew Engelke, *How to Think Like an Anthropologist* (Princeton: Princeton University Press, 2018), 257.

Alexander Coe Stewart's contribution on wild animals, plants, and places in the book of Amos is a welcome addition to the usual focus on urbanism and urban spaces in prophetic literature.[4] He surveys an almost indecent amount of material in an attempt to classify and categorize various aspects of spatiality and wilderness in the book. Following the consensus of the volume, Stewart defines "wild" as something beyond human management and control. He rightly sees domestic and wild spheres as an integral part of the literary composition and is able to show that aspects of wild life and wilderness are not pointing to places "outside" the book, but are in it. Stewart argues that wild animals serve metaphorically to characterize the other. This might be so, but I wonder whether domestic animals cannot function in a similar way as, for example, the cows of Bashan in Amos 4:1.[5] This aspect of othering, in my opinion, becomes problematic, when he turns his attention to God in Amos. Stewart comes down safely on the side of othering Yahweh and I have wondered whether this is really the case. Much rests on his view of Amos 1:2 and Amos 3:4-8. The roaring of God in Amos 1:2 is, of course, because he has made some prey—this can only be interpreted in the light of the destruction of Judah and Samaria. Maybe the lion-like behavior is simply an indication of power and strength. It is doubtful whether Yahweh is really portrayed as a terrifying lion king in Amos. Two of the earliest sayings of the prophet Amos (Amos 5:19 and Amos 3:12) use lion imagery albeit in a different context.[6] The stress seems on the inescapability of judgment and it is clear that the judgment originates in Yahweh. However, the wild animals are used to underscore this inescapability.[7] Especially Amos 5:19 attests to the fluidity of the borders between the domestic and the wild, when an animal of the wild (נחש) encroaches upon the

---

4. See, e.g., Lester L. Grabbe, "Sup-Urbs or only Hyp-Urbs? Prophets and Populations in Ancient Israel and Socio-historical Method," in *"Every City shall be Forsaken": Urbanism and Prophecy in Ancient Israel and the Near East*, ed. Lester L. Grabbe and Robert D. Haak, JSOTSup 330 (Sheffield: Sheffield Academic, 2001), 95–124, and the contributions in Aaron Schart and Jutta Krispenz, eds., *Die Stadt im Zwölfprophetenbuch*, BZAW 428 (Berlin/Boston: De Gruyter, 2012).

5. On the problem surrounding the interpretation of the phrase שמעו הדבר הזה פרות הבשן אשר בהר שמרון, see Rainer Kessler, *Amos*, IEKAT (Stuttgart: Kohlhammer, 2021), 115–18, who rejects a cultic interpretation and rightly notes that the phrase פרות הבשן cannot be interpreted as a derogatory term.

6. Here Amos 5:19 is an addition to an older *Weheruf* (cf. Reinhard Müller, "Der finstere Tag Jahwes zum kultischen Hintergrund von Amos 5,18–20," ZAW 122 [2010]: 576–92) incorporating an older proverb stressing that no one will escape the day of Yahweh; cf. Yair Zakovitch, "'As a Man Flees …' (Amos 5:19)—On a Proverb and Its Contexts," in *Eigensinn und Entstehung der Hebräischen Bibel: Erhard Blum zum siebzigsten Geburtstag*, ed. Joachim J. Krause, Wolfgang Oswald, and Kirsten Weingart, FAT 138 (Tübingen: Mohr Siebeck, 2020), 409–18.

7. This becomes especially clear in Amos 3:12-15 when a prophetic saying (v. 12) is transformed into an utterance of Yahweh (v. 15); cf. Reinhard Gregor Kratz, *The Prophets of Israel*, Critical Studies in the Hebrew Bible 2 (Winona Lake, IN: Eisenbrauns, 2015), 47–8.

domestic space. Amos 3:12 offers a similar perspective. If the situation is rooted in pastoral law, as is generally assumed on the basis of Exod. 22:9-11,[8] we would have an indication here for the necessity to negotiate the boundaries of domesticated and wild space as the sphere of the shepherds seems to form an area—a third space, to use a term coined by Homi Bhaba—where fluidity is more prevalent, creating a form of hybridity that incorporates aspects of wild and domestic space.[9]

The close proximity of the two realms ("domestic" and "wild") as well as the continuous interaction between them, stressed by Dalit Rom-Shiloni's application of critical spatial theory to the vocabulary of the wild (יער, מדבר and שדה), is further clarified in the detailed survey of human and natural landscape by **Dafna Langgut** and **Yuval Gadot**. This study emphasizes that land use represents the first major influence humanity has on the wild and that the transformation of the wild into a landscape sculpted by humans displays significant sociocultural characteristics. "Humans can therefore be treated as normal though highly manipulative (partly through being comparatively unspecialised biologically) members of the components of an ecosystem."[10] Here, the change in landscape seems to be directly linked to the influence of Assyrian rule in the southern Levant which results in a shift from a typical mixed Mediterranean agriculture to a more specialized one.[11] That the reshaping of the (wild) landscape is not simply a project of the past is highlighted by **Noam Levin's** careful survey of the continuing human activity in the desert and other lands formally labeled "wilderness." Levin remains skeptical whether the term "wilderness" can still be used, but notes that the desert as a place of spiritual self-discovery and connections with nature remains prevalent.[12] The desert as a place of spirituality is, of course, deeply rooted in the biblical tradition

---

8. Cf. Jörg Jeremias, *Der Prophet Amos*, ATD 24/2 (Göttingen: Vandenhoeck & Ruprecht, 1995), 41; Richard J. Coggins, *Joel and Amos*, NCB (Sheffield: Sheffield Academic, 2000), 112.

9. On the term "third space," see Homi K. Bhaba, "The Third Space," in *Identity, Community, Culture, Difference*, ed. Jonathan Rutherford (London: Lawrence & Wishart, 1990), 207–21, and Edward W. Soja, *Thirdspace: Journeys to Los Angeles and Other Real-and-Imagined Places* (Cambridge: Blackwell, 1996).

10. Ian G. Simmons, *Interpreting Nature: Cultural Constructs of the Environment* (London: Routledge 1993), 37.

11. This view from the Shephelah and the Judean hills explicated by Langgut and Gadot is supported by further evidence from Philistia; see Alexander Fantalkin, "Neo Assyrian Involvement in the Southern Coastal Plain of Israel: Old Concepts and New Interpretations," in *The Southern Levant under Assyrian Domination*, ed. Shawn Zelig Aster and Avraham Faust (University Park, PA: Eisenbrauns, 2018), 162–85. The evidence seems to favor a view that the "logic of the Assyrian world domination was based on the principle of maximum profit with minimal infrastructural investments" (Ariel Bragg, "Palestine under Assyrian Rule: A New Look at the Assyrian Imperial Policy in the West," *JAOS* 133 [2013]: 119–44 at 131).

12. A recent study calculates that Israel will lose 10 percent of its open spaces by 2050 unless urban planning improves and the birthrate drops; cf. https://www.haaretz.com/science-and-health/.premium-israel-to-lose-10-percent-of-open-spaces-by-2050-unless-birthrate-drops-experts-say-1.9943765 (accessed June 28, 2021).

itself. Levin succeeds in showing how such tradition shapes attitudes towards geography and space, and it may be fruitful for further discussion to include the political dimension since several voices have uncovered a "yearning for the empty horizon, unspoiled and unsullied by human hands," a process that "conveys much nostalgia but also a desire to escape from a cruel history, which has memorialized human conflicts on the face of the landscape."[13]

The physicality of the wild is also prevalent in **Dorit Pomerantz's** essay on the portrayal of wild animals in the Hebrew Bible. She uses the leopard (נמר; *Panthera pardus*) as a test case. With only seven attestations in the Hebrew Bible (Isa. 11:6; Jer. 5:6; 13:23; Hab. 1:8; Song 4:8; Dan. 7:6) and possibly no Mesopotamian tradition to follow,[14] the Hebrew Bible treats the animal as enemy that attacks suddenly. Though in the Hebrew Bible a connection to the divine realm is sparse with Song 4:8 being the exception to the rule,[15] we find evidence that the leopard (*nmrh*) can be part of a list of devourers sent by the gods against Arpad, when we read in KAI 222A:[16]

(30) … *wšlḥn 'lhn mn klmh 'kl b 'rpd wb 'mh [y 'kl p]*	(30) May the gods send every sort of devourer against Arpad and against its people! [May the mou]th
(31) *m ḥwh wpm 'qrb wpm dbḥh wpm nmrh wss wqml w'[—yhww]*	(31) of a snake [eat], the mouth of a scorpion, the mouth of a bear, the mouth of a panther. And may a moth and a louse and a [… become]
(32) *'lh qq btn …*	(32) to it a serpent's throat![17]

Pomerantz favors local knowledge of the wild, which may be the result of personal experience. That such experience does not necessarily lead to a detailed classification or accurate zoological description can be seen from a passage like Hab. 1:8 when the use of נמר seems to relate to a swiftness more commonly

---

13. Meron Benvenisti, *Sacred Landscape: The Buried History of the Holy Land since 1948* (Berkeley: University of California Press, 2000), 64.

14. According to Martin J. Mulder, "Art. נָמֵר nāmer," *TWAT* 5 (Stuttgart: Kohlhammer, 1986), 463–68, at 465; however, the animal is connected to Ištar of Arbela and to Inanna in Sumerian literature.

15. See Othmar Keel, *The Song of Songs: A Continental Commentary* (Minneapolis: Fortress, 1994), 158.

16. The passage is reminiscent of Jer. 5:6 but seems to use hyperbole as "there is no other passage with the triple parallelism of these three animals" (William L. Holladay, *Jeremiah 1: A Commentary on the Book of the Prophet Jeremiah Chapters 1–25*, Hermeneia [Philadelphia: Fortress, 1986], 179).

17. English translation according to *CoS* II, 214 (Joseph A. Fitzmyer).

associated with the cheetah.[18] If the use of well-known phenomena from the animal world as well as from interaction with it is used to enrich the text, the ever-present (wild) animals would be part of a continuum of metaphors that brings stability to discourse.[19]

Metaphorical language plays an important role in **Martien Halvorson-Taylor's** contribution. Using a revolutionary proposal by the anthropologist Eduardo Kohn, Halvorson-Taylor argues that the direction of metaphor runs both ways as "encounters with other kinds of beings force us to recognize the fact that seeing, representing, and perhaps knowing, even thinking, are not exclusively human affairs."[20] Such an interpretative model tallies well with the overall concept of fluidity when it comes to wild and domestic spaces. Furthermore, she notes the pluriform expression and manifestation of the wild and proposes that the wild is not defined in Song of Songs "since a definition has an air of finality for which the Song will never settle." I have to admit that I struggle with such a proposal as space—under which I would subsume the "wild"—plays an important part in the conception and description of a literary reality. Furthermore, Halvorson-Taylor rightly allows for a relationship between the domestic and the wild in Song of Songs and I wonder how such a relationship is possible without a definition.[21] Because the boundaries of space are porous does not mean that they elude borders. I have argued elsewhere that the creation of alternative spaces beyond the public and private or town and countryside dichotomy enables the man and the woman of Song of Songs to contest and renegotiate boundaries and cultural identity.[22]

18. See Lothar Perlitt, *Die Propheten Nahum, Habakuk, Zephanja*, ATD 25/1 (Göttingen: Vandenhoeck & Ruprecht, 2004), 55. Much of the interpretation of the verse depends on the phrase וחדו מזאבי ערב; see the discussion in Walter Dietrich, *Nahum, Habakuk, Zefanja*, IEKAT (Stuttgart: Kohlhammer, 2014), 113, and Heinz-Josef Fabry, *Habakuk/Obadja*, HThKAT (Freiburg: Herder, 2018), 200–201. One notes, however, how knowledge of the wild influences the comparison when two groups of animals are chosen that hunt at dusk.

19. On the question of ever-present animals, see Othmar Keel, "Allgegenwärtige Tiere: Einige Weisen ihrer Wahrnehmung in der hebräischen Bibel," in *Gefährten und Feinde des Menschen: Das Tier in der Lebenswelt des alten Israel*, ed. Bernd Janowski, Ute Neumann-Gorsolke, and Uwe Gleßmer (Neukirchen-Vluyn: Neukirchener, 1993), 155–93.

20. Eduardo Kohn, *How Forests Think: Toward an Anthropology Beyond the Human* (Berkeley: University of California Press, 2013), 1. Here we have to note, however, that Kohn only uses the concept of metaphor when describing dreams: "In a metaphoric human dream people recognize a gap between their mode of perception and that of the animal masters. Through dreaming, they are able to see how the forest really is—as the domestic gardens and fallows of the dominant animal masters. This, however, is always juxtaposed to how they see the forest in their waking life—as wild" (149).

21. Similarly, Elaine T. James (*Landscapes of the Song of Songs: Poetry and Place* [Oxford: Oxford University Press, 2017], 79) has argued that the wild spaces of the Song "are not entirely separable from the domestic spaces."

22. See Anselm C. Hagedorn, "Place and Space in the Song of Songs," *ZAW* 127 (2015): 207–23.

Halvorson-Taylor seems to move in a similar direction when she observes that throughout Song of Songs the wild is subsumed into the domestic. This is certainly the case in her example from Song 2:8-17, but I wonder whether such a perspective can be maintained for those passages that explicitly situate the beloved in the wild.[23] Here Song 4:8 comes to mind:

אתי מלבנון כלה אתי מלבנון תבואי	With me from Lebanon, bride, come with me from Lebanon,
תשורי מראש אמנה מראש שניר וחרמון	descend from the peak of Amana, from the peak of Senir and Hermon,
ממענות אריות מהררי נמרים	from the dens of lions, from the mountains of leopards.

In this verse the beloved clearly resides in the wild and inaccessible mountains—far removed from the domestic sphere. However, the combination with lions and leopards points to a construction of nature beyond the simple representation of the wild.[24] Instead, issues of mythical places and awesomeness are stressed, highlighting that the "awe the woman inspires is part of her attraction, and so her presence in this fantastic setting transforms it into a place of terrible beauty and enchantment."[25] Furthermore, the choice of Lebanon here may be determined by its connection to cults relating to Adonis.[26] It seems that we have left the metaphorical language here altogether and entered the sphere of theomorphic language and mythical remains that permeates love poetry.[27]

I agree that in Song 2:8-17 the male lover belongs to the wild but the question remains how wild this landscape or nature really is. In the passage the "wild" is intriguingly close to the domesticated world as the use of terms like window (חלון), lattice (חרך), and pruning (זמיר) indicate, and Christopher Meredith has highlighted the fact that "the space beyond the window ceases to be an exterior world at all."[28] What we have here is a truly fluid border between the wild and the domesticated

---

23. As far as Song 2:14 is concerned (יונתי בחגוי הסלע בסתר המדרגה הראיני את מראיך השמיעיני את קולך כי קולך ערב ומראיך נאוה) Halvorson-Taylor uses the verse—together with Song 2:7, 9—as an example of how the lovers express their wild self. This is surprising as she also acknowledges (fn. 5) that the linguistic evidence points to issues of inaccessibility, etc.

24. See Oswald Loretz, "Cant 4,8 auf dem Hintergrund ugaritischer und assyrischer Beschreibungen des Libanons und Antilibanons," in *Ernten, was man sät: Festschrift für Klaus Koch zu seinem 65. Geburtstag*, ed. Dwight R. Daniels, Uwe Gleßmer, and Martin Rösel (Neukirchen-Vluyn: Neukirchener, 1991), 130–37.

25. J. Cheryl Exum, *Song of Songs*, OTL (Louisville: Westminster/John Knox, 2005), 169.

26. See Lucian, *Syr. d.* 6–9 (Greek text and English translation in Jane L. Lightfoot, *Lucian—On the Syrian Goddess* [Oxford: Oxford University Press, 2003], 250–53), followed by Hans-Peter Müller, "Das Hohelied," in *Das Hohelied—Klagelieder—Das Buch Ester*, 4th edn, ATD 16/2 (Göttingen: Vandenhoeck & Ruprecht, 1992), 45–46.

27. See Othmar Keel, *Deine Blicke sind Tauben: Zur Metaphorik des Hohen Liedes*, SBS 114/115 (Stuttgart: Katholisches Bibelwerk, 1984), 39–45.

28. Christopher Meredith, "The Lattice and the Looking Glass: Gendered Space in Song of Songs 2:8-14," *JAAR* 80 (2012), 365–86, at 379.

realm, leading to the question whether the man or, in fact both, protagonists of the Song have an existence outside the wild? Maybe a purely metaphorical reading of the limits and boundaries between nature/culture or wild and domestic spaces distorts the imaginary landscape the Song so carefully crafts.[29]

The above ruminations hopefully attest to the richness of the issues presented in the current volume. By way of closing I will take the liberty to suggest some avenues of further research or, better, aspects where the insights from this collection could be fruitfully applied. My first suggestions would relate to the integration of anthropology. Issues of place, space, and anthropology of landscape have long been debated in social and cultural anthropology, and the debate about wild and domestic spaces in the Hebrew Bible could benefit from this discussion.[30] Since anthropologists often see the beauty of their field lying in its fluidity, "its resistance to tight compartmentalization and territorialization" making it, "in essence, an interstitial discipline," such observations would tally well with the observed fluidity prevalent in the biblical text.[31] Though an anthropology of nature may indeed be an oxymoron, the discussion in the field moves towards a scientific enterprise with no definite boundaries.

> Once the ancient nature-culture orthogonal grid has been disposed of, a new multi-dimensional anthropological landscape may emerge, in which stone adzes and quarks, cultivated plants and the genome map, hunting rituals and oil production may become intelligible as so many variations within a single set of relations encompassing humans as well as non-humans.[32]

My second suggestion is related to the anthropological angle. Several contributions have highlighted the stability of the concept of the wild and its inhabitants in the Hebrew Bible. This would suggest that the concept is part of a *longue durée*. If that is the case, aspects and characteristics of wild animals would offer a perspective of an integration of (literary) history into anthropology, making the wild in itself

---

29. James, *Landscapes*, 75–80 argues that we only have mere glimpses of the wild in the Song and that "wildness is a relatively attenuated theme" (79).

30. See, e.g., Eric Hirsch and Michael O'Hanlon, eds., *The Anthropology of Landscape: Perspectives on Place and Space*, Oxford Studies in Social and Cultural Anthropology (Oxford: Clarendon Press, 1995); Hamish Forbes, *Meaning and Identity in a Greek Landscape: An Archaeological Ethnography* (Cambridge: Cambridge University Press, 2007).

31. Vincent Carpozano, *Imaginative Horizons: An Essay in Literary-Philosophical Anthropology* (Chicago: University of Chicago Press, 2004), 5.

32. Philippe Descola, "Constructing Natures: Symbolic Ecology and Social Practice," in *Nature and Society: Anthropological Perspectives*, ed. Philippe Descola and Gisli Palsson (London: Routledge, 1996), 82–102, at 99; see also Kirsten Halstrup, "Nature: Anthropology on the Edge," in *Anthropology and Nature*, ed. Kirsten Halstrup, Routledge Studies in Anthropology (London: Routledge, 2014), 1–26.

part of a cultural continuum.[33] In turn, changes in the portrayal could point to changes in the cultural environment. This would warrant a diachronic analysis of the concepts.

My last suggestion pertains to the role of the divine and its relationship to the spheres of "domestic" and "wild." If we assume that topography influences the placement of sanctuaries, any association of certain kinds of natural space would allow a community to recognize the divine protection or divine character of aspects of the natural world.[34] Despite the fact that Yahweh was a deity of the North-West Semitic storm-god type,[35] the Hebrew Bible and much recent scholarship connects the origin of Yahweh to the wilderness.[36] To become, for example, a god connected to the city of Jerusalem, several borders had to be crossed between the wild and the domestic, and I think it would be fruitful to have a more detailed look at such concepts of borders. Only in passing will we mention a passage like Exod. 22:28-30. Here Yahweh declares that the reason for the slow expulsion of the Canaanites is the fact Israel is not yet numerous enough to be able to push back the wild animals that would begin to occupy the land after the demise of the Canaanites. Such issues would relate to the question how the deity conquers or rules the wild (and its inhabitants) and how transformations between the domestic and the wild are linked to the sovereignty of Yahweh.

Bibliography

Benvenisti, Meron. *Sacred Landscape: The Buried History of the Holy Land since 1948*. Berkeley: University of California Press, 2000.

Bhaba, Homi K. "The Third Space." In *Identity, Community, Culture, Difference*, edited by Jonathan Rutherford, 20-1. London: Lawrence & Wishart, 1990.

---

33. On the concept in anthropology, see Joel Robbins, "How Long is a *Longue Durée*? Structure, Duration, and the Cultural Analysis of Cultural Change," in *A Practice of Anthropology: The Thought and Influence of Marshall Shalins*, ed. Alex Golub, Daniel Rosenblatt, and John D. Kelly (Montreal; Kingston: McGill-Queen's University Press, 2016), 40–62.

34. Cf. Susan G. Cole, *Landscape, Gender, and Ritual Space: The Ancient Greek Experience* (Berkeley: University of California Press, 2004), 21.

35. See Henrik Pfeiffer, "The Origin of YHWH and its Attestation," in *The Origins of Yahwism*, ed. Jürgen van Oorschot and Markus Witte, BZAW 484 (Berlin: De Gruyter, 2017), 115–44.

36. See Martin Leuenberger, *Gott in Bewegung: Religions—und theologiegeschichtliche Beiträge zu Gottesvorstellungen im alten Israel*, FAT 76 (Tübingen: Mohr Siebeck, 2011), 10–33; Thomas Römer, *Die Erfindung Gottes: Eine Reise zu den Quellen des Monotheismus* (Darmstadt: WBG Academic, 2018) and Theodore J. Lewis, *The Origin and Character of God: Ancient Israelite Religion through the Lens of Divinity* (Oxford: Oxford University Press, 2020).

Bragg, Ariel. "Palestine under Assyrian Rule: A New Look at the Assyrian Imperial Policy in the West." *JAOS* 133 (2013): 119–44.
Carpozano, Vincent. *Imaginative Horizons: An Essay in Literary-Philosophical Anthropology*. Chicago: University of Chicago Press, 2004.
Coggins, Richard J. *Joel and Amos*. NCB. Sheffield: Sheffield Academic Press, 2000.
Cole, Susan G. *Landscape, Gender, and Ritual Space: The Ancient Greek Experience*. Berkeley: University of California Press, 2004.
Descola, Philippe. "Constructing Natures: Symbolic Ecology and Social Practice." In *Nature and Society: Anthropological Perspectives*, edited by Philippe Descola and Gisli Palsson, 82–102. London: Routledge, 1996.
Dietrich, Walter. *Nahum, Habakuk, Zefanja*. IEKAT. Stuttgart: Kohlhammer, 2014.
Engelke, Matthew. *How to Think Like an Anthropologist*. Princeton: Princeton University Press, 2018.
Exum, J. Cheryl. *Song of Songs*. OTL. Louisville, KY: Westminster/John Knox, 2005.
Fabry, Heinz-Josef. *Habakuk/Obadja*. HThKAT. Freiburg: Herder, 2018.
Fantalkin, Alexander. "Neo Assyrian Involvement in the Southern Coastal Plain of Israel: Old Concepts and New Interpretations." In *The Southern Levant under Assyrian Domination*, edited by Shawn Zelig Aster and Avraham Faust, 162–85. University Park, PA: Eisenbrauns, 2018.
Forbes, Hamish. *Meaning and Identity in a Greek Landscape: An Archaeological Ethnography*. Cambridge: Cambridge University Press, 2007.
Grabbe, Lester L. "Sup-Urbs or only Hyp-Urbs? Prophets and Populations in Ancient Israel and Socio-historical Method." In *"Every City shall be Forsaken." Urbanism and Prophecy in Ancient Israel and the Near East*, edited by Lester L. Grabbe and Robert D. Haak, 95–124. JSOTSup 330. Sheffield: Sheffield Academic, 2001.
Hagedorn, Anselm C. "Place and Space in the Song of Songs." *Zeitschrift für altestamentliche Wissenschaft* 127 (2015): 207–23.
Halstrup, Kirsten. "Nature: Anthropology on the Edge." In *Anthropology and Nature*, edited by Kirsten Halstrup, 1–26. Routledge Studies in Anthropology. London: Routledge, 2014.
Hirsch, Eric, and Michael O'Hanlon, eds. *The Anthropology of Landscape: Perspectives on Place and Space*. Oxford Studies in Social and Cultural Anthropology. Oxford: Clarendon, 1995.
Holladay, William L. *Jeremiah 1: A Commentary on the Book of the Prophet Jeremiah Chapters 1–25*. Hermeneia. Philadelphia: Fortress, 1986.
James, Elaine T. *Landscapes of the Song of Songs: Poetry and Place*. Oxford: Oxford University Press, 2017.
Jeremias, Jörg. *Der Prophet Amos*. ATD 24/2. Göttingen: Vandenhoeck & Ruprecht, 1995.
Keel, Othmar. *Deine Blicke sind Tauben: Zur Metaphorik des Hohen Liedes*. SBS 114/115. Stuttgart: Katholisches Bibelwerk, 1984.
Keel, Othmar. "Allgegenwärtige Tiere: Einige Weisen ihrer Wahrnehmung in der hebräischen Bibel." In *Gefährten und Feinde des Menschen: Das Tier in der Lebenswelt des alten Israel*, edited by Bernd Janowski, Ute Neumann-Gorsolke, and Uwe Gleßmer, 155–93. Neukirchen-Vluyn: Neukirchener, 1993.
Keel, Othmar. *The Song of Songs: A Continental Commentary*. Minneapolis: Fortress, 1994.
Kessler, Rainer. *Amos*. IEKAT. Stuttgart: Kohlhammer, 2021.
Kohn, Eduardo. *How Forests Think: Toward an Anthropology Beyond the Human*. Berkeley: University of California Press, 2013.
Kratz, Reinhard G. *The Prophets of Israel*. Critical Studies in the Hebrew Bible 2. Winona Lake, IN: Eisenbrauns, 2015.

Leuenberger, Martin. *Gott in Bewegung: Religions- und theologiegeschichtliche Beiträge zu Gottesvorstellungen im alten Israel.* FAT 76. Tübingen: Mohr Siebeck, 2011.

Lewis, Theodore J. *The Origin and Character of God: Ancient Israelite Religion through the Lens of Divinity.* Oxford: Oxford University Press, 2020.

Lightfoot, Jane L. *Lucian—On the Syrian Goddess.* Oxford: Oxford University Press, 2003.

Loretz, Oswald. "Cant 4,8 auf dem Hintergrund ugaritischer und assyrischer Beschreibungen des Libanons und Antilibanons." In *Ernten, was man sät: Festschrift für Klaus Koch zu seinem 65. Geburtstag,* edited by Dwight R. Daniels, Uwe Gleßmer, and Martin Rösel, 130–7. Neukirchen-Vluyn: Neukirchener, 1991.

McNeil, Maureen. "Nature". In *New Keywords: A Revised Vocabulary of Culture and Society,* edited by Tony Bennett, Lawrence Grossberg, and Meaghan Morris, 235–9. Oxford: Blackwell, 2005.

Meredith, Christopher. "The Lattice and the Looking Glass: Gendered Space in Song of Songs 2:8-14." *JAAR* 80 (2012): 365–86.

Mulder, Martin J. "Art. נָמֵר nāmer." In *TWAT* 5, edited by G. Johannes Botterweck, Helmer Ringgren, and Heinz-Josef Fabry, 463–8. Stuttgart: Kohlhammer, 1986.

Müller, Hans-Peter. "Das Hohelied." In *Das Hohelied – Klagelieder – Das Buch Ester,* Hans-Peter Müller, Otto Kaiser and James A. Loader, 3–90. ATD 16/2. 4th edn. Göttingen: Vandenhoeck & Ruprecht, 1992.

Müller, Reinhard. "Der finstere Tag Jahwes: Zum kultischen Hintergrund von Am 5,18-20." *ZAW* 122 (2010): 576–92.

Perlitt, Lothar. *Die Propheten Nahum, Habakuk, Zephanja.* ATD 25/1. Göttingen: Vandenhoeck & Ruprecht, 2004.

Pfeiffer, Henrik. "The Origin of YHWH and its Attestation." In *The Origins of Yahwism,* edited by Jürgen van Oorschot and Markus Witte, 115–44. BZAW 484. Berlin: De Gruyter, 2017.

Robbins, Joel. "How Long is a *Longue Durée*? Structure, Duration, and the Cultural Analysis of Cultural Change." In *A Practice of Anthropology: The Thought and Influence of Marshall Shalins,* edited by Alex Golub, Daniel Rosenblatt, and John D. Kelly, 40–62. Montreal; Kingston: McGill-Queen's University Press, 2016.

Römer, Thomas. *Die Erfindung Gottes: Eine Reise zu den Quellen des Monotheismus.* Darmstadt: WBG Academic, 2018.

Schart, Aaron, and Jutta Krispenz, eds. *Die Stadt im Zwölfprophetenbuch.* BZAW 428. Berlin/Boston: De Gruyter, 2012.

Simmons, Ian G. *Interpreting Nature: Cultural Constructs of the Environment.* London: Routledge, 1993.

Soja, Edward W. *Thirdspace: Journeys to Los Angeles and Other Real-and-Imagined Places.* Cambridge, MA: Blackwell, 1996.

Strathern, Marylin. *The Gender of the Gift: Problems with Women and Problems with Society in Melanesia.* Studies in Melanesian Anthropology. Berkeley: University of California Press, 1988.

Zakovitch, Yair. "'As a Man Flees …' (Amos 5:19)—On a Proverb and Its Contexts." In *Eigensinn und Entstehung der Hebräischen Bibel: Erhard Blum zum siebzigsten Geburtstag,* edited by Joachim J. Krause, Wolfgang Oswald, and Kirsten Weingart, 409–18. FAT 138. Tübingen: Mohr Siebeck, 2020.

INDEX OF AUTHORS

Ackermann, Oren 58, 59, 60
Adams, Matthew J. 59, 60
Aga, Nuha 59
Aguilar, Enric 108
Albenda, Pauline 39
Allen, Spencer L. 23
Alpert, Pinhas 108
Amar, Zohar 80
Amiran, Ruth B. K. 71
Amir, Ayala 62
Amit, David 63, 71, 73
Amit, Yairah 137
Anderson, Bernhard W. 11
Anderson, Francis I. 17, 23
Asadpour, Ali 78
Aster, Shawn Z. 140
Avner, Uzi 39
Avni, Gideon 97
Avni, Yoav 97
Ayali-Darshan, Noga 130
Ayalon, Avner 61

Bar-Matthews, Miryam 61
Bar-Oz, Guy 39
Barton, John 23
Baruch, Uri 66, 67, 68, 83
Baruch, Yuval 77
Barzilai, Omry 59
Barzilay, Eldad 70, 78
Beck, Hylke E. 106, 107, 108
Beeri, Ron 63
Bellwood, Peter 94
Ben-Ari, N. 70, 80
Ben-Dor, Eyal 100
Benvenisti, Meron 154
Benzaquen, Mordechay 59, 60, 64
Berlejung, Angelika 58, 141
Berlin, Adele 32
Berquist, Jon L. 2, 6, 122, 123, 147
Beusen, Arthur 94
Bhaba, Homi K. 153
Billig, Ya'akov 70

Bintliff, John 57
Blenkinsopp, Joseph 128
Bloch, Ariel 53
Bloch, Chana 53
Bloch, Guy 61
Bocher, Efrat 70, 71, 82
Boda, Mark J. 151
Boulding, Kenneth E. 108
Bragg, Ariel 153
Bruins, Hendrik J. 106
Bryant, Vaughn M. 65
Bunimovitz, Shlomo 63, 79
Butzer, Karl W. 57

Camp, Claudia V. 2, 123
Carpozano, Vincent 157
Carver, Stephen J. 95
Chaney, Marvin L. 76
Chapman, Cindy 53
Chiknui, Mark 76
Cinamon, Gilad 73
Coetzee, Narelle J. 96
Coggins, Richard J. 153
Cole, Susan G. 158
Colgan, Emily Jane 96
Conder, Claude Reignier 98
Cooper, Alan 23
Cooper, Jerrold S. 142
Crivellaro, Alan 65
Cronon, William 22
Crouvi, Onn 59

Dale, W. Manor 79
Dalley, Stephanie 60
Dan, Joel 59
Davidovich, Uri 62, 63
Deckers, Katleen 65
De-Groot, Alon 70, 76, 77, 78, 80
Descola, Philippe 157
De Villiers, Gerda 122, 139, 141
Diamond, Jared 94
Dietrich, Walter 155

Dobbs-Allsopp, F. W. 51
Dorman, Michael 110
Dor, Menachem 35, 36
Dozeman, Thomas B. 2
Dunayevsky, Immanuel 71

Edelstein, Gershon 69
Eidevall, Göran 23
Ein-Mor, Daniel 64, 78
Eitam, David 79
Elgart-Sharon, Yelena 63
Ellis, Erie C. 95
Engelke, Matthew 151
Eniukhina, Maria 63, 79, 80
Exum, J. Cheryl 49, 54, 156

Fabry, Heinz-Josef 155
Falk, Marcia 43
Fantalkin, Alexander 153
Fauna, Dor 35
Faust, Avraham 81
Feldt, Laura 1
Felix, Yehuda 35, 39
Feiltelson, Eran 109
Fick, Stephen E. 99
Finkelstein, Israel 59, 60, 64, 68, 70, 78, 82, 83, 97, 98
Fischer, Hans 100, 102
Fishbane, Michael 47, 49
Foley, Jonathan A. 94
Forbes, Hamish 157
Foster, Benjamin R. 39
Fox, Michael 46, 47, 49
Frantzman, Seth J. 101
Freedman, David Noel 17, 23
Fretheim, Terence E. 19
Freud, Liora 70
Fritz, Steffan 95
Frumin, Suembikya 65
Frumkin, Amos 64

Gadot, Yuval 4, 63, 65, 68, 70, 71, 73, 78, 82, 149, 153
Galai, Yoav 109
Galilee, Emir 100, 101, 109
Garrett, Duane A. 16, 23
Gault, Brian P. 46
George, Mark K. 2, 3
Ghorbanzadeh, Omid 101
Gibson, Shimon 57, 69

Gitin, Seymour 79, 81, 82
Goldewijk, Kees Klein 94
Goodchild, Michael F. 113
Gophna, Ram 60
Gordon, Cyrus 51
Gorelick, Noel 109
Grabbe, Lester L. 152
Greenberg, Moshe 124
Greenberg, Raphael 73
Greenhut, Zvi 70, 78
Gross, Boaz 80
Guthe, H. 100, 102

Haddad, Eli 80
Hagedorn, Anselm C. 6, 15, 43, 44, 155
Halstrup, Kirsten 157
Halvorson-Taylor, Martien 4, 149
Hareuveni, Nogah 96, 140
Hayes, John H. 23, 24
Hayssen, Virginia 36
Hecke, Pierre Van 18
Heidel, Alexander 130
Helman, David 110
Hiebert, Theodore 11
Hijmans, Robert J. 99
Hirsch, Eric 157
Hochman, Assaf 108
Holladay, William L. 35, 154
Hope, Edward R. 15, 21
Hopf, Maria 59
Horowitz, Aharon 65, 68
Horowitz, Wayne 139
Horvath, Ronald J. 95
Houston, Walter 25

Irwin, Robert 97

James, Elaine T. 43, 155, 157
Janowski, Bernd 141
Janssen, Peter 94
Jeremias, Jörg 23, 153
Jobling, David 14
Johnson, Mark 46
Jones, Kendall R. 104

Kagan, Elisa Joy 61, 83
Kallner, David 100
Kark, Ruth 100, 101, 109
Karnieli, Arnon 110
Keel, Othmar 47, 53, 154, 155, 156

Kennedy, Christina M. 104, 105
Kessler, Rainer 152
Khalaily, Hamoudi 59
Kiepert, Heinrich 100, 102
King, Philip J. 15
Kislev, Mordechai E. 64
Kitchener, Herbert 98
Koch, Ido 82
Kochva, Elazar 13
Kohn, Eduardo 51, 155
Kramer, Samuel N. 140
Kratz, Reinhard Gregor 152
Krispenz, Jutta 152
Krutzen, Paul J. 94
Kuffer, Monika 101

Laato, Antti 13
Lakoff, George 46
Langgut, Dafna 4, 59, 60, 61, 64, 65, 66, 67, 68, 78, 80, 83, 149, 153
Lauer, Donald T. 109
Laufer, Berthold 39
Laugomer, Ben 61, 80, 83
Lavie, Smadar 113
Leal, Robert Barry 96, 121
Lederman, Zvi 63, 79, 80
Lefebvre, Henri 2, 122, 123, 124
Lessing, R. Reed 23
Lesslie, Robert G. 103, 105
Leuenberger, Martin 158
Levin, Noam 5, 100, 101, 102, 103, 105, 109, 110, 150
Lev-Yadun, Simcha 57, 60, 64
Lewis, C. S. 19
Lewis, Theodore J. 158
Li, Linna 113
Lipschitz, Nili 64, 78
Lipschits, Oded 58, 60, 70, 80
Lipscomb, Anthony I. 13
Litt, Thomas 61, 66, 83
Loewen, Nathan 14
Longley, Paul A. 103
Loretz, Oswald 156
Lorimer, Jamie 94

Mackey, Brendan G. 103
Maeir, Aren M. 63, 79, 80
Malkinson, Dan 39
Marlow, Hilary 23, 24
Master, Daniel M. 81

Mazar, Amihai 61, 79
McCarter, P. Kyle 133, 138
McCloskey, Michael J. 95, 103
McKee, Emily 109
McKinny, Christopher 99
McNell, Maureen 151
Mendelsohn, Heinrich 35
Meredith, Christopher 43, 156
Michalowski, Piotr 142
Migowski, Claudia 61
Milgrom, Jacob 137
Minghi, Julian V. 109
Morain, Stanley A. 109
Morin, Efrat 108
Mulder, Martin J. 121, 125, 154
Müller, Hans-Peter 156
Müller, Reinhard 152
Murphy, Roland 47, 49

Na'aman, Nadav 81, 82
Nadel, Dani 39
Naess, Marius Warg 106
Nahkola, Aulikki 13, 14
Nash, Roderick F. 1, 22, 95, 121, 139, 141
Naveh, Zev 59

Oelschlaeger, Max 22
Ofer, Avi 83
O'Hanlon, Michael 157
Oksanen, Juha 113
Onozuka, Takuzo 63

Parker, S. Thomas 97
Paul, Shalom M. 18, 23
Paz, Yitzhak 59
Perino, Andrea 94
Perlitt, Lothar 155
Pfeffer, Karin 101
Pfeiffer, Henrik 158
Pomerantz, Dorit 4, 34, 149
Pope, Marvin 48
Porat, Naomi 62, 63, 97
Portnov, Boris A. 108, 109
Preece, Kathryn M. 103
Pritchard, James B. 76
Propp, William H. 130
Pyper, Hugh S. 18

Qimron, Elisha 136

Rabinowitz, Dani 113
Rainbird, Paul 58
Rappaport, Uriel 37
Riehl, Simone 57, 59
Robbins, Joel 158
Roberts, J. J. M. 35
Ricoeur, Paul 47
Rogerson, John W. 11
Römer, Thomas 158
Rom-Shiloni Dalit 5, 6, 147, 148
Ron, Zvi 64
Rosen, Arlene Miller 59
Rosen, Steve A. 97

Safriel, Uriel N. 108, 109
Salmon, Frederick John 101
Salomonson, Vincent V. 109
Sanderson, Eric W. 104
Sapir-Hen, Lidar 70, 82
Sapir, Neria 70
Schaffer, Gad 100, 102
Schaller, George B. 14, 21
Schart, Aaron 152
Schmidt, Joshua 113
Schweingruber, Fritz Hans 65
Seifan, Merav 110
Siegal, Zehava 110
Silberman, Neil Asher 83
Simmons, Ian G. 153
Sliuzas, Richard 101
Soffer, Arnon 109
Soffer, Tamar 58
Soja, Edward W. 2, 122, 123, 124, 138, 144, 153
Soskice, Janet 47
Spalding, Heather 103
Spiegel-Roy, Pinhas 59
Srebro, Haim 58
Stager, Lawrence E. 81
Stein, Andrew Brett 36
Stern, Ephraim 82
Stewart, Alexander Coe 3, 27, 148, 152
Stith, D. Matthew 18
Storchan, Benyamin 70
Strathern, Marylin 151
Strawn, Brent A. 14, 15, 18, 21
Stuart, Douglas K. 23
Swirski, Shlomo 109
Szanton, Nahshon 77

Talmon, Shmaryahu 121
Talshir, Zipora 136
Taylor, S. G. 103
Thareani, Yifat 82
Thöne, Yvonne Sophie 43
Tigay, Jeffrey H. 136
Tsoar, Haim 110
Tucker, Compton J. 110
Tucker, Gene M. 11, 22
Tzionit, Shaul 64

Uriely, Natan 113
Ussishkin, David 82

Vaks, Anton 113
Vardi, Jacob 59
Venter, Oscar 104

Wallis, Gerhard 121, 133
Wassermann, Nathan 130
Watanabe, Chikako E. 39
Watson, James E. M. 94, 104
Webb, Barry G. 137
Weems, Renita 49
Weinberg-Stern, Michal 76, 77
Weinfeld, Mosche 24, 25
Weippert, Helga 19
Weiss, Ehud 59, 64, 81
Welberg, Erika 57
Welch, Eric L. 63, 79, 80
Whitekettle, Richard 11
Williamson, Hugh G. M. 76
Winderbaum, Ariel 82
Wirzba, Norman 22
Wolff, Hans Walter 23
Wuebbles, Donald J. 108

Yahel, Havatzelet 109
Yechezkel, Azriel 64
Yezerski, Irit 63, 73
Yom-Tov, Yoram 35
Yosef, Yizhak 108
Younger, K. Lawson 82

Zakovitch, Yair 37, 152
Zinger, Avraham 81
Ziv, Baruch 106
Zohary, Daniel 59
Zohary, Michael 58, 110

INDEX OF REFERENCES

HEBREW BIBLE

Genesis

1:20-21, 24	11
1:28	11, 45
1:30	11, 134
2:5	134
2:7	11
2:19-20	11, 134
3	93
3:1	11, 45
3:8	50
3:14	11
3:17-19	93
3:18	131
4:1-5	98
4:8	45, 136
6:7, 20	11
7:8, 23	11
8:17, 19	11
9:2	11, 134
10:9	38
18:19	24
21:14	129
23:17	132
24	133
25:13	48
25:27	38, 94, 135
25:29	135
27:3	38
27:37, 40	94
29:2	136
30:14, 16	134
31:39	18
32:4	132
35:4, 8	128
37:7	131
37:15	124, 135
37:17	124
37:20, 33	11, 15
37:25	135
39:5	130
41:48	131
44:28	15
47:24	131
49:27	15

Exodus

1:14	133
3:1	96
8:9	130
9:3	19, 21–22, 25 131, 135
9: 31-32	131
10:5	131
13:15	12
16	133
16:4 21-30, 31-36	134
22:4-5	131
22:9-11	153
22:10	12
22:12	15, 18
22:19	12
22:28-30	158
23:11	11
23:16	131
23:29	11, 97

Leviticus

1:2	12
5:2	11
11:46	11
14	137
17:5	136
17:13	38
19:9, 19	131
20:25	11
23:22	131
24:21	12
25:3	51, 131
25:4, 5	131
25:7	11
25:12, 31, 34	131
26	131
26:4	131

26:5	143	20:31	128
26:6	11, 142, 143	21:10-12	131
26:20	131	21:11-12	130
26:22	11, 142	21:12	132
27:16	131, 132	24:26	128
27:22	132		

Numbers

		Judges	
22:4	131	5:4	132
22:23	135	5:19	130
23:14	130, 135	6:3-5	98
31:30	12	6:4-5	40
32:16	40	8:7	128
		9:27	131
		9:37	128

Deuteronomy

		9:39-45	137
4:17-18	11	13:9-10	137
5:21	130	14:5	14
11:11-17	31	15:4	32
11:15	131	20:6	132
12:22	38	20:31	135, 137, 140
14:4	12		
14:22	131	*1 Samuel*	
19:5	141	4:2	137
21:1	136	6:1	132
22	136	8:14	131
22:23-29	136	10:3	128
22:25	140	11:5	131, 135
22:25-27	45, 136	14	128
24:19	131	14:4-5, 15	137
28:3	130	14:25	124, 128, 137
28:4	12	15:12	20
28:16	130	17:34-35	18
28:38	131	17:34-36	38
29:18	24	17:43	11
32:10	97	17:44	134
32:13	129	17:46	11
33:20	15	19:3	133
		20:5	133, 135

Joshua

		20:11	133
8:15	125	20:24	133, 135
8:24	125, 137	20:36	133
8:24-29	133	22	129
9:17	128	22:5	128
9:32, 43	131	23:19, 24	121
15:15	97	24	129
15:21-62	99	25	129
15:48-55	20	25:2	20, 129
17:15, 18	21, 121, 128, 141	25:2-18	20
18:21-28	99	25:5, 7	20

25:15	20, 133, 135	4:39	134
25:21	20	7:1-2, 12	137
		8:12	15
2 Samuel		9:10	134
1:21	130	9:25	132
2:18	32	9:36, 37	134
5:11-12	140	14:9	134
7	47	15:16	15
7:2, 7	47	19:23	20, 128, 140
8:15	24	19:26	134
10:6-8	137	25:4	39
11:11, 23	137		
14:6	136	*Isaiah*	
17:8	134	5:1-7	76
18:6	31, 124, 125, 128, 133,	5:6	51
	137, 138, 141	5:7	26
18:8	45, 128, 141	5:8-10	142
18:9	128	5:29	35
20:11-12	135, 137	6:11-12	31
21:10	11, 134, 136	7:23-25	143
23:11	131, 138	7:24	38
23:20	38	9:6	24
24	139	10:18	20, 21
25	139, 140	11	35
26	139	11:4-5	24
		11:6	34, 35, 154
1 Kings		11:7	35
3:6	24	13:21	135
5:15-26	140	14:17	143
6	47	16:1	143
6:9, 10	47	16:5	24
6:14-22	140	16:8	143
6:15	47	16:10	20
7:2-12	140	21:13	128
10:22	39	24:16	51
11:29	135	24:18	38
11:29-39	136	25:5	51
14:11	134	27:10	143
16:4	134	29:17	20, 21
17–18	20	31:4	32, 41
18:19-20	20	32:2	40
18:42	20	32:9-14	142
21:1-4	132	32:14	31
21:23, 24	134	32:15	20, 21, 31, 143
		32:16	20, 143
2 Kings		32:19	128
2:24	15, 21, 32, 139	33:9	20
2:25	20, 140	33:15	24
4:25	20	34:13	40, 135

35:1	121, 143	16:4	134
35:2	20	16:16	38
35:6	143	17:3	130
37:24	140	18:14	129, 130
40:3	143	19:7	39
41:18	96	21:14	139, 141
43:19	143	22:13, 15-16	24
43:20	11, 121, 125, 135, 143	23:10	19, 143
45:8	26	23:15	24
45:19	24	25:33	134
50:2	143	26:18	21, 124, 143
51:3	143	27:5	134
51:20	38	27:6	11, 134
56:9	21, 128, 129	32:15	130
59:4, 8-9	24	32:17-18	130
		33:12	19
Jeremiah		35:6-9	130
1:1	129	39:4	39
2:2	96	46:18	20
2:6	97, 129, 139, 140	48:33	20
2:7	20	48:43-44	38
2:15	35	49:16	45
2:23	128	50:12	143
2:24	16, 128	50:19	20
2:31	139	51:38	14
4:11	143	51:43	31
4:17	129		
4:26	20, 143	*Ezekiel*	
5:6	15, 34, 35, 36, 139, 154	5:17	11
5:16	21	6:13-14	143
5:17	40	7:15	130, 137
6:25	137	12:13	38
8:2	134	14:15, 21	11
9:9	19, 31, 143	16:1-8	135
9:10	31, 143	17:8	131
9:11	143	17:24	134
9:15	24	19:1-9	14
9:21	134	19:3, 6	15
9:23	24	20:32-38	142
12:8	21, 31	21:2	124, 128
12:9	31, 134	21:3	128
12:10, 12	143	22:25, 27	15
13:23	34, 36, 154	25:13	97
13:27	130, 136	26:6, 8	137
14:1-6	135	29:5	125, 134
14:3-4	40	31:6, 13	134
14:5	34	32:4	134
14:6	16, 34	33:27	136, 137
14:17-18	130, 137	34:4	40

34:5	40, 41, 134	1:2	9, 16, 17, 19, 20, 26, 27, 152
34:6	40		
34:8	41, 134, 136	1:6, 9	16
34:10	18	1:11, 13	15, 16, 27
34:25	11, 21, 124, 128, 143	2	15, 18
34:25-30	143	2:1, 6	16
34:27	131	2:7	16, 27
36:30	131	2:10	9, 22, 27
38:20	11, 134	2:15	12
39:10	124	3	16, 19, 21
		3:3-6	15
Hosea		3:3-8	9, 26
2	48	3:4	9, 11, 14, 15, 16, 18, 19, 21, 128
2:3	31		
2:5	143	3:4-8	152
2:14	21, 124, 134, 143	3:5	11, 38
2:15-24	142	3:8	11, 17, 18, 27
2:16-25	143	3:12	3, 9, 11, 12, 16, 18, 27, 152, 153
2:20	11, 134		
4:13	128	3:12-15	152
5:1	38	4	22
5:14	15	4:1	12, 16, 27, 152
6:1	15	4:2, 3	16, 27
10:4	24, 26, 129	4:4-5	12
10:12, 13	26	4:9	9, 11, 21, 26, 27
12:12	129	4:10	9, 12, 21, 26
13:7	13, 34, 35, 41	5	12, 25
13:8	11, 13, 15, 34, 35, 41, 135	5:7	9, 22, 24, 25, 26, 27
		5:11	16, 21, 27
13:15	143	5:17	21, 27
13:16	15	5:18	12, 13
14:5-9	48	5:19	9, 11, 12, 13, 16, 19, 26, 27, 152
Joel		5:22	12
1:10	131, 132	5:24	24
1:11-12	131	5:25	9, 12, 22, 27
1:18	11, 12	6:4	12
1:19	19, 31, 125, 134, 143	6:12	3, 9, 12, 22, 24, 25, 26, 27
1:20	11, 19, 31, 125, 134, 143	6:14	9, 22
2:3	143	7:1	9, 11, 21, 26, 27
2:21-27	143	7:2	9, 21, 26, 27
2:22	11, 19, 125, 129	7:14	12, 21
2:23	26	7:15	12
4:19	143	8:1-2	27
		8:4	16, 27
Amos		9:3	9, 11, 20, 21, 26
1	15, 18, 19, 22	9:11-15	143
1:1	12, 19, 20, 129	9:13-15	26, 27

Obadiah
3	45
19	132

Jonah
3:7	12

Micah
1:6-7	142
1:8	135
2:2	130
3:12	21, 124, 143
4:10	45
5:7	11, 15, 21
7:14	20

Nahum
1:4	20
2:12	14
2:13	14, 15

Habakkuk
1:8	35, 154

Zephaniah
1:3	11
2:13	31, 143

Zechariah
1:16-17	143
8:1-3	143
8:8	24
11	41

Psalms
1:11	130
7:3	15
8:8	11, 129
8:9	11
9:9	24
17:12	15
22:14	15
32:9	12
33:5	24
42:1-2	32
49:13, 21	12
50:10	21
50:11	129, 134
58:2	24
65:10-14	143
65:13	19
72:1-2	24
72:6, 7	26
73:22	12
76:5	37
77:21	18
78:12	132
79:2	11
80:13-18	143
80:14	21, 128, 129
83:11	134
85:12	24, 25, 26
89:15	24
92:11	32
95:2	51
96:12	129
97:6	24
98:9	24
99:4	24
104:11	11, 129, 134, 135
104:12	11
104:18	32
104:20	21, 45
104:21	45
104:22	21, 45
107:36	130
107:37	131
119:54	51
125:2	68
132:6	128
148:10	11

Proverbs
8:20	24
23:10	45
24:27	45
30:2	12

Job
5:23	134
12:7-8	11
18:3	12
20:16	24
24:5	16
30:29	135
35:11	12
38:26	142
38:40	21

39:1	34	*Daniel*	
40:20	130, 134	4:9	11
		4:13	12
Ruth		5:21	12
4:5	132	7:6-7	37
		6:17	39
Song of Songs		7:6	154
1:2-6	48		
1:16-17	53	*Nehemiah*	
2:3	45	3:5	19
2:7	45	3:15	39
2:8-17	49, 54, 149, 156	5:3, 11	130
2:9	53, 54		
2:12	53	*1 Chronicles*	
3:1-5	54	16:32	129
3:4	53		
3:5, 6	45	*2 Chronicles*	
4:8	21, 140, 154	20:20	19
5:2-8	54	25:12	15
7:6	20	26:10	20, 31, 40, 129
7:12	45		
8:2	53	ANCIENT NEAR EASTERN SOURCES	
8:5	45		
		CoS	
Lamentations		II, 214	154
1:6	32		
3:15	24	*Gilgamesh*	
3:52	32	M. iv 10	129
4:9	129	Y. vi 261	129
5:18	31, 40		
		RINAP	
Ecclesiastes		3/1: 178 Sennacherib	
3:18-19	12	22, col. Iii, lines 11	140
		3/2: 308-10, Sennacherib 222	140

www.ingramcontent.com/pod-product-compliance
Lightning Source LLC
Chambersburg PA
CBHW051526230426
43668CB00012B/1749